Right to the Juke Joint

MUSIC IN AMERICAN LIFE

*A list of books in the series appears
at the end of this book.*

Right to the Juke Joint

A Personal History of American Music

PATRICK B. MULLEN

UNIVERSITY OF
ILLINOIS PRESS
Urbana, Chicago, and Springfield

Publication of this book is supported by the
Lloyd Hibberd Endowment of the American
Musicological Society, funded in part by the
National Endowment for the Humanities and the
Andrew W. Mellon Foundation, and by a grant
from the L. J. and Mary C. Skaggs Folklore Fund.

Library of Congress Cataloging-in-Publication Data
Names: Mullen, Patrick B., 1941– author.
Title: Right to the juke joint : a personal history of
    American music / Patrick B. Mullen.
Description: Urbana : University of Illinois Press,
    2018. | Series: Music in American life | Includes
    bibliographical references and index.
Identifiers: LCCN 2018006598 | ISBN 9780252041648
    (hardcover : alk. paper) | ISBN 9780252083280
    (pbk. : alk. paper)
Subjects: LCSH: Popular music —United States
    —History and criticism. | Folk music —United
    States —History and criticism.
Classification: LCC ML3477 .M78 2018 | DDC
    781.640973 —dc23
LC record available at https://lccn.loc.gov
    /2018006598

Contents

Acknowledgments

Several years ago, my wife, Roseanne, suggested I write about the music that's been so important to me all my life, both personally and professionally. From childhood to adulthood, I loved country, rock 'n' roll, blues, jazz, and such, and I listened to music as often as I could. Following Roseanne's advice, I started writing the book outline the next day. She has continued to help me by editing the entire manuscript and encouraging me throughout the writing process. Other family members and friends were supportive as well; I especially want to thank Roseanne's brother Vic Rini; my brother, David Mullen; my sister Linda Katz, and her husband, Bobby, for all the music we've shared and their interest in my articles and books throughout my scholarly career.

I also would like to acknowledge several good friends and colleagues who have discussed music and gone to concerts and other music venues with me over the years: David Brose, Charley Camp, Bob Cantwell, Cece Conway, Larry Doyle, Kathy Greenwood, John Hellmann, Amy Horowitz, Charley Jackson, Bob Jones, Tony Libby, Bill Lightfoot, Tim and Barbara Lloyd, Brian Lovely, Mark Lutz, Janice and Tom Mitchell, Barry Pearson, Dudley Radcliffe, John Reese, Jim Scarff, Curt Schieber, Jack Shortlidge, Martha Sims, Kyle and Nancy Smith, and Art Thornton. I hope I haven't forgotten anyone.

The readers for the University of Illinois Press, Stephen Wade and an anonymous scholar, provided useful commentaries that were essential in revising the manuscript. I'm especially indebted to Professor Wade for his close reading and detailed suggestions. Laurie Matheson, the director of the University of Illinois Press, was very helpful and supportive throughout the process of turning an early draft into a publishable book. Thanks to all of you.

Right to the Juke Joint

....

CHAPTER 1

They All Go Native on a Saturday Night

Civilized versus Native in American Vernacular Music

Country Roots

When I was seven years old, my family drove across Texas from our hometown of Beaumont to my father's new construction job in Levelland. It was a long way on two-lane highways from the bayous and swamps of the southeast Texas Gulf Coast, through the piney woods, and out to the plains. As we went farther west, everything got drier and drier, and we finally ended up in a place where dust storms were a regular occurrence and I ate sand in my Cheerios every morning. Mama and Daddy and my older sister, Carol (always Sissy to everyone in the family), my little brother, Bubba (David), baby sister, Linda, and I were making our first long trip in the new Chevrolet. We'd stop to eat barbecue or chicken-fried steak with cream gravy, mashed potatoes, and okra and tomatoes; all those dishes now seem one with the music we heard on the café jukeboxes and on the car radio.

One song I remember was Red Foley's "Tennessee Saturday Night."

> Now, listen while I tell you 'bout a place I know
> Down in Tennessee where the tall corn grows
> . . . .
> Civilized people live there all right
> But they all go native on Saturday night.
> (Transcribed by the author)

It was a big country hit in 1947; people must have liked the idea of "going native." The song continues,

They do the boogie to an old square dance.
The woods are full of couples lookin' for romance.
Somebody takes his brogan knocks out the light.
Yes, they all go native on Saturday night.

The song refers to drunkenness, sex, and violence in sometimes indirect ways, but the country audience knew that getting "kicks from an old fruit jar" meant drinking moonshine, and that the "couples looking for romance" in the woods were doing more than smooching. The violence is more explicit:

When they really get together there's a lot of fun.
They all know the other fella packs a gun.
Everybody does his best to act just right
'Cause there's gonna be a funeral if ya start a fight.

The music seems pretty tame now, an arrangement straight out of 1930s and '40s western swing, pre-honky-tonk in style if not by date. And Red Foley brought his trained voice to the mix, further civilizing the lyrics. (More on this song in chapter 2.)

Another song I remember hearing on the radio on that trip was "Oklahoma Hills." It was written by Woody Guthrie and sung on the 1947 hit record by his cousin Jack Guthrie. The song is set in the period when Oklahoma was Indian Territory before it became a state.

Way down yonder in the Indian Nation
Cowboy's life is my occupation
In them Oklahoma Hills where I was born.
(Transcribed by the author)

The words must have stuck in my mind because my father was born in Oklahoma in 1912, five years after the Indian Territory became a state. Plus, my brother, David, and I loved cowboys; we went to see Gene Autry, Lash Larue, and Red Ryder movies every Saturday morning in Lubbock, a twenty-two-mile drive from Levelland but worth the trip for the whole family. I was especially thrilled by the opening of the Red Ryder movies, when Red and Little Beaver step out of a book.

I loved to read as much as I loved listening to music on the radio, and I read lots of books and comics about cowboys and Indians, outlaws, and sweethearts of the rodeo. There's a family picture of Bubba and me standing on a boulder in the Rocky Mountains a year after moving to Levelland with Daddy holding Linda next to us. When Mama—the family photographer—took this picture, I was eight and Bubba was seven, and we're wearing Roy Rogers cowboy shirts. In later years, Sissy and her husband, Bob, kept one of those shirts hanging in the family den at their home in Missoula, Montana, along with a western print by Remington, photographs of a winter cattle roundup at the ranch Bob's father owned near Ovando, and some paintings of ranch landscapes by a local artist or someone in the family, I don't remember which.

But I do have vivid memories of Sissy, eighteen at the time, driving the car to Daddy's next construction job after Levelland in 1949, this one in Devon, Alberta, Canada, where the company Daddy worked for was building a gas plant. Daddy had gone ahead to start the job, and Sissy drove Mama crazy by sticking her left foot out the window while driving the car and singing along with Hank Williams's "Lovesick Blues" on the radio. The song is about a man whose "baby" has left him, and he is moaning the blues.

> Lord, I don't know what I'll do.
> All I do is sit and sigh, oh Lord.
> That last long day she said good-bye
> Well, Lord, I thought I would cry.
> (Transcribed by the author)

From Beaumont through Wichita Falls, Texas; Raton, New Mexico; Loveland, Colorado; Casper, Wyoming; Billings, Montana; and Calgary, Alberta; all the way to the town of Devon, just southwest of Edmonton; it took five or six days to drive that far, and we heard Hank Williams all the way. The words of the song on the page don't even begin to evoke the feelings that Hank's voice raised in me and even more in Sissy, who had left a boyfriend back in Texas. I liked Red Foley and Jack Guthrie's singing, but Hank Williams's voice was something new and exciting. I became a fan of honky-tonk long before I ever set foot in one.

The three songs I remember best from my childhood were about cowboys roaming free in Oklahoma, country people going wild in Tennessee, and a lovesick boy going crazy from losing his girl in Texas (I imagined). I've been listening to those songs again recently. In some ways they led to my career as a folklorist because they remained in my consciousness and influenced me to study folklore in college. I still play such songs in folk music classes I teach now.

Urban Developments

I'm one of those lucky people who teach what they love—country music and all the different kinds of American music I heard growing up. I watched *Your Hit Parade* on television in the early 1950s and liked Perry Como and Jo Stafford, but as a teenager I heard Ray Charles, Big Joe Turner, and LaVern Baker on the radio and was transformed into a different person. Rhythm and blues opened up my musical tastes to Elvis Presley, Carl Perkins, and Jerry Lee Lewis, part of a non-ironic brave new world of Chuck Berry and Buddy Holly, Gene Vincent and Bo Diddley. White and black, pop and folk, country and rock—currents of music were swirling all around me and helping to form me and "my generation" way before the Who.

My fascination with music didn't stop with R&B and rock 'n' roll though; in my last year of high school in 1958–59, I had a friend named Scott who played piano and introduced me to jazz, in particular two albums: Duke Ellington's *Hi-Fi Ellington Uptown* (Columbia, CL 830, 1953) and Ahmad Jamal's *Live at the Pershing* (Green Corner, 200892, 1958), adding sophistication to the down-home sounds I was already immersed in. Later in 1959, when I started college, I heard B. B. King's "Sweet Sixteen," a two-sided six-minute song released six years before Bob Dylan's famously long "Like a Rolling Stone." That same year at Lamar Tech in Beaumont, the black kitchen workers were playing Bobby "Blue" Bland's "I Pity the Fool" on the dining-hall speakers, and I was listening to the black radio station KJET. What blues scholar Charles Keil termed "urban blues," a close relative of the rhythm and blues I had been listening to since junior high, became part of the mix. When white kids partied, then as now, black music was the thing. In college during the blues revival of the late 1950s and early '60s, we "discovered" country blues, an older form of African American music recorded in the 1920s and '30s.

The first of these country blues artists I heard was Robert Johnson (for more on this legendary artist, see chapter 5). My friend Brady Parker drove up from Port Arthur one night, ran into my dorm room with the LP *King of the Delta Blues Singers* (Columbia, CL 1654, 1961) in his hand, and said, "You have to hear this." We put it on the record player and listened to a few cuts, and I instantly knew where all my musical tastes had come from. I bought the LP the next day, and I still have it. I pulled it off the shelf as I was writing this so I could hear it again on vinyl.

These musical experiences were all different yet all related, and the range of music created openness in me toward other forms of American vernacular music: folk revival, bluegrass, conjunto, Cajun, and zydeco. These various kinds of ethnic music had already been influenced by blues, jazz, country, and pop music, and new hybrids emerged from the mixing of these regional/ethnic styles with rock and roll and country, including country rock, blues rock, Cajun rock, and a conjunto-country-rhythm-and-blues-rock hybrid in bands such as Los Lobos and Los Lonely Boys.

This book is about the music from my perspective as a fan and a researcher/teacher. It covers all the kinds of music I've mentioned plus some others, arranged in a rough chronology but jumping around in time to trace particular musical threads. I focus attention on individual genres but emphasize even more the blending of music from different ethnic, regional, and racial groups. Much of what I write is in narrative form—the story of my life as a fan—but at times the researcher/scholar comes out, and I delve into some analysis of the music and what it meant not only to me but also as a cultural history of my generation and the music we loved. This book is not an exhaustive study, though—I don't know much about eastern European ethnic music in the United States, and I know very little about Native American music or Asian American music. What I know starts with country and folk and goes through the rest of what many people today call American roots music.

The Civilized and the Native

"Tennessee Saturday Night" introduced a musical theme into my life, the "civilized" and the "native," which connects all the different kinds of music I was fascinated by later. To one degree or another, blues, jazz, rock and roll, conjunto, Cajun, zydeco, and the rest represent the native side of the dichotomy with various civilized elements. They all contain some element of dance that encourages abandoning all restraint. "They all go native on a Saturday night" could describe different American cultural groups, although not all of them would consider their own music and dance traditions native. That category is an invention of white Europeans who also imagined civilized as the other side of the dichotomy, and both concepts have profound class, race, and ethnic implications. Several terms are roughly analogous to native, including folk, primitive, and exotic: they all suggest the opposite of *civilized*, and all are grounded in historical concepts of the "other," meaning other than white European elites whether those others are encountered in Europe as rural peasants or on other continents as colonized tribal people. American vernacular music can't be thoroughly understood except in the hierarchical terms of us/them, elite/folk, civilized/primitive, urban/rural, educated/uneducated, literate/illiterate, and print/oral cultures. Even after groups designated as folk or primitive became more educated and literate and migrated to cities, some of the same associations with them were maintained, and those attitudes and assumptions colored the general public's responses to their music.

My parents were one generation removed from tenant farmers of North Texas on my mother's side and "hillbillies" from the Ozark Mountains of Arkansas on my father's. Both families ended up in my hometown of Beaumont because of the oil boom of the early twentieth century. My parents had high school educations, and my father worked as a house carpenter and later in heavy construction building refineries and chemical plants. If folklorists at the time had studied them, they would have classified my family as folk because of their rural and working-class backgrounds. They liked country music, which itself was considered working-class and close to folk roots. My paternal grandfather, Benjamin Harrison Mullen, "Big Daddy" to family and most of the people at our church, learned traditional ballads growing up in the Ozarks and sang them to us when we were kids while crossing his leg and giving us a pony ride on his foot. He wrote down many of them as a young man in 1907 following the tradition of the "ballad book," and my Aunt Ocie encouraged me to copy them ten or twelve years after his death after I had become a professional folklorist.

My grandmother on my mother's side, whom we called "Nanny," grew up on a tenant farm near Waxahachie, Texas. Her name was Lillian Overstreet, and she married my grandfather John Terry, "Pappy" to his grandchildren and the men he worked with in the oil fields, when she was sixteen and he was thirty-six. The marriage was arranged by her father, and after having seven children (one boy, Earl, died in an accident when he was nine), she divorced Pappy before I was born. I only learned recently from my Aunt Hally that he had been a philanderer, or as Hally said, he "ran around on her." After the divorce, Nanny worked scrubbing floors in the Goodhue office building in downtown Beaumont. From my earliest memories, she walked with a stoop.

She used to tell a story about how her father migrated to Texas from Alabama after getting into a fight with his brother while they were chopping weeds in the cotton field. He was afraid to face their father, who had threatened them with a whipping if they fought again, so he started walking west and ended up in Texas. Traditionally this is known as a GTT (gone to Texas) story. Having this kind of family story and traditional ballads performed by southern rural people with a somewhat limited education (Nanny dropped out of school when she married at sixteen, and Big Daddy finished high school and took a summer of normal school) would be enough for folklorists to label them American folk.

But, of course, we never considered ourselves folk. Folk is an invention of an educated elite and applied to others who are different in terms of class, ethnicity, race, or location. It was originally an academic term from the German *Volk* (one meaning of which is "peasant") that has come to mean common people. No matter what class you belong to in America, however, you usually don't consider yourself folk; they are always someone else, usually someone you consider beneath you in some way. White urban or suburban middle-class pop music is not folk music; folk music is played and enjoyed by someone else: those Cajuns or Appalachians out in the sticks, or African Americans and hillbillies who moved to the city, or college students who learned it from those traditional sources or who play music they composed in that acoustic style.

There are some self-identified folk, though, especially within the context of the cultural politics of identity—those groups who see a need to band together as a minority in order to protect their rights against the power of the majority. They will take up traditional musical instruments, costumes, food, and dance as a means of fostering group solidarity and ethnic or racial pride. This has happened at various historical points with African Americans, Cajuns, Mexican Americans, recently arrived immigrants from Europe, migrants from the dust bowl who went to California during the Depression, and so on, and it continues today.

But for my family of upwardly mobile white people in the 1940s and '50s, it was not necessary to think of ourselves as folk. We took our rural background and musical tastes for granted; country music was part of our cultural identity, but we didn't think of it self-consciously in that way. That changed for me as I began to study folklore, and coming from the folk became a badge of authenticity. I imagined myself as a better folklorist because

I had a romanticized notion of the folk. I could be both educated and folk, act civilized during the school week and "go native on a Saturday night."

Big Daddy and Pat Boone

Big Daddy was a house carpenter and a ballad singer; he was born and raised in the Ozark Mountains, and as I already said, he was someone outsiders might have considered a hillbilly. One of Big Daddy and Big Mama's favorite comic strips was *Snuffy Smith*, whose main character fulfilled the common notion of a hillbilly, but they did not fit that stereotype. They both read a lot; from what I could tell staying at their house on Grandberry Street, they read the *Beaumont Enterprise & Journal*, *Reader's Digest* condensed books, and plenty of other books that fascinated me—one about Teddy Roosevelt and the Rough Riders, another about Abraham Lincoln, probably Carl Sandburg's biography. Big Daddy knew everything about the Korean War and would argue persuasively about it. He had finished high school in Arkansas and gone to normal school one summer in order to be certified to teach. Big Mama had a certificate to teach second grade, but I don't know if she ever taught. I do know Big Daddy taught for a while in a one-room schoolhouse before going off to work in the oil fields of Oklahoma and Wyoming, finally ending up in southeast Texas.

After Big Mama died in 1956, Big Daddy came to see us in Delaware, where my father was working construction on a new Getty oil refinery. I was fifteen and in the tenth grade, and already a rabid rock 'n' roll fan. Big Daddy's favorite music was the hymns we sang at the Highland Avenue Church of Christ in Beaumont, where he was a respected elder. He had a good voice and sang loud. There were no musical instruments in the church since it was a southern evangelical denomination that literally interpreted the Bible as forbidding instruments in the worship service. Some of my favorite hymns were "Have Thine Own Way, Lord," "Drifting Too Far from the Shore," and "Why Not Tonight?," the hymn they were singing the night I went forward at the age of sixteen to be saved at a revival meeting (for more on this experience, see chapter 2). Big Daddy was proud to welcome me into the fellowship of those who had been born again. He would have been disappointed to learn that I began to "backslide" at the very moment I should have been saved and eventually became an agnostic while maintaining emotional ties to my religious upbringing.

While he was visiting us in Delaware, we took a trip to New York City, only a few hours drive up the New Jersey Turnpike from where we lived. We went for the weekend, and on Sunday morning he insisted on finding a Church of Christ in Manhattan. There was only one, on the Upper East Side, and we went to its worship service. I immediately recognized the man who was leading the singing. It was Pat Boone, who already had a string of hit records covering black rhythm and blues performers—Fats Domino's "Ain't That a Shame," Little Richard's "Tutti Frutti," Ivory Joe Hunter's "I Almost Lost My Mind," and Big Joe Turner's "Chains of Love." My grandfather had no idea who Pat Boone was, but he liked his hymn singing. Big Daddy and I went up to talk with him after the service. Big Daddy complimented him on his voice and song selection, and we had a short chat with him. I was thrilled to meet my first famous person, but Big Daddy didn't know we had met a celebrity until we left the church building. And even then it didn't faze him.

I didn't know it at the time, but Pat Boone was married to Red Foley's daughter Shirley. Now I think of that meeting as another symbolic expression of my southern musical world that included songs about Saturday night sin and Sunday morning salvation.

I was so deeply immersed in "real" rock 'n' roll at the time that I disdained Pat Boone's covers of rhythm and blues tunes, although I liked his slow make-out songs like "Love Letters in the Sand" better. I already had the 45 records of the original "Ain't That a Shame" by Fats Domino and "Tutti Frutti" by Little Richard, and I thought Pat Boone's versions were pale imitations. I was already a devoted fan of Fats Domino, Little Richard, Big Joe Turner, Chuck Berry, and other black performers, and I was equally enamored of Elvis Presley, Carl Perkins, Jerry Lee Lewis, and Johnny Cash, white rockabilly singers. For me, rockabilly, unlike most music by white singers like Pat Boone and Georgia Gibbs, had the edge and excitement of black performances.

Woody Guthrie, Pete Seeger, and Me

Woody Guthrie wrote "Oklahoma Hills" while in Los Angeles in the late 1930s, and he sang it on his hillbilly radio show and at bars in LA in 1937 and '38. He wrote new lyrics using the melody of an old folk song, "The Girl I Loved in Sunny Tennessee."

On a morning bright and clear
To my old home I drew near
Just a village down in sunny Tennessee.
I was speeding on a train
That would bring me back again
To my sweetheart that was waiting there for me.
(Transcribed by the author)

Guthrie borrowed more than the melody from the old folk song; he also incorporated the pastoral romanticism that was part of American folk and country music from their beginnings. Nostalgia for Tennessee becomes nostalgia for Oklahoma, and the song would have resonated with other Okies in California. But he was writing more than hillbilly songs in the 1930s; this was also the period when he began to write the protest songs that he became famous for later, including "Talking Dust Bowl" and "Do-Re-Mi." Woody Guthrie heard "The Girl I Loved in Sunny Tennessee" growing up in Oklahoma, and Big Daddy heard it in Arkansas and included it in his ballad book; it was one of many experiences shared by Woody Guthrie, my grandfather, and my father.

My father and Woody Guthrie were both born in Oklahoma in 1912, Woody in Okemah and Daddy in Tomaha, less than a hundred miles to the east. They came from the same region, liked the same kind of music, and shared some important early life experiences, but their later experiences led to different political beliefs. Daddy was not a big talker, but one time he told me that as a teenager he hopped a boxcar in Beaumont and went all the way to the West Coast. Woody also rode the rails to California as a young man, but while he was in Los Angeles beginning his career as a professional singer and political activist, "Moon," as my father was called by his friends since he was a teenager (based on the comic strip character Moon Mullins and the honky-tonk singer/piano player Moon Mullican), was in Beaumont in the 1930s working as a carpenter building houses; when that slowed, he worked on shrimp boats out in the Gulf for a short time. He had learned some carpentry from Big Daddy and bought a series of books on carpentry to learn more, books I wish I had kept after he died. He joined the carpenter's union and paid union dues the rest of his life, but he never took up the leftist politics associated with union organizing. In fact, he became more conservative with upward mobility.

During the Second World War, Daddy worked in the shipyards in Beaumont building cargo ships to carry war materials to the front (I inherited his framed photo of one of those ships in the Neches River Turning Basin, which now hangs on the wall above my desk), and when the war ended, he went to work for C. F. Braun, an Alhambra, California, construction company that built refineries and chemical plants all over the world. His first job was building a natural gas plant near Levelland, where we were headed when I heard "Oklahoma Hills" and "Tennessee Saturday Night" on the car radio. He worked his way up from craft supervisor to general superintendent with corresponding raises in salary. As he traded in the Chevrolet for an Oldsmobile and the Oldsmobile for a Cadillac, he became more conservative politically. I think he voted for Roosevelt and Truman, but by the 1950s he was voting for Eisenhower along with lots of other Democrats, and he eventually became a Republican. By the 1970s he was an ardent defender of Richard Nixon.

Moon and Woody came from similar class and cultural backgrounds, but Woody's politics went in the opposite direction. His experiences with other Okie migrants in California and his exposure to socialist and Communist political ideas in Los Angeles led him to develop a more populist leftist ideology, expressed in songs such as "Do-Re-Mi," which describes the dilemma of poor people migrating to California who think they're headed for the sugar bowl but must face a harsh reality.

> But if you ain't got the do-re-mi, boys,
> If you ain't got the do-re-mi,
> Better go back to beautiful Texas,
> Oklahoma, Kansas, Georgia, Tennessee."
> (www.woodyguthrie.org)

Woody experienced the same disillusionment with the American dream among Okie migrants in California that prompted John Steinbeck to write *The Grapes of Wrath*, and Steinbeck saw Guthrie as a political ally and kindred spirit.

> Woody is just Woody. Thousands of people do not know he has any other name. He is just a voice and a guitar. He sings the songs of a people and I suspect that he is, in a way, that people. Harsh voiced and nasal, his guitar hanging like a tire iron on a rusty rim, there is nothing sweet

about Woody, and there is nothing sweet about the songs he sings. But there is something more important for those who will listen. There is the will of a people to endure and fight against oppression. I think we call this the American spirit.

The "American spirit" that Steinbeck refers to is directly expressed in the best known of Woody's songs, "This Land Is Your Land," which doesn't emphasize the flaws in American politics and culture as much as the ideal of American democracy that we often fail to live up to.

> This land is your land, this land is my land,
> From California to the New York island,
> From the redwood forest to the Gulf Stream waters,
> This land was made for you and me.
> (www.woodyguthrie.org)

The leftist romantic idealism that suffuses many of Woody Guthrie's songs influenced several generations of Americans beginning during the Depression and continuing through the 1960s and beyond. I was one of those affected in the sixties, having first been opened up to liberal ideals by a junior high civics teacher in Newark, Delaware, and by the civil rights movement. The leftist folk song revival strongly influenced me and millions like me. What we call the folk revival of the late 1950s and early '60s had its roots in the Popular Front political movement of the 1930s, and Woody Guthrie's songs were one of the strongest musical currents of that antifascist, pro-labor-union, Communist-influenced movement.

In the early 1940s, Woody joined Pete Seeger, Bess Lomax, Millard Lampell, Arthur Stern, and Sis Cunningham to form the Almanac Singers, the urban folk music group that best exemplified Popular Front political ideals. Woody Guthrie had written a song earlier, "Union Maid," that became one they often used in union organizing. It describes a heroic woman labor organizer who faced "deputy sheriffs" and "company finks," but "she always stood her ground."

> Oh, you can't scare me I'm sticking to the union,
> I'm sticking to the union, I'm sticking to the union,
> Oh, you can't scare me I'm sticking to the union,
> I'm sticking to the union, till the day I die.
> (www.woodyguthrie.org)

Pete Seeger sang lead, and the rest of the group joined in on the rousing chorus. In its day it must have emotionally stirred union members at rallies and reinforced their solidarity just as it did for me decades later when I began to play the recording in my folk music classes far from the front lines of the struggle.

Where did I learn to be emotionally and intellectually engaged by such leftist sentiments? Not from my father but from Woody Guthrie and Pete Seeger. Music was an important political learning experience for me whether it was civil rights anthems, Woody Guthrie songs, or protest songs by Bob Dylan. I was affected not always by the original versions first but by covers by other singers. I learned to like "Do-Re-Mi" not from Guthrie's version but from a Ry Cooder recording in 1976, a rendering that took the 1930s song and broadened it to another ethnic group. Cooder is a guitarist/singer/ songwriter who recorded albums that could have been produced by an ethnomusicologist thanks to his ability to unearth ethnic and regional songs and musicians from Hawaii to Texas and from Mississippi to Cuba (see chapter 6). He does "Do-Re-Mi" in conjunto style with the help of famed Mexican American accordionist Flaco Jiménez (see chapter 8). It's an inspired take on a 1930s protest song since playing it conjunto style suggests new meanings in terms of another oppressed group of migrant workers.

Conjunto is working-class music for both Mexican American musicians and audience, and a number of the songs from the tradition deal with problems of illegal migrant workers from Mexico such as Flaco Jiménez's "Un Mojado Sin Licensia" ("A Wetback without License"), a song I talk more about in chapter 8. Ry Cooder's "Do-Re-Mi" shows how adaptable Woody Guthrie's songs have been over the years with such covers as the Byrds'"Pretty Boy Floyd," Willie Nelson's "Philadelphia Lawyer," Bruce Springsteen's "Vigilante Man," and innumerable versions of "This Land Is Your Land."

Pete Seeger carried on Woody Guthrie's protest song tradition, surviving the Communist blacklist in the 1950s, promoting the civil rights movement and inspiring Bob Dylan in the 1960s, and finally becoming an elder musical spokesman for the Left in the twenty-first century. When I was a graduate student in Austin, I heard Pete Seeger in person for the first time at a 1965 concert during a tour he made with the Freedom Singers. I wasn't a big fan at the time because I was more of a rocker than a folkie, plus he didn't sound like the "real" folk to me. *Folk* meant the genuine article, and *folkie* meant college students who took up the banjo or sang old ballads.

I preferred singers and musicians who had grown up in a West Virginia holler or on a Mississippi tenant farm. I was what I now think of as a "populist elitist." That may sound like an oxymoron, but it makes sense as a description of people who think that lower-class folk roots are culturally superior to middle- and upper-class education and privilege. My parents were working-class Texans, and Pete Seeger's were fairly well off and highly educated New England elites; his father was the well-known ethnomusicologist Charles Seeger. I didn't know at the time that the Seegers were such committed leftists that they lived a Spartan existence when Pete was growing up in order to experience poor and working-class life firsthand. Thinking that Pete was totally upper class and his denim overalls an affectation, I allowed my class bias to prevent me from completely accepting his music, but on that night in 1965 I was caught up in romantic leftist idealism as never before.

The concert was in an old arena in Austin that I think was used for rodeos. The only other concert I had attended there had been a performance by James Brown and the Famous Flames. That was special too since I had never seen Brown in person before. Friends from North Texas came down for the show. Kyle and Nancy Smith and my then-wife, Caroline, and I were thrilled by the chance to display our white liberal credentials by going to see a black performer with a mainly black audience. There was a clear connection between the Freedom Singers' and James Brown's concerts because of their shared roots in African American gospel. The difference concerned the purposes of the music. This concert took place before James Brown's "I'm Black and I'm Proud" political statements, and his performance was more like that of his famous "Live at the Apollo" concert, recorded in 1962—passionate, melodramatic, with Brown collapsing on the stage, an assistant bringing out a cape, covering his shoulders, and helping him off, only to have him throw off the cape and start screaming again. Fantastic. It was from the church, but the purpose was strictly secular.

The Freedom Singers and Pete Seeger also used gospel music, but they kept the religious connotations and combined them with political intent much as Martin Luther King Jr. had been doing for years. In this case, it was preaching to the converted since the audience was made up of black people already active in the civil rights movement and like-minded white students and faculty from the University of Texas. The James Brown audience was almost entirely black, but the Pete Seeger and Freedom Singers' concert had already accomplished one of its goals by attracting an integrated audience.

The Freedom Singers' concert was emotionally moving all the way through, but the peak moment came at the end, when the singers were all leaving the stage. The audience spontaneously began to sing "We Shall Overcome," and the singers returned to the stage to sing along with us. This was a watershed moment for me, bringing together my beliefs about racial equality with my love of music. This must have been happening for black and white people all over the country during that period, and I feel privileged to have been part of it. In retrospect I realize that ideology and aesthetics were fused at that moment, and they have remained intertwined in my musical experiences ever since.

Almost forty years later, in 2004, I heard Pete Seeger in person again. In fact, while a professor at Ohio State University, I "became" Pete Seeger for a short period of time. Another folklorist at Ohio State, Amy Horowitz, was making a documentary film about music as protest, and she invited Pete Seeger, Harry Belafonte, Bernice Johnson Reagon, and Holly Near to take part in a discussion that included singing excerpts from tunes about their experiences as singers and political activists. The discussion was held at the Southern Theatre in Columbus, Ohio, with an invited audience, and the entire event was filmed. The day before the concert, Amy and another folklorist, Amy Shuman, asked me to help with the preparations by being a stand-in for Pete Seeger during the lighting setup. There I was sitting with the other pretenders while the film crew worked around us. I must have been chosen because of my gray hair and beard, my only resemblance to Pete Seeger except for our similar tendency to dress in denim and other working-class attire.

The discussion was intellectually stimulating, musically exciting, and politically inspiring, everything I had hoped it would be. Holly Near represented the women's and lesbian rights movements and recounted the difficulties she had faced in spreading their message at a time when there was strong homophobic resistance. She sang excerpts from her own songs that perfectly illustrated how significant music can be as political protest. Harry Belafonte was as charismatic as I had imagined he would be; his voice still powerful and emotionally affecting at seventy-eight, his message still as true and significant as it had been when he began his career in the 1950s. At the time of the filming, he was a major critic of the war in Iraq and the Bush administration. Bernice Johnson Reagon spoke of her experiences in the civil rights movement, and how effective African American hymns had been in the fight for freedom. She sang snatches of songs that she had performed over the years with the group Sweet Honey in the Rock, illustrating exactly what that metaphor means. Pete Seeger drew on his vast experience in the Popular Front of the 1930s, as a member of the Almanac Singers in the 1940s, as a demonstrator for civil rights in the 1950s and '60s and against the Vietnam War in the 1960s and '70s to express the power of music as a weapon against oppression, conjuring up images of Woody Guthrie's guitar, which had "This Guitar Kills Fascists" written on the front.

My wife, Roseanne, and I went back stage after the concert and met the four singers, which was a thrill for us as longtime admirers of all of them. Alfonso Hawkins, a former graduate student of mine who was writing his dissertation on Belafonte, had come all the way from Birmingham, Alabama, by Greyhound bus to observe the filming. Alfonso was more formal than I am and always called me Dr. Mullen, even though I asked all my graduate students to call me Pat. He had lunch with Belafonte and had the chance to talk with him at length. Later when Alfonso introduced me to Belafonte as "Dr. Mullen," Belafonte said, "Hi, Doc," immediately relaxing everyone, including me, since I had been in awe of him all my life. My response to him was much like the young Bob Dylan's when he first saw Belafonte at a party in Greenwich Village in the early 1960s: "Harry was that rare type of character that radiates greatness, and you hope that some of it rubs off on you. The man commands respect. You know he never took the easy path, though he could have."

After talking with him briefly, Roseanne and I went to a backstage room where food was being served to the performers and guests. I saw that there was a vacant chair next to Pete Seeger, and I sat down and introduced myself. He was so gracious and open that he also made me feel totally comfortable in his presence. We talked about music for about a half hour. At one point he pulled a song out of his pocket that someone had sent him by e-mail, and he sang it for me—an incredible experience for someone who considered him an American legend.

I could echo John Steinbeck's description of Woody Guthrie in giving you my impression of Pete Seeger that night: "Pete is just Pete. He is just a voice and a banjo. He sings the songs of a people and I know that he is that people." My earlier sense of him as a populist elitist was completely wiped out after I met him; his singing, what he said, and the way he acted had erased any class distance I had imagined. His consistent commitment over the years to the rights of oppressed minority groups and the poor and working-class people of America and his presence at that moment convinced me that "he is that people." I know—it's hero worship on my part with both Pete Seeger and Harry Belafonte. I have a persistent streak of romantic idealism that won't go away no matter how disillusioned I become about American politics. My approach to American vernacular music contains an entire range of attitudes from disillusionment to romanticism. (Pete Seeger died on January 27, 2014, at the age of ninety-four. The tributes were global and astounding in their respect and love for him and his music.)

Another significant influence on my political approach to American music was folklorist Archie Green. He wrote a monumental book on working-class folk music that influenced everything that followed, *Only a Miner: Studies in Recorded Coal-Mining Songs*. His political approach to folk music went beyond academic folklore studies; he was an activist who lobbied the United States Congress to pass the American Folklife Preservation Act, which was the basis for the American Folklife Center at the Library of Congress. Folklore studies in general have benefited from his activist approach. (Archie Green died on March 22, 2009.)

Authentic Folk and Real Rock and Roll

Pete Seeger changed from a folk wannabe to a real folk musician in my mind. These culturally imagined categories also fit a singer like Pat Boone, who was never a "real" rock and roll singer to me (I won't go into his current right-wing politics), but Little Richard was and continues to be real (as outrageous as his makeup and costumes might be). What does that tell us about authenticity in vernacular music? The judgments we make are directly related to how we feel about the music, and the question of authenticity is part of our understanding of that aesthetic. Finally, what is real or genuine or authentic is subjective; it exists in our minds and is not intrinsic to the music. We could argue all day about whether Joan Baez is an authentic folk singer (see chapter 6), but finally it is a subjective opinion, a relative matter and not absolute. The argument about authenticity would be all wrapped up in how we conceived of tradition itself, how we interpreted the past from the perspective of the present. Tradition as a concept doesn't exist in the past; it is a way of viewing the past from the present, and there will always be differences in the way we look at the past and arguments about what it means.

At one time, folklorists thought that to be authentic the folk had to be rural, isolated, and uneducated; now academic folklorists see the folk as including those who are educated and live in cities. There are now studies of the folklore of lawyers and computer users. Over time the social and intellectual context in which we make such distinctions changes, and the concepts change to fit changing circumstances. As I tell my students, we have to ask ourselves, "Authentic to whom and for what reasons?" In other words, questions about what is the "real thing" in music have to be examined in ever-changing social and political contexts. In this sense, the categories are important historically and politically, and we need to keep discussing and arguing about them.

In another sense, the categories don't make any difference: Hank Williams and Johnny Cash, Ray Charles and Aretha Franklin are great artists no matter what label is put on their music. But if we want to understand the cultural meaning of their music, we should interpret it in the contexts in which it was first performed and in the various contexts in which it has subsequently been heard. The categories people create for music reveal their perceptions of it and their attitudes toward not only the music but also toward the ethnic, racial, and regional groups of those who play the music. This is where the old elite and folk, civilized and native dichotomies come in. This categorization is all part of the cultural politics of vernacular music and to me essential to understanding the music itself.

I remember hearing Johnny Cash's Sun recording of "I Walk the Line" on a Wurlitzer jukebox at a café in the Mississippi Delta as my family was driving back to Texas from Delaware in 1956. I was amazed by the booming deep bass sound rumbling out of the jukebox through the worn wood floor and up my body. I thought of it as rock and roll *and* country, no problem for a fifteen-year-old who grew up on country and who had been enjoying rock 'n' roll since 1954. I spent years trying to replicate the sound of that jukebox on record players, not even coming close until sometime in the early 1970s when I could afford the audio equipment to give me a bass that was close to the sound (and as a result Roseanne still complains from the kitchen below my study). The sound of "I Walk the Line" was rock 'n' roll *and* country to me and still is.

Johnny Cash was a lot of things to different people: he was selling records to a country music audience at the time, and later Columbia promoted him as a folk singer in an attempt to take advantage of the folk revival boom. He has all the folk qualifications in terms of background—poor family, hardscrabble farming in Arkansas, learning songs and musical instruments in a traditional community setting, and so on. But there are plenty of country singers who came up around the same time in places like Memphis, Houston, and Los Angeles, and urban backgrounds have not disqualified them from folkness, nor has middle-class status. The whole argument becomes meaningless since the criteria for authenticity are so fluid and subjective over time, but I would argue that those labels are still significant in understanding Johnny Cash's appeal, the meaning his music has for his audience, and his ultimate enshrinement as an American demigod. Vernacular music can tell us something about what it means to be American.

CHAPTER 2

Yes Indeed

Race, Revival, and Rock 'n' Roll

My family lived all over the United States and Canada while I was in school, but Beaumont, where I spent my first seven years and have frequently visited throughout my life, shaped my musical tastes more than any other place. Southeast Texas has many different kinds of music, including large helpings of Cajun and zydeco, but the kinds of music I knew first were country and rhythm and blues, two genres that suggest the importance of race in American vernacular music. The very earliest was Anglo-American country music (see chapter 1), and I'm still a fan, but in 1954, when I first became conscious of African American rhythm and blues, it and emerging rock 'n' roll became the dominant music in my life. The immediate appeal of black vernacular music took place within the context of race relations in Beaumont when I was growing up.

My hometown was totally segregated in 1941, the year I was born, and it continued to be segregated until the civil rights movement of the sixties. Southeast Texas was culturally a part of the old Deep South, and the segregation extended to housing, schools, and all facets of social life. I remember the "colored" drinking fountains at the White House and the big downtown department store, the "colored" waiting room at the Greyhound bus station, and "Negroes" in the back of city buses. There was a large black population in Beaumont, but the only black person I knew as a child was Melissy, the woman who did the ironing for everyone in our family.

One day when I was six or seven, Melissy was in the dining room ironing, and I was in the kitchen eating lunch. I was playing with the salt and pepper shakers and said, "This one is white, this one is a nigger." My mother scolded me, pointing to the other room where Melissy could hear me. I remember feeling ashamed because I might have hurt Melissy's feelings. I had been taught to say "colored" or "Negro" and to be kind to black people in the patronizing way that polite southern whites had at the time.

Melissy did ironing for both of my grandmothers and most of my aunts, and they had a genuine concern for her well-being. As was the custom, we gave our old clothes to her and her family, and she would sometimes take leftovers home. Black people were all around us, but as far as I could tell then, there was no cultural contact except for these paternalistic interactions. At the time, I was innocent about the violent forms of racism that existed in Beaumont, which later we especially associated with the town of Vidor just across the Neches River. Vidor had the reputation of a place where black people had to be out of town by sundown. It was sort of a scapegoat for Beaumont residents who did not want to be associated with violence driven by racism, but both places had plenty of racist behavior.

We went to the two black neighborhoods closest to us fairly often—taking Melissy home across the railroad tracks to the northeast where part of the drive was on Railroad Avenue, which had tracks down the middle of the street. Much to the delight of my brother and me, we were often driving next to boxcars, tankers, and locomotives as we went down the street. When going to the black neighborhood to the west, we crossed another railroad track on the way to the place that cleaned and refrigerated ducks Daddy had shot on hunting trips. The other black-owned business there was Patillo's Barbecue on Washington Boulevard, later Martin Luther King Drive. Patillo's was where I developed my taste for barbecued brisket, smoked for eight hours over hickory wood. Cuisine was like music in being a cultural connector between black and white, and for me another means of romanticizing black culture through the international language of music and food. Washington Boulevard connected our all-white neighborhood of South Park with Pear Orchard, the black neighborhood to the west. South Park is now mainly black, and all my family has moved to other parts of town. My parents returned to South Park after Daddy's retirement in the seventies, and they had black neighbors next door. Desegregation had been a slow and difficult process, but by the seventies everyone seemed to get along fine.

Growing up in the forties, I learned certain racial stereotypes from my white cultural surroundings. As a result of segregation and cultural differ-ence, we imagined black people as strange and mysterious. Driving the few blocks into the black neighborhoods, we felt as if we had entered another country, maybe in my mind an African country—an image that I found later in white folk song scholar John Lomax's work from the thirties and forties. White and black people might live in close physical proximity, but an unbridgeable gap caused by perceptions of racial difference separated them. This idea was the beginning of what I later learned was the white racial notion of blacks as "exotic other," taking the reality of cultural differences and skin color and imagining African American culture as something strange and essentially biologically racial.

After my father went to work in heavy construction, we started moving all over North America, from Beaumont to Levelland, Bay City, Lake Jackson, Houston, and Baytown in Texas; to Baton Rouge and Lake Charles, Louisiana; Lakewood, California; and Newark, Delaware; and to Devon, Alberta, and Oakville, Ontario, in Canada. I went back to Texas for college, but every summer I went home to work in construction wherever my parents happened to be living—Long Beach, California; Quilcene, Washington; Woodbury, New Jersey; Joliet, Illinois; and Moundsville, West Virginia. From elementary school through high school, no matter where we lived, no black kids attended the schools that I did. Even in the East, North, or West, we might as well still have been in the segregated South as far as any direct contact with blacks was concerned.

I remember only a few exceptions to this isolation from blacks. When I was in the fourth grade in Bay City, a barbershop around the corner from our house employed a black shoeshine man. He sometimes brought a son my age with him to work, and the two of us would play in the empty lot next to the barbershop. In the ninth and tenth grades in Delaware, the high school in Newark was all white, but we had football games and track meets against black schools. I competed against black athletes in sports but otherwise had no social interaction with them.

Late in 1956, when I was halfway through the tenth grade, we moved back to Beaumont, where sports were still totally segregated. White people would go to black football games, and the best players from the region seemed to come from black schools, Charlton-Pollard east of South Park and Hebert High to the west; many of the really good ones later went to colleges in the North to play. Bubba Smith was probably the best known of them. I remember hearing the bands play when the black schools had a night game at the white high school stadium in South Park. The sounds traveled throughout the neighborhood, and I was intrigued by what I heard—the black bands didn't just play marches; they played current rhythm and blues hits. When I returned to Beaumont to go to college in 1959, I remember hearing a black marching band playing the Coasters' "Poison Ivy" while in my Aunt Ocie's house, where I stayed until the dorms opened in the fall.

When I was in the eighth grade, first in Baton Rouge and then in Baytown in 1954–55, I heard black rhythm and blues for the first time that I remember. The schools were still segregated, but white kids were listening to black radio. The first time I heard a white cover of a rhythm and blues song was in Baton Rouge, the Crew-Cuts' version of the Chords' "Sh-Boom," and I liked it as what was then called a novelty song, but the real thing soon grabbed me on another, more intense level.

We moved from Baton Rouge to Baytown, and like many white southerners my age, I became fascinated by African American culture when at the age of thirteen I heard Ray Charles sing "I Got a Woman," LaVern Baker sing "Tweedle-Dee," and the Penguins sing "Earth Angel." I think "I Got a Woman" was the very first and the most significant of the three. I had no idea at the time what a breakthrough song it was in the development of American vernacular music. Most rock critics and music scholars now see it as one of the first tunes blending rhythm and blues with gospel to create a new form of music that later became soul music. At the time I couldn't hear enough of it or play the radio or record player loud enough, starting a conflict with my mother that lasted until I went away to college. My junior high interest in rhythm and blues led to high school and college discoveries of blues musicians Robert Johnson, Leadbelly, and B. B. King, and eventually to jazz musicians—Duke Ellington, Charlie Parker, and John Coltrane—all of it laying the groundwork for my later interests as a folklorist.

It was no accident that in the 1950s white thirteen-year-olds were attracted to black music; right at puberty, right as we were developing sexually and becoming conscious of sexuality, we discovered this sexy music. As a teenager, I was fairly innocent of sexual innuendos in R&B and rock songs; I didn't even know that when Little Richard sang "gonna ball all night long" he was singing about sex. I thought he meant dancing, and I didn't think of dancing as a metaphor for sex although I definitely knew on a literal level that dancing was sexually exciting. School and church officials knew it too. The "dirty bop" was banned at junior high dances in Baytown, and my family's church banned dancing altogether, which made me love it that much more. I worked on my dirty-bop moves listening to my small 45 rpm record player in the privacy of my bedroom and rarely got a chance to dance with a girl—I was too shy to ask. A few years later I recognized Elvis Presley's moves on stage as growing out of the dirty bop, and it was still considered obscene by those who saw rock 'n' roll as sinful.

We didn't care where it came from; we didn't analyze the racial, religious, and cultural implications; we just wanted to listen and dance to it. We didn't see a "desire" to be African American as the basis for our attraction to black music as scholars like bell hooks later theorized. It seems obvious now that desire was part of it; the white middle-class sexually repressed society we grew up in made us ripe for perceiving another culture as exotically sexual, for seeing a darker people as mysterious and earthy, for conceiving of their music as liberating, for imagining black people as exotic other. And we were not the first; this process of inventing the "primitive other" has a long history in European civilization, especially in the history of colonialism, and American history, which is filled with instances of representing black people in ways that fit preconceived white notions about difference. Segregation aided in this process; having little contact with black people, white teenagers were free to imagine what blacks were like through their music. We didn't know many actual individual human beings to contradict generalizations about the culture or the stereotypes that had been around for generations. Our parents and grandparents had some of the same attitudes we did, although each generation worked out its own particulars.

Our attitudes about black people reflected right back on what it meant to be white, although that was never apparent to anyone. Looking back from the perspective of my readings on race over the last twenty-five years, I can see that whiteness must have meant repression and restraint, especially in sexual terms, although this idea was totally off the radar on a conscious level at the time. I can remember certain girls repeatedly going forward in the evangelical church I attended to publicly confess their "sins," not explicitly stated but I imagined them as sexual sins, and they may have been as innocent as a French kiss (which the first time I tried was rejected by the girl's clenched teeth). If black music represented freedom from repression, then white music (in church and popular music on the radio) must have seemed to repress sexuality, covering it up with romantic images of moonlight and the lush sound of strings although these approaches sometimes overlapped in white pop and black R&B. Never mind that some religious African American parents were probably just as restrictive with teenagers as white parents. That possibility did not enter into our thinking about race; in imagining what whiteness and blackness mean, details that don't fit are simply left out.

"O Why Not Tonight?"

I was saved at a Monday-night revival meeting at the Church of Christ on Highland Avenue in Beaumont, Texas, when I was sixteen. The visiting preacher had already called for the sinners to come forward, confess their sins, and be born again. I had been thinking about taking that step for several months but had always chickened out at the last minute. The congregation sang the song of invitation, "Why Not Tonight?"

> O do not let the Word depart,
> And close thine eyes against the light;
> Poor sinner, harden not your heart,
> Be saved, O tonight.
> O why not tonight?
> O why not tonight?
> Wilt thou be saved?
> Then why not tonight?
> (www.cyberhymnal.org/htm/o/w/owhynott.htm)

After the song ended, I breathed a sigh of relief that once again I could not make myself take that first step. But the preacher looked out at us and said, "I know you're out there, and I know you felt relief at not having the courage to come forward and accept Christ as your savior. We'll sing another verse and give you one more chance to be saved." Without thinking about it, I left my seat and walked to the front of the church. The congregation rejoiced, and I was taken to a room behind the altar where I changed into white overalls and stepped down into the baptismal pool with the preacher. The curtains parted, and the preacher said, "I baptize thee in the name of the Father, the Son, and the Holy Ghost," placed his hand over my nose and lowered me completely under the water. When I came up, I didn't feel different; I didn't feel new; I didn't feel reborn. As I've told the story since that night, the only thing different was that my hair was wet. I was saved and lost in the same moment—saved because I went through the ritual, lost because it didn't take; I experienced it only physically, not emotionally or spiritually.

In some ways I was more emotionally invested in music than in religion. At sixteen I was a die-hard rock 'n' roll fan. Rhythm and blues, rockabilly, and rock 'n' roll had already provided me with a revival experience, and not just me but millions of other teenagers. I can now admit what fundamentalist preachers were saying all along: rock 'n' roll was undermining faith (mine).

Or perhaps music was not so much undermining religion as replacing it with something else. I thought the experience I would have the night of my baptism would be more like the feeling I sometimes had listening to rock or rhythm and blues. The sounds coming from my 45 rpm record player and the radio, lo-fi as they were, carried me somewhere else.

During my baptism, I remained right there in the blond brick church on Highland Avenue at the corner of Threadneedle Street, where we lived in a white two-story house. The new self, cleansed of sin and one with Christ that I was supposed to be, just didn't happen. I missed my chance to become a new spiritual person at least partially because I had already created a new self listening to rhythm and blues and rock 'n' roll, one that was firmly grounded in the physical world, one directly related to my sexual development already in progress for several years. The music started the transformation, but I created a new self in my own imagination.

I had already been to another revival, a larger one involving thousands and then millions of teens listening to rock music and being transformed. The music freed us from our traps, largely imaginary but real to us. One of the differences between the baptism into Christ and the one into rock 'n' roll was that friends and family were gently pushing me into the church, but no one tried to make me a rhythm and blues fan. I heard the message and responded. Family and church and school were trying to influence me in their direction, and that was one of the traps I was trying to escape or thought I needed to escape. The music was just out there, part of the sounds all around us; it felt free, and it made me feel free in ways that my religious revival experience had not.

The Three R's: Race, Rock, and Revival

The history of American vernacular music from the late forties onward can be seen as a series of revivals. There were rockabilly revivals in the seventies, eighties, and nineties, but the original birth of rock and rockabilly in the fifties was itself a musical revival. White and black singers and musicians were reviving and reinterpreting existing music while at the same time creating something new. This process had been going on for over a hundred years—black rhythm and blues and white country music can trace their roots directly to folk in the nineteenth century. Music revivals have had complex cultural, emotional, and psychological meanings all along. Inherent in revivals whether sacred or secular is a need to be someone else that originates in dissatisfaction with who you are. You look for a new spiritual self in religious revival, but in secular music revivals you look to an idealized past to find the model for your new identity, or you look at an other—a romanticized racial, ethnic, cultural, class, or regional group—for a new style and image.

Race is so important to American vernacular music revival and in the corresponding need for a new self that we need to examine its complexities in much more depth and detail. Black and white performers participated in the revival process in different ways in the 1950s. Big Mama Thornton, Ruth Brown, Ray Charles, Chuck Berry, Little Richard, and other African American singers and songwriters were a significant and essential part of the invention of rock 'n' roll, but since they were reinterpreting their own musical heritage—already a mixture of African and European music—they were not so much seeking a new identity as reshaping their own. But Elvis Presley, Jerry Lee Lewis, Carl Perkins, and other white male singers were imitating African American musical style and, on a deeper level, emulating an imagined black masculinity.

Part of rockabilly's appeal for white teenage boys was grounded in the same desire to be black that arose from dissatisfaction with their white middle- or working-class identity. When we listened and danced to the music, we were transformed into someone else. This transformative power is not just true of rockabilly and rock 'n' roll, though; all music revivals share this symbolic meaning—the folk music revival of the fifties, the blues revival of the sixties, the old-time string band revival of the seventies, the Americana alt-country roots revival of the early twenty-first century, and everything in between.

But the revival experience of rock 'n' roll in the fifties had the fullest racial and religious dimension in terms of the direct influence of African American gospel music. Thomas A. Dorsey was the most important figure in the creation of gospel, which was then developed by other singers and musicians who followed him. He began his musical career in secular music as a blues piano player known as Georgia Tom, and he later produced a new style of religious music by merging blues and jazz elements with Christian hymns. Dorsey was born in Georgia in 1899 and later moved to Chicago, where he became the music leader of the Pilgrim Baptist Church from the 1930s to the 1970s. His innovative compositions were recorded by white country and western singers such as Red Foley, who made "Peace in the Valley" a hit, and by the great gospel singer Mahalia Jackson, who immortalized "Take My Hand Precious Lord." The generation of singers, songwriters, and musicians who developed rhythm and blues and rock 'n' roll in the fifties—Ray Charles, Little Richard, Elvis Presley, and Jerry Lee Lewis, among others—were profoundly influenced by Dorsey's music.

Little Richard was steeped in the gospel music of the Seventh-Day Adventist Church he grew up in, and his breakthrough recordings of "Tutti-Frutti," "Long Tall Sally," and "Lucille" are filled with gospel intensity. He secularized his gospel influences with sexual lyrics and his own exotic personality to the point that a teenage listener like me was barely aware of the church source. Ray Charles, on the other hand, expressed his gospel origins more directly in his singing and his piano playing, although I wasn't aware at the time of how religious it was. Gospel was there in the first Ray Charles song I remember hearing, "I Got a Woman" in 1954, but only many years later did I realize that you could substitute *Jesus* for *woman* and *He* for *she* in the lyrics and make it a religious song. "I got Jesus," "He's good to me," and in the last stanza:

Ah don't you know He's alright
Ah don't ya know He's alright
He's alright He's alright
Oh yeah oh yeah oh.
(Transcribed by the author)

By 1958 Ray Charles overtly and very consciously linked gospel, rock 'n' roll, and emotional intensity together in "Yes Indeed." The structure of the song is the traditional African American call-and-response pattern with Ray calling out a line and the Raylettes responding with "Yes indeed." The song opens with a very churchy sounding organ, and the gospel-like emotion of a rock 'n' roll performance is stated directly in the lyrics:

Well I know (Yes indeed)
If it hits you (Yes indeed)
. . . .
You'll get a feeling down in your soul
Every time you hear that good ol' rock and roll.

This could be about feeling the Christian spirit until the last three words of the last line. The horn section of the band responds gospel-like on some of the lines, but a sexual-sounding sax solo in the middle, as well as the reference to "good ol' rock and roll" in the last line, reminds us of the secular nature of the experience.

Ray describes one of the ways to express the ecstasy of the moment: "I know you'll dance all over the floor" and "You will be jumping til' they close the door." When I was sixteen, the song made me dance all over the floor of my room until my mother closed the door to keep the "noise" from the rest of the house. The music made teenagers feel what he was describing in the lyrics, and we expressed it with our bodies as we listened. It was the closest thing to a religious experience I had ever felt—"down in your soul."

"Yes Indeed" is also related to rockabilly songs that celebrated their own music and dancing. We could call this meta–rock 'n' roll or meta-R&B, in which the lyrics of the song refer to the kind of music it is. Just as literary critics call fiction about fiction "metafiction," in the musical case, meta-rock music was self–referential— celebrating itself in the lyrics, causing listeners to act out what was being described in the songs and demanded by the music. Except that rockabilly songs like "There's Good Rockin' Tonight," "Whole Lotta Shakin' Going On," and "Tear It Up," while influenced by gospel, are all more secular in words and music. Ray Charles was the first to express the parallels between religious music and rock 'n' roll directly and the first to use gospel to evoke a similar secular revival response in his listeners.

"Yes Indeed" was not the first time a Ray Charles song had used gospel to make white kids experience something new. In 1954, at age thirteen, when I first danced the dirty bop to "I Got a Woman" (significantly not too long after my sexual awakening), I was feeling not like myself as I had existed up to that point but like someone else, someone I didn't recognize, someone who wanted on an unconscious level to be black. All the evidence of African American cultural difference is there in Ray Charles's voice, in the rhythm of the music, in the saxophone solo, and in the lyrics. We teenage fans imagined this as racial difference in a biological sense, un-aware that what we heard was the result of hundreds of years of cultural history going back to Africa and mixed with European Christianity. Race was part of our white cultural background, which led us to observe black people and imagine them as different biologically, often as inferior, but it was also part of a cultural process that went back to the first contacts between black and white people during the history of colonialism. But in 1954 in the South, the music was imagined as expressing racial difference more than cultural.

Despite our awareness of racial difference, the lyrics sung by African Americans somehow sounded familiar to us in ways that made the transference of imagined black identity easier: "I got a woman way cross town that's good to me."

It seems obvious now that this quintessential African American song shares an attitude toward women with other kinds of European American vernacular music, with rockabilly and popular culture in general, and it is obviously sexist from a postfeminist perspective. "I Got a Woman" is grounded in black experience, but black music was already a hybrid of black and white influences.

The musical sound of "I Got a Woman" is most obviously derived from black gospel and rhythm and blues, but Ray Charles was also influenced by white pop crooners and early on emulated Nat King Cole's white-influenced style. Charles had absorbed white country music as he grew up, something most of us were not aware of until we heard *Modern Sounds in Country and Western* (ABC-Paramount, ABC-410) in 1962 even though he had given us hints with his earlier cover of Hank Snow's "I'm Movin' On." (He has also listed swing bandleader Artie Shaw and country music singer/songwriter Willie Nelson among his musical favorites in the liner notes to *Ray Charles: Music That Matters to Him* (Hear Music, OPCD-1991, 2003). The racial divide was not as great as we thought it was; "they" weren't as radically different as we imagined, and the racial boundary was permeable through a history of cross-cultural influences and social and sexual interactions including during slavery.

The white desire to be black was based on white perceptions of blackness, not on the reality of black life. The music sprang from black experience, but when white kids heard it, we imagined something else, a pure, primitive, unrestrained sexuality, pleasures we thought were denied us by our white middle-class inhibitions. When I and my friends first heard Ray Charles sing the country song "I Can't Stop Loving You" in college, we liked it and the other songs on *Modern Sounds in Country and Western*, but we also thought Ray Charles had sold out and preferred the earlier Atlantic-label Ray with an R&B band and the Raylettes to the ABC/Paramount Ray with lush strings and a chorus, conveniently forgetting that he had also recorded with strings on Atlantic (side 2 of *The Genius of Ray Charles*, Atlantic, SD 1312, 1962). From the perspective of our imagined blackness, his music was now too white. By romanticizing black life as pure freedom from puritanical restrictions, we overlooked the fact that black people and white people had always interacted, and that there was no pure black or pure white either racially or culturally.

Most American music revivals have always had a racial dimension. Even the seemingly white folk music revival of the late fifties and early sixties depended on a racialized concept of the folk (see chapter 6). When I first heard the Kingston Trio sing "Tom Dooley" in my junior year of high school, I didn't know that the song was a traditional ballad that had been sung earlier by Frank Proffitt from the Appalachian Mountains of North Carolina, but I knew it was folk music. It was the first song that defined folk music for many of my generation, and even though it was never stated, on some level we knew that it was "white" folk music. So how could the folk revival have anything to do with race except on the most obvious level that white and black folk singers, including Josh White, Brownie McGhee, Odetta, Bob Dylan, and Dave Von Ronk, sang blues?

The connection is in the unstated and unacknowledged dynamic interaction between our assumptions about whiteness and blackness. Black creates white and white creates black and have done so since the beginning of American slavery. African American novelist Toni Morrison expresses this eloquently in her book *Playing in the Dark*. She starts from the premise that racial difference is not biological fact but culturally imagined. There are physical differences, including skin color, among different groups of people in the world, but these differences are strictly surface. As Mollie Ford, an elderly black woman I interviewed in southern Ohio in 1978, said, "There ain't but one race created on earth, and that's the human race." Our DNA is the same; there is no scientific support for dividing humans on the bases of these superficial differences. Just look at the shades of skin colors and try to mark the exact boundary where one race ends and another begins.

Once we have established this scientific fact, all the stereotypes about difference based on race become imaginary. There are differences in intelligence among humans, but they have nothing to do with race; some people dance better than others, but that has nothing to do with race. Rather, we dance better or have a better sense of rhythm based on cultural factors—for instance, whether we listen to rhythmic dance music within the cultural groups we grow up with. The racial superiority of black people as dancers and the racial inferiority of black people as primitive are both white social constructions, to use some of the scholarly jargon.

There are, then, *cultural* differences between people of different skin colors and other physical features, and these cultural factors are often misinterpreted as *racial* in a biological sense. As I mentioned earlier, the stereotype that black people have "natural rhythm" suggests that this trait is biologically inherent when it is actually culturally learned. This fact seems obvious, but it still persists as a white perception of blackness. This misperception seems positive, but underneath lurks a remnant of primitivism, black as exotic other and ultimately more animalistic than white. Not all black people are good dancers; it depends on cultural and social background. Did they grow up in a home where dance music was on the radio or stereo and they were held up as babies and moved in time to the music? Or did they grow up in a home where classical music was played and they took ballet lessons? Cultural difference is sometimes based on class difference within the black community, or white or brown communities. African American culture is not monolithic but is made up of many different cultures. Again, this seems obvious but has to be stated because racial stereotypes persist.

In the early seventies, I knew a black couple who exemplified this cultural and class difference. Nate was a lawyer and Hyacinth was a college professor, but they came from different social-class backgrounds (names and places have been changed). She grew up in a professional family in Baltimore, and he grew up in a working-class family in Ohio. Nate loved the blues, and we often listened to Albert King's album *King of the Blues Guitar* (Atlantic, SD 8213, 1969) and other blues records on his state-of-the-art stereo. Hyacinth grew up in a home where blues was considered lower class, and her parents discouraged her from listening to it. As part of our education in the blues, we all went to hear a B. B. King concert on the Ohio State Fairgrounds, and Nate and I went backstage to talk with B. B. King while Hyacinth stayed in our seats. On another occasion, they invited me over for dinner one night when Hyacinth was learning how to cook one of Nate's favorite dishes, chitlins. She and I had never had them before, and neither of us was converted. By the way, they were both good dancers.

In some sense, because of their different class backgrounds, Hyacinth was "whiter" than Nate, but we all understood that to mean cultural socioeconomic-class whiteness, not as biologically race-based. By the same token, his "blackness" was culturally learned. You can see from this example that cultural assumptions about different races interacted; one was dependent on the other. Hyacinth and Nate perceived me in racial/cultural terms as part of defining themselves, and I did the same—my whiteness was at least partially defined in contrast to their blackness. And music and dancing and food were ways we expressed our cultural differences and similarities.

That brings us back to Morrison's point about white creating black and black creating white: racial identity is based in culture and is determined through an oppositional process. As I said earlier, people often consider these cultural traits to be biological, and thus racial concepts of black and white determine each other. White as "civilized" depends on black as "primitive"; the stereotype of black as inherently criminal implies white as inherently lawful. All of this is directly relevant to white teenagers' need for a new identity because so often the teen's new self was based on an imagined blackness that was exotic and outside white middle-class conventions. Finally, one of Morrison's most important ideas is that this process is part of the creation of what we conceive as American. And I would add that imagining whiteness and blackness is also the key to understanding American vernacular music and how teenagers found a new identity in a new music that was really hundreds of years old.

"Hang Down Your Head, Tom Dooley": Whiteness and Revival

"Tom Dooley" was white, the Kingston Trio was white, and most of the teenagers and college students who made the song a hit were white. Although it was unspoken and likely subconscious, folkies attracted to traditional Anglo music were drawn to the identification with pure whiteness, a purity that existed in the imagined past. The new identities they sought existed not within ethnic or racial groups in the present, as they did for fifties rock and R&B fans, but in their own Anglo-Saxon past (also an imagined identity). The whiteness of the performers, audience, and subjects of "Tom Dooley" was never stated because whiteness is the assumed "norm" in American culture, a norm so pervasive that it does not need to be expressed overtly. "Tom Dooley" is an old American ballad from the Appalachian Mountains, and in the American imagination, Appalachian equals white. No need to say it; it just is.

Despite the historical facts of large minority populations of African Americans, eastern European ethnic groups, and American Indians, the Appalachian region until recently has been imagined as an Anglo-American enclave—more British than the British Isles, an isolated area that has retained archaic speech: ancient English, Irish, and Scottish ballads and old British folk tales. The mountain musical tradition gave birth to hillbilly music through such performers as Clarence Ashley, Gid Tanner and the

Skillet Lickers, and the Carter Family—singers and musicians who along with southern flatlanders such as Jimmie Rodgers established the foundation for American country music. That is only part of the history though; it leaves out black Piedmont blues singers and guitarists such as John Cephas and Archie Edwards and black banjo and fiddle players like Dink Roberts, Odell Thompson, and Joe Thompson, who continued African American tradition in the mountains. All were unintentionally neglected or ignored in cultural representations of the region, thus maintaining the popular image of Appalachia as pure Anglo-Saxon and, without saying it, white.

I think we can generalize from this regional, cultural, and musical example to all American vernacular music. Many genres of popular music are not labeled as white but are assumed to be because they are not associated with black or other racial groups despite African American influence on them. This would include Broadway show tunes, popular love songs, country, bluegrass, and polka and other European ethnic music. Some of the qualities associated with these "white" genres take on meaning within a cultural context that contrasts them with qualities considered nonwhite, usually black, because of the pervasive popularity and influence of African American music on other genres. This simple dichotomy becomes a lot more complicated when we recognize how much African American music has affected everything else. Despite the influence of black music on blues and jazz especially but also on genres such as country and bluegrass, these genres continue to be thought of as white. Because rock 'n' roll was so directly and obviously derived from black rhythm and blues, it has continued to be thought of as a hybrid. The rise of rap and hip-hop as popular music has reinforced the blackness of rock 'n' roll even when performed by white singers and musicians. On the other hand, most music from the fifties folk revival was thought of as white, especially in the beginning.

The Kingston Trio was made up of three young, middle-class white men; two were from Hawaii and the other from California. Their button-down shirts and chino pants evoked the Ivy League for teenagers and college students in the fifties, and Ivy League schools suggested white Anglo-Saxon Protestant (for a fictional representation of this notion, read John Updike's 1964 short story "The Christian Roommates"). And as if the Kingston Trio's appearance wasn't white enough, the acoustic banjo and bass and the Appalachian melody of "Tom Dooley" sang out the performance's whiteness as did the references in the lyrics to Tennessee and the mountain where

Tom meets Laura Foster, the girl he later kills and whose murder he is condemned to die for.

I had never detected any African American sound in "Tom Dooley" until the early nineties, when I read an essay on the folk revival by Bob Cantwell: "'Tom Dooley' had a rhythmic shuffle and a vocal countermelody strongly reminiscent of rhythm and blues, and a pronounced syncopation in the lyric." The sound was also influenced by calypso music, which was popular at the time (this was pointed out to me by folk music scholar Stephen Wade). I listened to the record again, and I hear it now, but in 1958 when I was in the eleventh grade in Oakville, Ontario, and first heard "Tom Dooley," I thought of the song and the performance as the antithesis of the wild, drunken good times evoked by rhythm and blues, rockabilly, and calypso. "Going native" meant something different in the folk revival because at first the folk were imagined as white, which meant repressed instead of oppressed. The singing on "Tom Dooley" is sad and restrained in keeping with the moral of the story, "Poor boy you're bound to die," the opposite of the hedonistic anything-goes amorality of rockabilly and R&B songs like "Dixie Fried" and "Drinkin' Wine Spo-Dee-O-Dee" (see chapter 3).

I couldn't hear anything black in "Tom Dooley" because it sounded so unlike the songs on the 45s I was buying during my high school years such as "Sweet Little Sixteen," "Why Do Fools Fall in Love?," and "Bo Diddley." I preferred black music, and even though I liked "Tom Dooley," I never bought the record. It may have sounded "authentic" but not in the same way as Howlin' Wolf's "Smokestack Lightnin'," which was the opposite of the restrained singing and expression of emotion on "Tom Dooley." I listened to folk revival music on the radio and at parties, but if you couldn't dance to it, I didn't need to buy it. I was a rocker, not a folkie.

"That'll Be the Day": White Teenagers Make Rock 'n' Roll Their Own

In the early to mid-fifties, white teenagers of my age and aesthetic sensibilities were listening mainly to black R&B, but gradually as more white singers started singing rockabilly and covers of R&B songs and writing songs of their own, our music became more like us. Race was still a significant factor, but the norm of whiteness began to envelop the music we identified with. Pretty quickly African American singers such as Ray Charles, Big Joe

Turner, Chuck Berry, Bo Diddley, and Little Richard were joined by the Anglo-American Elvis Presley, Gene Vincent, Buddy Holly, and the Everly Brothers in the pantheon of rock 'n' roll favorites.

In junior high we danced to Johnny Ace ("the late and great"), the Clovers, the Charms, and Big Joe Turner—all black singers and groups. The white imitators were just starting, and the first one I remember hearing was Bill Haley and the Comets, who caused a sensation with "Rock around the Clock" in the 1955 movie *Blackboard Jungle*, when I was thirteen—a big year for me with my first dance, first date, and first kiss all wrapped up in the merging of sexuality and music. I can't convey in words the electricity that ran through that Baytown, Texas, movie theater full of teenagers when "Rock around the Clock" was played. We already knew Ray Charles and the rest, but this was something new because it was white guys playing it. I loved "Rock around the Clock" so much that I asked my older sister Carol to buy the record for me even though I didn't have a record player. The record was a 78 and broke before I was given a record player, but I soon replaced it with a 45 followed by hundreds more of those round black vinyl saucers (you could fly them across the room with a quickly developed backhand sweep) through junior high and high school.

Radio was the most important influence on my likes, and there was a radio station in Baytown that mainly played black rhythm and blues at night. All the kids I knew listened to it. I guess this was pre–rock 'n' roll, during a brief period when we were not listening to white covers of the songs because our favorite local radio station played only African American R&B. It was Hank Ballard and the Midnighters' explicit version of "Work with Me Annie" and not the cleaned-up cover by Georgia Gibbs, "Dance with Me Henry." I don't think there was a white cover of Big Joe Turner's "Shake, Rattle, and Roll" with these lines: "You're wearin' that dress, the sun comes shinin' through / I can't believe my eyes all that mess belongs to you."

I liked LaVern Baker, Ruth Brown, and other women R&B singers and even some white women pop singers, but not with the same intensity as I liked Ray Charles and Elvis Presley. It was musical male bonding, identifying with them and their singing in a way that I couldn't with women singers. So part of what I'm talking about here is the significance of gender in trying to understand music, especially R&B and rock 'n' roll. As I was passing from childhood into adolescence, I was finding models for masculinity in the music I was listening to, in the singing, the music, the lyrics, and the movements on stage.

The first rockabilly singers were six or seven years older than I was, but we shared a fascination with African American music and culture. This is where the personal and the cultural connect; I was one of hundreds of thousands of white teenagers who were attracted to African American music in the early fifties, and the number grew to the millions when white singers started to imitate black styles and sing rhythm and blues songs. Pat Boone and other white singers were important in this growth from a regional vernacular music to a national pop culture phenomenon, but I think there were many white teenagers like me who rejected the watered-down pop versions of black songs and grabbed onto rockabilly as an acceptable reinvention of the form. I loved Carl Perkins's version of Chuck Berry's "Roll Over Beethoven," but as I said in chapter 1, I hated Pat Boone's cover of Little Richard's "Tutti Frutti." Maybe we thought Pat Boone was a little "fruity," or that he didn't have the edge that was defining masculinity for us (doubly ironic given Little Richard's ambiguous gender style). In this preference for "the real thing," I was caught up in the cultural romanticizing of African American life that was already a part of popular music, movies, and fiction in the fifties—Marlon Brando's cool in *The Wild One*, James Dean's in *Rebel without a Cause*, and Sal Paradise's yearning to be black in *On the Road* (see chapter 3).

Rock, R&B, blues, doo-wop, rockabilly—the categories didn't consciously mean that much to me in the mid- and late fifties; the important thing was that the music grabbed you, and you could dance to it. As the kids on *American Bandstand* always used to say, "It's got a good beat. I give it an 85." We danced to black and white singers, to Bo Diddley and Buddy Holly, the Everly Brothers and Chuck Berry, Frankie Lymon and the Teenagers and Dion and the Belmonts. By the second half of the fifties, rock 'n' roll was coming from all over the country, from Long Island to Lubbock to Los Angeles and back again. Some of my fifties favorites included the singers and songwriters who were later recognized as unique and innovative, the ones who invented something new out of something old, the ones who influenced everything that followed in the sixties including the Beatles, James Brown, the Beach Boys, Aretha Franklin, the Rolling Stones, and Marvin Gaye. My response to fifties R&B and rock 'n' roll was probably typical of most kids my age, and on some level it was related to race, revival, and my shifting identity. Ray Charles started it for me, but Chuck Berry soon took over because he was so good at writing great songs that both captured and created my teenage emotions, first with "Brown-Eyed Handsome Man" and then with "School Days."

The "Brown-Eyed Handsome Man" Goes Back to "School Days"

The first song I remember hearing by Chuck Berry was "Oh, Maybellene" when I was in junior high in Newark, Delaware, in 1956, but the one that imprinted on my soul was "Brown-Eyed Handsome Man." In the tenth grade at South Park High School in Beaumont in 1957, around the same time I first heard Buddy Holly and was baptized, they let us dance in the gym during lunch break, and the high school DJ played "Brown-Eyed Handsome Man" every day. Because we had moved back to Beaumont in the middle of the school year, I didn't know many other kids; I don't remember knowing any girls, and I was too shy to ask one of them to dance anyway. I stood on the sidelines feeling like I was dancing, moving around just a little bit, and imagining that I was the brown-eyed handsome man. I "hit a high fly into the stand / Rounding third I was headed for home / I was a brown-eyed handsome man." I knew Chuck Berry was black, but I imagined that the brown-eyed man was white because he was me.

I'm sure there were black teenage boys dancing to the song at that same moment at Charlton-Pollard and Hebert High Schools just a couple of miles away across the railroad tracks to the northeast and the west, and that they were imagining themselves as the hero of the song (and Mexican American teenagers in South Texas and Asian Americans in Southern California). Looking back and knowing how talented Chuck Berry was as a songwriter and performer, how aware he was of his audiences, I think he must have known that the hero of the song was both black and white simultaneously. He had integrated his audience on some unconscious, imaginative level even as the entire country was starting to be influenced by the early civil rights movement. Rock 'n' roll and rhythm and blues were starting to change a generation of white teenagers and in many ways preparing them for the social and political shifts of the sixties.

Chuck Berry was the right age to be the "Brown-Eyed Handsome Man" (thirty in 1956, when the record was released), but he had a knack as a songwriter to imagine what it was like to be a teenager. In the summer of 1957, could any song fit a teenager's life better than "School Days"? That summer Daddy had my brother, Bubba, and me help him fix up our house on Threadneedle Street in Beaumont. Houses along the Gulf Coast back then were built on blocks because the ground was so swampy, and our house had begun to sink, so Daddy jacked it up and had a truckload of dirt dumped next to the house. Bubba and I crawled underneath to spread it one shovelful at a time. He also painted the house that summer, and we scraped the old paint off one of the few two-story houses (to our regret) in the neighborhood. While we worked, I had a portable radio outside playing the hits on deejay J. P. Richardson's KTRM radio show. The song that had the most meaning for me that summer was "School Days":

> Up in the mornin' and out to school
> The teacher is teachin' the Golden Rule
> American history and practical math
> You study 'em hard hopin' to pass.
> (Transcribed by the author)

I could identify with that and feel the need to escape, whether it was from sitting in the classroom or from scraping paint off the house, and Chuck Berry's song was an imaginative escape in both its music and its lyrics:

> Soon as three o'clock rolls around
> You finally lay your burden down
> Close up your books, get out of your seat
> Down the halls and into the street
> Up to the corner and 'round the bend
> Right to the juke joint you go in.
>
> Drop the coin right into the slot
> You gotta hear something that's really hot
> With the one you love you're makin' romance
> All day long you been wantin' to dance
> Feelin' the music from head to toe
> 'Round and 'round and 'round you go

And then at the end, it became an anthem:

> Hail, hail rock 'n' roll
> Deliver me from the days of old
> Long live rock 'n' roll
> The beat of the drum is loud and bold
> Rock, rock, rock 'n' roll
> The feelin' is there body and soul.

Clearly one of those "meta-rock" songs—the line "Deliver me from the days of old" says a lot about the appeal of rock 'n' roll: rejection of the old, escape to the new. Unlike the folkies, who sought their new identities in the Anglo-Saxon past, we rockers loved the present moment of imagined African American abandon. Like Ray Charles in "Yes Indeed," Chuck Berry tapped into the teenage desire to escape through music, through our music, rock 'n' roll. Dancing was a physical escape that was also spiritual: "The feelin' is there body and soul." This was yet another experience that shows how much rock 'n' roll music was like a religious revival for me and other teenagers. Ray and Chuck were no longer teenagers, but they were imaginative, creative, market savvy, and able to connect with teenage consciousness—in spite of the racial and cultural differences between African American performers and Anglo-American fans.

Chuck Berry died on March 18, 2017. The obituaries all recognized his role as one of the founders of rock 'n' roll and his importance as an inventor of rock electric-guitar style. I dug out my Chuck Berry CDs and played all his numerous hits as my private tribute to him. "Long live rock 'n' roll."

· · ·

Then along came a white singer just out of his teens who appealed more directly to white teenagers. The first time I heard Buddy Holly was when he was the lead singer in a group called the Crickets, and the song was "That'll Be the Day." It made such an impression on me that I remember the exact setting. My whole family was in the car on the way to Rettig's ice cream parlor on Park Street in Beaumont. I was in the tenth grade, and it was 1957, the same year when I was almost saved at the Highland Avenue Church of Christ, which we drove by on the way to Rettig's. I remember the lyrics vividly.

> You say you're gonna leave me,
> You know that's a lie
> Cause that'll be the day ay ay when I die.
> (Transcribed by the author)

They were tough lyrics with the threat apparent in Buddy Holly's voice. I had never heard anything so emotionally complex in a love song, and I'm not sure I fully understood it at the time, but that edge was part of the appeal. When I heard the song, I immediately recognized the link to rockabilly. Buddy Holly had recorded another song earlier, "Rock Around with Ollie Vee," which is perfect rockabilly with all sorts of Elvis vocal effects. It even has the typical meta-rockabilly self-reference—"Ollie Vee comes from Memphis, Memphis,

Tennessee" and "I'm gonna wear my blue suede shoes tonight." But other qualities in "That'll Be the Day" went beyond rockabilly—the ringing guitar; Buddy Holly's vocal, which sounded younger and fresher than Elvis and Carl, more like a teenager's voice; and something else, what I later thought of as more pop than Memphis rockabilly, most apparent in the "wooo" at the end of a line that later reemerged in the Beatles. And that pop sound came out even more in two of his other hits, "Everyday" and "Peggy Sue."

The teenage quality was part of the appeal, and I know now that it was easier for me to identify with Buddy Holly because he was white. His style was white, even nerdy, although I don't think the word had been invented yet. He wore horn-rimmed glasses and so did I; he sang about his longing for a girlfriend in ways that expressed exactly what I was feeling. And the fact that he was from Lubbock, Texas, where Bubba and I went to see Gene Autry movies in the second grade, made me feel that much closer to him. Hearing Buddy Holly records took me away; the song coming from the car radio on the way to get ice cream made me forget everything else in ways that my baptism a few months later did not.

"Sweet Little Sixteen"

We moved from Beaumont, Texas, USA, to Oakville, Ontario, Canada, in the fall of 1957, as I was beginning the eleventh grade. I was still a Buddy Holly fan and had accumulated nine of his 45s; I know it was nine records because I still have them. It was February 3, 1959, in the middle of my senior year, when I heard the news on the radio about the plane crash that killed Buddy Holly, Richie Valens, and the Big Bopper. I owned 45s by all three of them—most of Buddy Holly's records, Valens's "La Bamba"/"Oh Donna," and the Big Bopper's "Chantilly Lace." I felt as if I knew the Big Bopper, whose real name was J. P. Richardson, because he was from Beaumont and had been my favorite disc jockey back in the tenth grade. He had an afternoon radio show on KTRM as himself and a late afternoon hour as the Big Bopper.

Race was an obvious factor in Richardson's performance; when he played the Big Bopper, his voice became an exaggerated mimicry of black dialect, a throwback to Amos and Andy of the 1930s and '40s radio, especially of King-fish, whose "Oh, Sapphire, what I gonna do?" became "Oh, baby, you know what I like" in "Chantilly Lace." While we were in Beaumont, Richardson tried to break some kind of radio marathon record by broadcasting for six days without sleep. Before it was over, he became punchy and incoherent, and I felt sorry for him, the frail person behind the boisterous and outrageous Big Bopper character. I loved his Big Bopper show not so much for the dialect act but because he played mostly African American music—the Coasters, Ray Charles, Little Richard, and Fats Domino. I liked "Chantilly Lace" and I bought it, but I knew it for what it was, a novelty act, obvious mimicry, and not the real thing.

Two Texans I felt close to died in that plane crash; the third singer on the plane was a Mexican American from Southern California whom I didn't know as well, but Richie Valens's song "La Bamba" got me interested in Mexican music and paved the way for my later love of conjunto (see chapter 8) and the Latino rock 'n' roll of Los Lobos. Several months after the deaths of Holly, Valens, and Richardson, a rock 'n' roll show came to Oakville, and I heard that it was the continuation of the Buddy Holly tour. The concert was held in the town hockey rink, and I was excited about hearing Jimmy Clanton, who was from Baton Rouge, where I had been in the eighth grade and whose hit "Just a Dream" I liked. But I ended up being disappointed; Clanton was fine, but the Kallen Twins were too much like the fake rockers I had already rejected, and I couldn't help thinking about missing out on Buddy Holly live. I never knew if the concert was really a continuation of the previous tour, although I read later that after the plane crash Jimmy Clanton and Frankie Avalon did finish out the "Winter Dance Party" tour in the upper Midwest with Holly's backup band and Dion and the Belmonts.

Listening to a rock concert while standing on the ice in a skating rink was a new experience for me, and so was Blakelock High School in Oakville. Influenced by the British educational system, it was more formal than South Park High School in Beaumont. The school color at both places was green, but it was the South Park "Greenies" and the Blakelock "Green Gaels." I'm sure most of my classmates in Beaumont didn't know what a Gael was, and neither did I until I moved to Canada. The Canadian students had different styles and interests and seemed more preppy to me, but there were still plenty of kindred spirits who were big rock 'n' roll fans. I heard new singers after we moved to Canada, but some of my old favorites continued to grab my attention. Besides Buddy Holly's 45s, I still bought the new Chuck Berry records.

In the spring of 1958, I was on the high school track team, ran the 440-yard relay, and was also a shot putter. I was the slowest guy on the relay team, but at 6 feet 2 and two hundred pounds not a bad shotputter, and I worked hard at it, physically and mentally. I watched the Olympic champion Parry O'Brien on film and tried to emulate the technique he had invented earlier in the fifties. At the district meet, it all came together, and I put the shot several feet farther than I ever had before. It felt so good; I knew it was my personal best even before they measured it—good enough for third place and the only medal I ever won in the shot put.

Afterward on that beautiful, sunshiny spring day, my teammates and I were lying around on the grass in the infield with the girls' team lounging nearby when "Sweet Little Sixteen" came on the transistor radio. I and the song and the moment were one; I had never felt better in my life. Just as the brown-eyed handsome man was the perfect me, sweet little sixteen was the perfect girl, "tight dresses and lipstick, sportin' high heel shoes"—the unabashed sexism of fifties teenage masculinity. Today, educated in feminism, I'm not so likely to objectify girls or women, although any honest liberated man of a certain age will admit to remnants of those reactions—the adolescent within.

There was another kind of escape in "Sweet Little Sixteen," one related to the wide world that was waiting out there. I liked Canada and my Canadian friends a lot, but I longed to go back to the United States when I heard Chuck sing,

> 'Cause they'll be rockin' on Bandstand in Philadelphia, PA.
> Deep in the heart of Texas, and round the 'Frisco Bay
> All over St. Louis, way down in New Orleans
> All the cats wanna dance with Sweet Little Sixteen.
> (Transcribed by the author)

I had never been to 'Frisco or St. Louis, but I had been to and loved the other two cities. I had visited New Orleans many times with my family when I was thirteen and we lived in Baton Rouge. We would wander around the French Quarter and go to the Audubon Zoo. And when we lived in Delaware, when I was fourteen, we drove up to Philadelphia to see my first Major League baseball game, the Phillies playing at the old Connie Mack Stadium. And when family came to visit from Texas, we would go see the Liberty Bell at Independence Hall. Finally, of course, listening to "Sweet Little Sixteen" I also yearned to be back deep in the heart of Texas. The song also offered the fantasy appeal of going to San Francisco to see the Golden Gate Bridge and to St. Louis to watch the riverboats go down the Mississippi. To me the place names in "Sweet Little Sixteen" conjured up the cities on an imaginary map of the United States and made me want to see all of them. America was where people were dancing in the streets, where the sweet little sixteens were always ready to dance.

Teenagers were dancing in Canada too, but things were definitely different. In some ways race seemed to have disappeared. Oakville was an all-white suburb of Toronto, and as far as I remember, we never saw any black people. For a southern white kid like me, there were still the black singers and musicians in rock 'n' roll and R&B. I think my tastes tended toward African American performers more than most of my friends. I was the DJ at high school dances and brought my own records, which included plenty of R&B hits, which were just as popular in Canada as they were in the United States. I would put the needle in the groove and jump off the auditorium stage onto the floor, where Judy Brown was waiting to dance (see chapter 4). She had learned my variation of the Texas bop, totally alien to everyone else in our Toronto suburb, although they may have noticed the similarity between my dancing and Elvis Presley's moves on stage. Once at a party, I even did an impression of Elvis singing "I Got a Woman" with a broom handle as my microphone stand that was filmed by one of my friends, Isabel Agnew. Somewhere there may still be a home movie of my Elvis gyrations. Not a bad example of taking on a new identity through emulation of different musical styles at an amateur level. Elvis was one of the first white rock 'n' roll singers to absorb black rhythm and blues and to demonstrate it in his singing and performance, a model for fifties white teenage boys who felt that unconscious need for a new identity.

The other kids didn't know rhythm and blues and the black side of rock 'n' roll as well as I did, and they didn't have my record collection acquired in Texas and Delaware, closer to the southern and black roots of the music; some of my 45s were on obscure labels like Gee and weren't even available in Canada, where most records from the States ended up on different labels such as Apex and Quality. There were no black students at Blakelock High School, and I became an expert on black music and played the role to the hilt, never hesitant to express my opinion about the superiority of black performers to the watered-down Pat Boones, Fabians, and Frankie Avalons. On some unexpressed, partially unconscious level, I was following the widespread unarticulated cultural pattern of defining white in relation to black, and white was lacking. White must have seemed puritanical to me, not a word I would have used then, but one that now seems appropriate when talking about white as repressed and black as free—"freedom" in a different sense, but still sadly ironic given the history of slavery and oppression of black people in America.

There was an underlying racial tension, then, in North American popular music in the fifties, one that continues to this very day. Black rhythm and blues and rockabilly and rock music derived from it were either condemned as primitive and animalistic or celebrated as energetic and unrestrained. Both interpretations were grounded in previous racial attitudes of black as exotic other, both reinforced existing stereotypes, and both images of blackness were inextricably intertwined with images of whiteness. Some of the nation's educated elite may have had a condescending view of country music, bluegrass, folk revival, and European ethnic, but the music was safe because it was white. The white performers who emulated black styles were either seen as threatening or embraced as avatars of a new identity for rebellious white teenagers, and rockabilly had provided the rebellious masculine model for the rock music that followed.

CHAPTER 3

Let's All Get Dixie Fried

*Sexuality, Masculinity,
Race, and Rockabilly*

Bobby Caruso, Susie Singleton, and Me

The cool, alienated outsider was part of the zeitgeist in the United States in the 1950s. The white hipster borrowed his cool style from black masculinity, and Jack Kerouac drew on his own experiences as a hipster in the late forties to chronicle what came to be called the Beat Generation. His fictional characters in *On the Road*, Sal Paradise and Dean Moriarty, were based on himself and his close friend Neal Cassady. He wrote *On the Road* in 1951, but it wasn't published until 1957, too late to influence the early development of the outsider image; however, movies were depicting cool, alienated young men in the mid-fifties. *The Wild One* with Marlon Brando as a rebel motorcycle-gang leader came out in 1954 and was followed in 1955 by James Dean as the protagonist in *Rebel without a Cause*.

For me and other adolescents in the fifties, cool models of masculinity were found in movies and music more than in written fiction. I saw movies about rebels and cool guys when they came out but didn't read books like *On the Road* until I was in college in the early sixties. Rockabilly provided the musical equivalents of young rebels in Elvis Presley, who was the first; Jerry Lee Lewis, who broke all the rules; and Gene Vincent, who was, as *The Rolling Stone Encyclopedia* succinctly puts it, "darker, tougher, greasier than Elvis." Sure, Elvis was a mama's boy and not as rebellious as we imagined at first, but the first impression was of someone who rejected our parents' and teachers' beliefs and values and did it in a way that attracted teenage girls.

James Dean's portrayal of the rebel without a cause was a special favorite of rockabilly performers and fans. We teenage boys began to imitate his style and looks from the movie. I was probably typical when I started wearing a white T-shirt with a red nylon jacket right after I saw James Dean's character wearing that outfit, and I daydreamed about wearing a black leather jacket and riding a motorcycle after seeing Marlon Brando in *The Wild One*. I wore the nylon jacket for a long time but lost my enthusiasm for motorcycles when in the fifth grade I met an older boy who walked with a pronounced limp from a motorcycle accident.

In 1954, when I was thirteen and in the eighth grade at Istrouma Junior High in Baton Rouge, my best friend, Bobby Caruso, was *the* cool cat. He was a year older and wore his Levi's low with a tucked-in, tight white T-shirt, his greasy hair swept up in a pompadour with a "ducktail" in back (also known as a "DA" or "duck's ass"), with a cigarette dangling from his lips. He was smart but indifferent to school, and the girls loved him. His father worked for the same construction company as my father so we got to see each other fairly often outside school. I started to emulate him as model of teenage masculinity in dress and hairstyle, but the cigarettes were what got me in trouble. Bobby was teaching me how to inhale instead of just "nigger lipping" the cigarette: in Baton Rouge in 1954, casual racism was part of the fabric of white social behavior.

I stole a pack of Camels from my father, and he found them in my desk and asked me where I got them. "From Bobby Caruso" (he was one of those people you always referred to by both names). My father caught me in the lie because he always bought his cigarettes on trips back to Beaumont, where they were cheaper, and his Camels had a Texas sales-tax stamp. I got a whippin' for lying, not for smoking, but the lesson stayed with me. I never smoked cigarettes again. Except for wearing my Levi's low and using Wildroot Cream Oil on my slicked-back pompadour, the Camels episode was about the extent of my adolescent rebellious behavior, but I continued to romanticize the cool teenage rebel and was ready for Elvis and the other hillbilly hipsters when they came along.

I left Baton Rouge and Bobby Caruso behind in the middle of the eighth grade when we moved for another job in Baytown, Texas, toward the end of 1954. I took all my adolescent ideas about coolness with me, and I was still trying to attract a cute girl by imitating Bobby Caruso. My new school was Horace Mann Junior High School, where I met Susie Singleton (not her real name), who was a cute drum majorette. Wow, she was "just a dream," as Jimmy Clanton later sang in his hit song. I had dreamed about cheer-leaders and majorettes from afar, never expecting to know one personally.

Then to my total surprise and delight one of Susie's girlfriends told me, in that time-honored junior-high way, "Susie likes you." I was still too shy to approach her, but Susie asked me out on a date.

How lucky could a thirteen-year-old boy be? I had never been on a date, much less with a majorette, and didn't know how to drive anyway, but she had a learner's permit. My mother said, "No." My grandmother Nanny, who was staying with us said, "Let him go." My mother agreed, but only if we didn't actually drive anywhere. It was a double date, and the boyfriend of Susie's girlfriend was older and had a regular driver's license, so he drove his car. They parked in front of our house. I went out, got in the back seat with Susie, and we sat in the car for I can't remember how long—fifteen minutes, an hour? They were making out in the front seat, and I awkwardly attempted to kiss Susie. I kissed her for the first time, clumsy and excited, and after that I didn't know what else to do.

I had one more "date" with her. Her girlfriend arranged for us to meet at the movie theater (where we all first saw *Blackboard Jungle*). We arrived separately, her girlfriend had me sit next to Susie, and the movie started; it was *Battle Cry* with Van Heflin, Aldo Rey, Mona Freeman, and in a supporting role Tab Hunter. The other couples started making out, and I sat there thinking, "I'm going to put my arm around her now," but I was frozen and couldn't move my arm. I wasn't even watching the movie, just agonizing over putting my arm around her. Finally one of her friends behind us said, "Why don't you put your arm around her, Pat?" My arm shot up in anticipation, and I smacked Susie in the face with the side of my hand. I dropped my arm back down and sat in embarrassing silence for the rest of the movie.

Obviously, at thirteen I didn't have a very good understanding of sexuality, whether in my own adolescent life or in the R&B and emerging rock 'n' roll I loved. I had no awareness that the music I listened to and the singers I liked were part of a complex personal, cultural, emotional, and psychological process in which I was growing up and developing my sense of masculinity. Fifty years later, in my mid-sixties, I started looking back at the music I grew up with and began to examine how it formed me, for better or for worse.

From Rhythm and Blues to Rockabilly

With Susie I had failed in my first attempt to be a cool guy with a girl. In fact, I was the exact opposite, the awkward nerd wearing horn-rimmed glasses, but I continued to dream about being as cool as Bobby Caruso.

Even though I wasn't consciously searching for models of masculinity in music, I look back now and realize that I was. R&B and rock 'n' roll meant so much to my emotional and imaginary life that I looked to my favorite singers for masculine attitudes and behaviors, both in the songs they sang and in their performing personas. I found them in white rockabilly singers like Elvis and Gene Vincent and early rock 'n' roll singers like Buddy Holly and Ricky Nelson. They provided the male template for my teenage ideal.

Race was again an important factor in the meaning of music for me and I think for other fifties teenagers as well. I didn't think of Ray Charles, Johnny Ace, Big Joe Turner, or other black singers in the same way I did the white ones. I was pulled deeply into black music, but the racial barriers kept me from identifying with the performers on such an intimate level. Besides, Ray Charles was blind; I had the same deeply ingrained attitude toward disabilities that nearly everyone had at the time—children, adolescents, and adults. Also, all these singers were older than me: Ray Charles by eleven years, Johnny Ace by twelve, and Joe Turner by a whopping thirty. When I first heard Johnny Ace's "Pledging My Love," he was already "the late, great Johnny Ace," having shot himself playing Russian roulette.

The white singers I liked were also too old in some ways; Elvis and Jerry Lee were six years older, and Carl Perkins nine, but I had no trouble identifying with their musical personas. So although I liked white and black singers equally and in most instances preferred rhythm and blues versions to rock 'n' roll covers, unexamined racial attitudes, for the most part, caused a thirteen-year-old southern boy to make heroes out of cool white rock 'n' roll singers, actors, and eventually fictional characters. The irony is that the style and sound of those white singers and bands were totally steeped in black rhythm and blues. From the white teenager's point of view, some black people, especially male singers, were seen as outsiders, and our playing their music was an act of rebellion and symbolic identification. But the identification had to remain symbolic; the desire to be black could be expressed indirectly, but direct identification with a black singer as a personal hero would cross the forbidden racial divide, at least for southern white teenagers like me.

The emulation by white singers, musicians, and songwriters of black masculine performance style is a historical process that can be traced back to nineteenth-century blackface minstrelsy and continues to the present. Race scholar Eric Lott says that white men who performed in blackface were engaged in "manly mimicry" and that they were attempting "to become black" in order "to inherit the cool, virility, humility, abandon . . . of black manhood." He is describing nineteenth-century behavior, but this also is true of white male singers' imitation of black performers in the twentieth century: country singer Jimmie Rodgers's emulation of African American blues singers in the twenties and thirties, Elvis Presley's blending of rhythm and blues and country in the fifties, Mick Jagger's mimicry of blues and soul music in the sixties, and white rapper Eminem taking on the cultural and musical style of black rappers starting in the late nineties. In all these cases and with the rockabilly singers I first heard in the fifties, this imitation is more than mimicking a musical style; it is also assuming a black masculine persona that white men imagined as both cool and more primitively sexual.

"They Do the Boogie to an Old Square Dance": Hillbilly Roots of Rockabilly

The racial and gender roots of rockabilly can be discerned in its immediate precursor, the hillbilly music of the late forties and early fifties; one song in particular reveals the source of certain cultural attitudes about masculinity and race. Red Foley's "Tennessee Saturday Night" (1947), which I discussed in chapter 1, was the first song I remember hearing on the radio as a child, and it seems to have nonracial lyrics.

> Now, listen while I tell you 'bout a place I know
> Down in Tennessee where the tall corn grows
> Hidden from the world in a bunch of pines
> Where the moon's a little bashful and it seldom shines
> Civilized people live there alright
> But they all go native on Saturday Night.
> (Transcribed by the author)

The key racial idea in the song is "going native" because it suggests primitivism, which has long been associated with blacks in the white imagination. There are no direct references to race, but "they all go native" is certainly understood as acting in a primitive way in opposition to "civilized people," who are linked to whiteness on some unconscious level. To "go native" in this case specifically refers to drinking ("They get their kicks from an old fruit jar"), fighting, dancing, and romancing in the woods. Going native seems pretty tame in the song until "somebody takes his brogan [and] knocks out the light" so that couples can sneak off to the woods. In the next stanza, there is the violence: "the other fellow packs a gun" and "Ev'rybody does his best to act just right / 'Cause there's gonna be a funeral if you start a fight." Black people are not mentioned in the song, but blackness in dancing is implied when "they do the boogie to an old square dance."

Boogie was historically derogatory white slang for a black person, and when used in a music and dance context, it meant derived from African American music. In vernacular usage the meaning of *boogie* broadened to mean "enjoy[ing] oneself thoroughly," the definition in *The Dictionary of American Slang*, reminding us that blackness is associated with the ability to enjoy, and whiteness is associated with restraint and an inability to let loose, as bell hooks has observed. Until their Saturday-night display of drunkenness, the people described in the song fit the widely accepted Anglo-Saxon Puritan cultural pattern of restraint and inhibition. Folk song scholar Alan Lomax directly contrasted this concept of whiteness with African American cultures, "which placed a high value on erotic and aggressive behavior and which provided [blacks] with vivid outlets for them in song, dance, and ceremonial."

Although country-music historian John W. Rumble says that "Tennessee Saturday Night" was "a milestone in country music's borrowing from rhythm & blues," to me the music doesn't sound nearly as uninhibited as 1940s R&B. It seems more closely aligned with western swing of the thirties and forties, which itself was influenced by R&B. Popularized by such bands as Bob Wills and the Texas Playboys, western swing brought together hillbilly music of the twenties with swing jazz of the thirties. Red Foley's vocal on the song reflects his background growing up near the small town of Berea, Kentucky, where his father ran a general store. His parents paid for him to have voice lessons in high school, and he received a voice scholarship from Georgetown College, where he was classically trained. His singing style was a blend of regional old-time music and formal training.

To me his vocal on "Tennessee Saturday Night" seems to embody the restraint in the line "Ev'rybody does his best to act just right." The guitar, fiddle, and pedal steel solos, while showing jazz influences, are played more in keeping with the "old square dance" than with the impulse to boogie, another implied dichotomy of white and black, civilized and native. There may have been a conscious effort to mimic rhythm and blues music in the recording, but the emulation also existed on a less obvious level as revealed in the coded references to race in the lyrics. This direct musical borrowing from African American music and subconscious underlying assumptions about racial difference continued in honky-tonk music of the forties and fifties and in rockabilly of the fifties.

"Honky Tonk Blues"

One year after my family's first long-distance move to West Texas in 1948, we were on the road again to northern Alberta, where my father was working on another gas plant near the small, newly built town of Devon. It took us five days to make the drive from Beaumont, and as I said in chapter 1, on the way we heard Hank Williams singing one of his first country hits, "Lovesick Blues," over and over on the car radio. The song was a Tin Pan Alley composition from 1922, but Williams was more directly influenced by Emmett Miller's 1928 recording with the Georgia Crackers, a group that included swing jazz instrumentalists Tommy and Jimmy Dorsey, Eddie Lang, and Leo McConville. The song was derived from African American blues, but the Georgia Crackers' music, like Red Foley's, was clearly white country in style, and Emmett Miller and all the musicians were white.

Another fascinating racial element here is that Emmett Miller sang and did black dialect comic routines in minstrel shows from 1918 until 1949, an indication of how long into the twentieth century blackface minstrelsy was a direct influence on American popular music. In fact, the recording of "Lovesick Blues" by Emmett Miller contains an opening dialogue of him and another white man doing a traditional minstrel show routine in which Miller speaks in a broad black dialect, so exaggerated and stereotypical that most listeners today would consider it racist and offensive. By the time Hank Williams recorded his version, the racist dialogue had been removed.

Hank Williams was influenced by these minstrel recordings, but he also had direct African American musical influences; he grew up in rural/small-town Alabama, where he learned to play guitar and sing from black street singer Rufus Payne, known locally as Tee-Tot. Hank mimicked black blues as a fourteen-year-old. He also listened to recordings by the "Blue Yodeler" Jimmie Rodgers, who learned blues from black men he worked with on the railroad. Hank's voice had more of a blues quality than Red Foley's or perhaps any previous white country singer's, yet he remained deeply hillbilly in his delivery. As far as I can tell, his lyrics do not make direct or coded references to African Americans, but the music is steeped in black blues.

Unlike "Tennessee Saturday Night," Hank's honky-tonk songs expressed a more complex, ambivalent attitude toward Saturday-night revels. A good example is another hit song of his, "Honky Tonk Blues," in which his voice expresses some of the emotional qualities of African American blues:

> Well I left my home down on the rural route
> I told my paw I'm going steppin' out and get the
> Honky tonk blues, hey the honky tonk blues
> Hey lord I got 'em, I got the honky tonk blues.
> (Transcribed by the author)

Instead of celebrating Saturday-night good times, the song uses the honky-tonk setting to represent the corruption of city life for a boy from the country. The sins are not mentioned specifically except for dancing, and dancing is definitely a sin to many southern evangelicals. The church I grew up in forbade dancing, and we went to a movie on prom night instead. Drinking, fighting, and carousing are only implied in the song, but then the country audience would know all about what went on at honky-tonks. Country and bluegrass are full of songs that celebrate Saturday-night drinking, fighting, dancing, and lovemaking, and just as many are about Sunday-morning regret and repentance. These elements were also part of the formation of rockabilly in the 1950s.

"Whole Lotta Shakin' Goin' On": The Invention of Rockabilly

The singers, musicians, songwriters, and record producers who created rockabilly in the mid-1950s grew up listening to hillbilly, western swing, and honky-tonk, but they were also listening to blues and R&B. The fusion of all these strains took place in and around Memphis, Tennessee, from 1953 to '54, spread throughout the mid-South region (Tennessee, Arkansas, Louisiana, Mississippi, and Texas) between 1954 and 1956, and finally became a national and international form of popular music from 1956 to 1958, when it was absorbed by a developing mainstream rock 'n' roll. Part of the transition from regional to national was a westward movement from Memphis to Lubbock, Texas (Buddy Holly) and Los Angeles (Gene Vincent and Eddie Cochran). Since then there have been periodic rockabilly revivals such as the one that influenced punk music in the late seventies and early eighties.

The early practitioners of rockabilly were southern white boys including the well-known ones I've already mentioned, plus lesser-known figures like Charlie Feathers, Billy Lee Riley, Sonny Fisher, and the Burnette brothers, Johnny and Dorsey. Sam Phillips, owner of Sun Records in Memphis, first recorded Elvis Presley, Carl Perkins, Jerry Lee Lewis, Johnny Cash, and Roy Orbison. He also recorded black blues singers such as Little Junior Parker, Howlin' Wolf, and Ike Turner, and he was, as legend has it (although it was never documented), trying to find a white man who could "sing like a nigger." He knew he had found him when he recorded Elvis Presley's first sides for Sun, and rockabilly was born.

I first heard Elvis on the Dorsey Brother's television show in March 1956; I know it was that show and not an earlier one because the March performance was the first time he sang "Heartbreak Hotel" on TV. I happened to be alone in the living room that night watching the grainy black-and-white TV when Elvis came on. I was mesmerized by him and the song. He was cool and hot at the same time, like nothing I had ever seen or heard before. It was as if I had been waiting for him since I first started listening to R&B and rock in 1954. It was as if Bobby Caruso had grown up and become a great rock 'n' roll singer. I was fourteen and in the ninth grade in the Newark, Delaware, junior high school. It was my first taste of Elvis's music, and I craved more.

My family had rented an old farmhouse outside the village of Christiana, and I had to wait until my mother drove me into Wilmington to buy the 45 of "Heartbreak Hotel." It was his first release on RCA, but I was soon buying his old Sun recordings, which were being reissued on RCA, and to me they were even better than "Heartbreak Hotel." "Mystery Train," "That's All Right," "I'm Left, You're Right, She's Gone," "Baby, Let's Play House," "Blue Moon of Kentucky"—rock 'n' roll and country and rhythm and blues and bluegrass all mixed up, and a new sound coming out of my little 45 rpm record player's speaker. I became a rockabilly fan before I ever heard the name. To me it was just the best rock 'n' roll, and I wanted to hear more.

Also in 1956, I heard Carl Perkins for the first time, his first big national hit "Blue Suede Shoes," the first rockabilly record I bought on the Sun label, and I loved the flip side, "Honey Don't," almost as much as the number 1 hit side. I still think of it as one of the best boogie recordings of all time. Carl Perkins's first hit came after Elvis, but to me he deserves as much credit for the invention of rockabilly since he had been playing a similar mix of country and R&B for years, and he was a direct influence on Elvis.

Later in '56, when I was fifteen, we moved back to our hometown in Texas; I was in the tenth grade when I first heard Jerry Lee Lewis on the radio. I went out and bought my second 45 rpm Sun record, another one I still have. "End of the Road" is on one side, an up-tempo, "pumping piano" number as is stated beneath Jerry Lee's name on the label. It was my favorite side, but I also loved "Crazy Arms," a slower country tune that was a cover of Ray Price's hit recording, which Jerry Lee made into his own.

Much later, as a grown-up who taught a course on folk music and did research on vernacular music, I thought about doing research on rockabilly, a labor of love. I was still listening to the music on 45s, LPs, and CDs, and at some point I decided to focus on two songs that seemed especially culturally significant; the titles suggest why—Jerry Lee Lewis's "Drinkin' Wine Spo-Dee-O-Dee" and Carl Perkins's "Dixie Fried." I recognized their connection to the earlier hillbilly song "Tennessee Saturday Night," all linked by their emphasis on men's wild drunken behavior at bars, dance halls, and honky-tonks, and they all describe fighting as an essential ingredient. I concentrated on two songs, but other fifties rockabilly songs reflect the same kind of excessive drinking and wild behavior, including "Ubangi Stomp" and "Jungle Rock" (both suggestive of primitivism again), "Whole Lotta Shakin' Goin' On," "Let's Get Wild," "Have Myself a Ball," "We Wanna Boogie," and "Tear It Up."

"Drinkin' That Mess, Their Delight"

"Drinkin' Wine Spo-Dee-O-Dee" was an R&B hit in 1949 in two different versions, the first by Stick McGhee backed up by his brother, Brownie, on guitar. The McGhee brothers were from Kingsport, Tennessee, in the middle of the Appalachian Mountains only twenty miles from Maces Springs, Virginia, home of A. P. Carter of the profoundly influential hillbilly or "old-time" country group the Carter Family, who according to folklorist (and old friend) Bill Lightfoot learned "their best attempt at the blues," "Oh, Take Me Back," from a group of black musicians that included the McGhee brothers and their father, George, as well as African American guitarist Lesley Riddle, who taught Maybelle Carter how to play guitar in a way that evolved into a major style in American folk guitar. All this interracial, intercultural interaction belies the supposed isolation of the southern mountains and indicates the porous barriers between the races when it comes to mixing musical traditions. In Louisiana-born-and-bred Jerry Lee Lewis's version of

"Drinkin' Wine Spo-Dee-O-Dee," we immediately recognize his mimicry of black music, but most people don't think of the Carter Family as directly emulating black blues on any of their songs. Their music is usually seen as the purest of the pure old-time Anglo-Saxon mountain music.

A more stereotypical home of the blues might be Ferriday, Louisiana, on the banks of the Mississippi River, where Jerry Lee Lewis was born and grew up. In 1949, when he was fourteen, his cousin Maudine gave him a record of Stick McGhee's "Drinkin' Wine Spo-Dee-O-Dee." Jerry Lee loved the record; he was already playing the piano and was especially crazy about the piano player on the recording, Big Chief Ellis. In November 1949, the local Ford dealer had an open house to introduce new car models, with a hillbilly band playing in the car lot. Jerry's father, Elmo, told the owner of the dealership that his son was a better piano player than the one in the band, and the dealer asked him to come up on stage and play. At Jerry Lee Lewis's public debut in 1949, he played his own speeded-up version of "Drinkin' Wine Spo-Dee-O-Dee," and the crowd loved it. Jerry Lee later recorded the tune and continued to play it throughout his career.

The song was widely popular among early rockabilly bands; besides Lewis, the Rock 'n' Roll Trio, Malcolm Yelvington, and Sid King and the Five Strings recorded it. The title refers to several African American drinking customs of the 1940s, but the one I remember best is literary and involves taking a shot of port wine, followed by a shot of whiskey, and another shot of port. "Nice sweet jacket for all that bad whiskey" as one black character in Jack Kerouac's *On the Road* says. Stick McGhee's 1949 release of the song reveals some of its appeal for rockabilly performers and their fans.

> Down in New Orleans, where ev'rything is fine
> All them cats is drinkin' that wine
> Drinking that mess, their delight
> When they gets drunk, start singing all night
>
> Drinkin' wine spo-dee-o-dee, drinkin' wine (bop ba)
> Wine spo-dee-o-dee, drinkin' wine (bop ba)
> Wine spo-dee-o-dee, drinkin' wine (bop ba)
> Pass that bottle to me
> (Transcribed by Todd Peach with revisions by the author)

African American dance music with lyrics that described wild drinking and partying appealed to rockabilly musicians and reflected their images of blacks as more natural and uninhibited than whites. The vague "native" of "Tennessee Saturday Night" was now more explicitly black in the minds of white rockabilly performers as they sang "Drinkin' Wine Spo-Dee-O-Dee." The lyrics of the versions by Stick McGhee and Jerry Lee Lewis have only a few minor differences, but the meanings could be very different with the shift from an African American to an Anglo-American context. More specifically here, my emphasis is on masculinity in the lyrics of "Drinkin' Wine" and "Dixie Fried," especially on white perceptions of black masculinity, not necessarily masculinity as black men would define it but as white men emulated what they imagined it to be. Masculinity is emphasized by the all-male setting in both the rockabilly and the R&B versions of the song. Women may be there, but Stick McGhee's version does not mention them at all, and in Jerry Lee Lewis's rendition he refers to his "honey" only once.

Rockabilly covers of African American rhythm and blues songs like "Drinkin' Wine Spo-Dee-O-Dee," Elvis's version of Roy Brown's and Wynonie Harris's "Good Rockin' Tonight," and Billy Lee Riley's take on Billy "The Kid" Emerson's "Red Hot" were the standard at first, but it was inevitable that white rockabilly performers would write their own versions of uninhibited drinking songs. Carl Perkins was one of the first rockabilly performers to write songs that were influenced by African American music and reflected a white perception of wild Saturday nights. His most famous song was "Blue Suede Shoes," but his "Dixie Fried" captured the essence of the crazy, drunken hillbilly rocker.

Perkins absorbed African American music while growing up in much the same way as Hank Williams and Jerry Lee Lewis did, hearing it directly and listening to it on radio and records. He was from a sharecropping family in western Tennessee and worked alongside blacks who sang as they worked in the fields. He later recorded a rockabilly version of Blind Lemon Jefferson's "Matchbox Blues," which he heard his father sing, and the Beatles covered the Perkins's version in the early sixties. "Dixie Fried" was recorded by Carl Perkins at Sun Studios in Memphis in 1956, not the first rockabilly recording but one that contains some significant qualities of the form, including racial implications.

> Well, on the outskirts of town, there's a little night spot.
> Dan dropped in about five o'clock.
> Pulled off his coat said, "The night is short."
> He reached in his pocket and he flashed a quart.

He hollered, "Rave on, children, I'm with you!
Rave on, cats," he cried.
"It's almost dawn, and the cops are gone.
And let's all get Dixie fried."
(Transcribed by the author)

Here again there is an all-male setting at the honky-tonk; Dan only refers to his "hon" while he's in jail. Also, as with "Drinkin' Wine Spo-Dee-O-Dee," this narrative, imaginary as it is, is still grounded in a real time and place. In an interview Carl Perkins described the violent behavior he had observed in southern honky-tonks: "I'm talking about rough places, where half the people went there to fight. . . . And a lot of these places had chicken wire around the juke box and us to keep the bottles from hitting." The interviewer asked him, "Are these the kind of clubs that inspired you to write your kind of songs?" Perkins replied, "Yep, there's no doubt about it. Yes sir." He must have had "Dixie Fried" in mind.

"Rave On, Cats": Drinking, Fighting, and Male Bonding

Clearly the lyrics and musical attitudes of both "Drinkin' Wine" and "Dixie Fried" project a strong sense of masculinity, especially the social bonding of men through drinking and fighting. We learn about male bonding at an early age. For instance, at twelve and thirteen, boys' social behavior already keeps them separate from girls while at the same time developing an intense interest in them. When I "dated" Susie Singleton in the eighth grade, my shyness kept me from having much social interaction with girls. I played touch football and playground baseball with other boys, and I went to movies and dances with male friends. Through the rest of junior high and high school, we bonded with other boys around our favorite R&B, rockabilly, and rock'n' roll music: we collected records, got together to listen to music, and talked about new music we heard on the radio the night before. At the time, I wasn't aware of girls bonding over their interest in popular music, but later in high school and college, I knew girls who were huge fans and socially bonded with other girls over music. There was more cross-gender socializing around music the older we became.

In my experience, being thirteen in 1954 meant no drinking of alcohol at all, but I do remember fighting among boys. The only fight I ever had was in eighth-grade gym class. Some kid pushed in front of me in the line to pick up towels, and I pushed back. We scuffled a little bit, and the coach came over and broke us up with the comment, "If you guys want to fight so much, put on the gloves and you can box." The other students made a circle, and coach refereed. I knew how to pose like a boxer but knew nothing about technique. I found out later that my opponent took boxing lessons at the YMCA, and he beat the shit out of me. A few weeks later, we agreed to another fight, and the coach put the gloves on us again. This time I decided I was not going to pretend I could box but just punch him as hard and as fast as I could. I weighed more, and I won. We shook hands and didn't get into any more fights. I think it was male bonding, not as significant as listening and talking about music with my male friends, but still a lesson in masculinity was learned: how to act tough and express it through fighting.

That was it for adolescent fighting, and I managed to keep out of fights for the rest of my adult life except for one fight in the spring of 1970, when I was twenty-eight. I had just moved to Columbus to start teaching in the English department at Ohio State. I was freshly divorced and sort of crazy during that time—drinking too much, staying up all night, dating different women including a black woman whom I became emotionally involved with. Gloria (not her real name) was recently divorced herself and had an eight-year-old son, whom I became very attached to. When I wrote my mother and told her I was dating a black woman, she handled it pretty well despite having grown up in a time and place of racial segregation and prejudice, but when she told my father, his response was, "Has Pat gone crazy?" Sounds like prejudice, but he was mainly concerned about the difficulties we would face as an interracial couple. Even in Columbus, which wasn't nearly as prejudiced as Beaumont, she and I did encounter some negative stares and whispering when we were together in public.

We dated for several months but finally broke up mainly because she seemed unable to open up to me emotionally. She had a hard time revealing her own thoughts and feelings about me or our relationship. We went to a lot of parties and had a good time, but she would often get mad at me for something I had said or done. I wanted to talk about what happened; I wanted to know exactly what I had done wrong, but she refused to talk about it. I knew I was at fault in some way, and I wanted to work on the problems and try to change, but I couldn't get her to talk. I don't think our problems had anything to do with race; they seemed to be mainly the result of our different personalities. Finally we decided to break up, and I had a tearful last talk with her son and never saw him or her again.

I was in a period of my life when I didn't have much self-control; I felt as if I had married too young and missed a chance to "sow some wild oats" as the old euphemism had it. I had dated only a few other women before I became engaged, and my wife and I were faithful to each other until we separated. After that I wanted to have sex with as many women as I could, and I started dating women graduate students in the English department. It was not considered appropriate behavior for faculty to date students, but lots of men professors did, in fact, do so. I started going to graduate student parties where there was loud rock music and dancing, and flirtations were part of the drunken atmosphere.

It started that way with Ellie, a graduate student's wife, but our flirting became more serious since she was in the process of breaking up with her husband, Phil (not their real names). They finally separated, and he moved out; she stayed in their house with their three little boys, whom I had become fond of. I spent more time at her house than I did at the one that my ex and I had bought when we moved to Columbus. By that time, my relationship with Ellie was completely out in the open. We would see her husband at parties, but we usually avoided each other. Finally, though, at a party at the house of one of my faculty friends, Phil's anger erupted. As usual we were all drinking. There was a beer keg on the screened back porch, and most of the English department faculty and grad students were in the backyard. Phil came through the house headed for the backyard. He had already been drinking, and as he passed me, he hit me in the face with his fist.

We started to fight, lost our balance, and fell through the screen door into the backyard. Everyone turned to see what was going on. We exchanged only a few punches before one of my friends in the department pulled us apart. My shirt was ripped, and I had a little blood on my face. Almost everyone in the English department had observed the altercation, and my first thought was a selfish one: "I'll never get tenure in this department." It was my first year in the department, and I knew several older profs who were very judgmental about young professors who were having affairs. One married couple had just broken up because the husband was having an affair with a student.

Ellie and I left the party and went back to her house. The incident became a part of department folklore; I was still hearing about it years later—notoriety but no dismissal; in fact, I received a promotion and tenure five years later. Phil left grad school at the end of the quarter. Ellie and I broke up within a few months when I went away to teach at a summer institute at the University of Wisconsin, Milwaukee, and started dating a woman I met there.

That was the last fight for me. Up to that point, I had followed a pattern that is well documented in the research on masculinity. As boys become men, fighting becomes more serious, especially when alcohol is added to the mix. Drinking and fighting are a performance of masculinity in the sense that they are a social display that has an audience. My personal example certainly fits that description, and in the case of country music and rockabilly this performance often takes place at a honky-tonk. As country-music historian Bill Malone says, "The honky-tonk was essentially a masculine retreat . . . a place to aggressively assert one's manhood." Often the fighting would be over a woman, but men were bonding even as they were fighting.

Another essential element in understanding masculinity in country music and rockabilly is the lower socioeconomic class context in which the music was played. Malone refers to honky-tonk music of this period as evoking "the ambience and flavor of the working-class beer and dancing clubs where the style was born." Those working-class honky-tonks have often been perceived as violent, places where drinking and fighting went together. All the singers and songwriters whom I'm writing about (with one exception, Red Foley) came from hardscrabble, rural, working-class backgrounds and played in bars with audiences from that same class. So we need to look more closely at social-class difference among young men at southern dance halls.

Both the R&B and rockabilly versions of "Drinkin' Wine Spo-Dee-O-Dee" are celebrations of male bonding through getting drunk and fighting. As I noted earlier, this "hell-raising" behavior is described as exclusively masculine, which might suggest that for men to really let loose, women as a civilizing influence must not be present. Their drunken fighting is represented as pleasurable and even referred to as "their delight." One feminist historian says that for men, drinking asserts "a glorious manhood unfettered by the nagging demands of women who would, had they their way, ensconce men at home, squander their wages, forbid them to drink—in short emasculate them." Men are celebrating their freedom from women's control and at the same time expressing their masculinity.

"Dixie Fried" presents another version of "going native" on Saturday night, but by 1956 rockabilly had transformed the fairly tame music of Red Foley's 1948 hit into a sound as raucous as the activities being described.

The hillbilly-sounding pedal steel guitar in "Tennessee Saturday Night" has been replaced by a blues-influenced rock 'n' roll guitar, and when Perkins switches from his narrator role to play Dan, his singing suggests that his raving is truly crazed. "Dixie Fried" is very close to "Drinkin Wine Spo-Dee-O-Dee" in the way it emphasizes drinking and fighting. Dan tosses a note to his "hon" through the jailhouse bars, but she isn't placed at the honky-tonk, only in the outside world where women and police could be coconspirators to keep men under control. The lack of women and dancing in the song again places the emphasis on male bonding.

There are no direct sexual references in "Dixie Fried," but plenty of alcohol and violence. The singer/narrator is someone who was there to observe Dan's actions firsthand; he admires Dan and seems to express the group's attitude toward him: "Now Dan was the bravest man that we ever saw / He let us all know he wasn't scared of the law." The attitude of the singer and group make Dan a rockabilly hero whose drunken behavior, including the flashing of a razor, is to be emulated. He pays for his transgressions by being arrested and thrown in jail, but in the end he is still unrepentant, hollering from his cell, "Rave on cats . . . I've been Dixie fried."

As rock critic Greil Marcus says, "Rockabilly fixed the crucial image of rock 'n' roll: the sexy, half-crazed fool standing on stage singing his guts out. . . . Rockabilly was the only style of early rock 'n' roll that proved white boys could do it all—that they could be as strange, as exciting, as scary, and as free as the black men who were suddenly walking America's airwaves as if they owned them." I don't think Marcus means to describe an all-male environment, but the elements are certainly here: "white boys could do it all"; they didn't need women to have a wild, uninhibited good time. There is a kind of narcissism here with the intended audience of women rendered invisible. The outsider rockabilly hero can be seen as dependent on the all-male setting, away from the societal control of women in a free-for-all atmosphere of drinking and fighting. Like all heroes, Dan is to be emulated by those who consider him a hero, reinforcing culturally learned masculine behavior.

Both "Dixie Fried" and "Drinkin' Wine Spo-Dee-O-Dee" are good examples of upbeat rockabilly dance music, and one of the ironies here is that the songs don't mention dancing at all. It's as if fighting has replaced dancing, and this seems appropriate given the implied meaning of the songs and the social environment in which they are set. Even though it's usually all right for women to dance with women, men can't dance with other men because that would be perceived as homosexual; fighting then becomes a violent replacement for dancing. Think of all the movies in which fighting is accompanied by rock music, and the connection becomes more apparent. Also, many men who go to honky-tonks without women *almost* dance with other men while standing around the dance floor watching the dancers. Moving in time with the music with another man is okay as long as you don't touch him, face him, or dance behind him, but keep your gaze on the dance floor.

In general male bonding can be found across socioeconomic class boundaries, from men's book discussion groups to pickup basketball games, from college fraternity parties to labor union meetings. But are there different perceptions of this bonding behavior in different social classes? For instance, how are fighting and drinking perceived differently by class? The middle and upper-middle class often perceive working-class men as being more violent. Since country and rockabilly music originally came from southern rural, working-class people and continues to be associated with them, the drinking and fighting depicted in lyrics still conjure up class images.

"Band Doll": The Need for Women

When I was in college in southeast Texas in the early 1960s, fighting and male-bonding behavior were still common. On Saturday nights, my friends and I would drive to Louisiana to go to the Big Oak, a rock 'n' roll bar where we could buy liquor at eighteen. It was similar to southern honky-tonks of the forties and fifties in terms of loud dance music played by local bands, excessive drinking, and frequent fighting. Most of the young men there, of whatever class background, came with other men, not with dates; there were some male-female couples but women also came mainly with other women. Some men asked women to dance, and on some occasions a woman asked a man to dance, but much of the social interaction was within two groups, one made up of women and the other of men.

There was a perceived class difference between the college boys and the local guys our age. We were in college, and they were already working at local refineries and chemical plants. We saw them as tough and pugnacious, ready to brawl at the slightest provocation. I don't know how they saw us, perhaps as "wimps," with good reason since we fit the stereotype. Fights broke out among the locals every time we went to the Big Oak, but our college group assiduously avoided them. Bouncers threw brawlers out, so most of the alterations took place in the parking lot, and when we college boys went back to our car, we carefully walked as far away from the fights as we could.

We did so despite the fact that most of us came from working-class backgrounds and were the first generation of our families to go to college. Upward mobility and going to college were enough to make us and our working-class age cohorts aware of class difference, even though we both behaved in similar ways, getting drunk and running in packs. Both socioeconomic groups were engaged in male bonding behavior, but the working-class guys seemed more likely to fight, at least that's how we perceived them. I don't want to generalize too broadly from this personal subjective example, but I suspect the pattern might be borne out more widely in American social-class behavior at the time.

We had fun, we got drunk, we danced on the sidelines, and all with little interaction with women. Not that we didn't want to be with women, to dance with them or take a woman out to the car to "make out." Whenever I tell personal stories about going to the Big Oak, I mention wanting desperately to dance with one girl from my college who was very cute and a great dancer—so good that one of the bands, Jay Richard and the Blues Kings, named a song after her, "Band Doll," obviously a sexist term, but the word *sexist* wasn't in our vocabulary or our consciousness at the time. I worked up the nerve to ask her to dance only once, and dancing with her was the highpoint of my Big Oak experiences. Our focus on her suggests a situation that might have led to fighting over her, but we college boys seemed to lack that fighting instinct.

From my observation, the locals behaved in similar ways—they drank, they hung out together, and periodically they would ask a girl to dance. The big difference was that they fought and we didn't. The masculine behavior of both male groups offers evidence to support the idea of fighting as male bonding, but it was also, in some ways, an expression of our social isolation from women (for more on the Big Oak experience, see chapter 4).

A power dynamic was at work in pretending we didn't need women, but this pretense also suggests a desire for women that we were denying. We were interacting with one another in ways that were clearly male bonding and at the same time coping with the lack of women in our lives. Our male friendships sent out a message that we didn't need women, but of course we did. Viewing women as unnecessary and even antithetical to the masculine urge to get drunk was a means of expressing dominance over them. This is also the case in honky-tonk and rockabilly lyrics that exclude women—the denial of needing women as an unconscious expression of the need for women. Men who think they don't need women usually don't recognize this subtext. I know I wasn't aware of it, but there is a deeper level of meaning that performers in the social drama are not always conscious of. Performing masculinity often obscures the meaning of the performance from the audience and the performer.

Rockabilly and R&B lyrics can be extremely sexist and at times racist, but ironically, as Nick Spitzer observes, American vernacular music itself undermines all the divisions that have been erected to keep us apart. This is because the music ignores the boundaries between class, race, gender, and sexual orientation and produces instead a wonderful mixture of ethnic, regional, class, gender, and racial elements in rock 'n' roll, country, R&B, jazz, hip-hop, Cajun, zydeco, conjunto, salsa, Latina, and on and on. James Baldwin has expressed this idea more eloquently than I ever could: "Each of us, helplessly and forever, contains the other—male in female, female in male, white in black and black in white. We are a part of each other."

CHAPTER 4

Take Me Higher

Dancing, Drinking, and Doing Drugs

Y ou can't write about rock 'n' roll, blues, R&B, and country music without talking about dancing. The most visceral appeal of rock 'n' roll in the fifties was its connection with dancing; whether we were doing the bop in junior high or imagining we were jitterbugging with a cute girl on *American Bandstand*, dancing was at the core of our response. The roots of rock 'n' roll—R&B, country, blues, and swing—insisted that people dance; and drinking always loosened people up for dancing—at juke joints, honky-tonks, and rock 'n' roll bars, places that were basic to the development of American vernacular music. And if you broaden the history to include Polish polka clubs in Milwaukee, Tex-Mex dance halls in San Antonio, Cajun and zydeco clubs in Lafayette, and blues bars in Chicago, dancing is still the great connector.

I wasn't a great dancer, but there was no doubt that I was having fun and my partners were too. Judy Brown and I were known by the other kids as crazy for dancing, out on the floor for nearly every fast song. I knew her in my last two years at Blakelock High School in Canada. She had a crush on me, I think, and I loved her in my own way. We were in that awkward teenage state of good friends with an underlying attraction that was never acted on. She wasn't as shy as I was, but we were both shy enough that the romance was always just beneath the surface. I also had a little flirtation going on with a dark-haired French Canadian girl named Shirley Patrick who finally asked me out on a date, where I experienced my first nonresistant French kiss. Despite Shirley's charms, Judy retains a special place in my heart. She enthusiastically learned the dance step I had brought with me from Texas, a modified dirty bop similar to Elvis's moves on stage.

Judy asked me to dance first, and she immediately started to pick up the moves of the Texas bop. Judy and I danced to Chuck Berry, "School Days"; the Cleftones, "Little Girl of Mine"; Ray Charles, "Yes Indeed"; Frankie Lymon and the Teenagers, "Why Do Fools Fall in Love"; and other records from my collection of 45s. I became the unofficial DJ at school sock hops. I brought a wooden box made especially for carrying 45s to the dance, put one on the turntable, jumped off the stage in the combination auditorium/ gym, danced with Judy, and jumped back on stage to change the record. Judy asked me to go to the prom with her. This was my first prom, having missed all the ones in high school in Texas.

Dancing became a regular enjoyable activity at Blakelock High School, especially significant for me because at the previous high schools and junior highs I attended, I had never worked up the courage to ask a girl to dance. I learned to dance by myself while listening to records at home starting in 1954, when we lived in Baytown, Texas, and I was in the eighth grade. In that same year I first heard Ray Charles, Johnny Ace, the Penguins, and Bill Haley and the Comets on the radio. Dancing and R&B music were one, and it was a natural transition to rock 'n' roll. In 1954 teenagers in Texas were dancing something that looked like jitterbugging from the forties, swinging your partner by the hand but with dirty-bop hip movements added—suggestive enough to have the dance banned at Horace Mann Junior High School. By 1956 in Beaumont, the same dance was accepted at South Park High School, where kids danced in the gym during lunch break to songs like Chuck Berry's "Brown-Eyed Handsome Man," and that style of dancing continued elsewhere throughout the fifties.

A new style of dancing came in the sixties: standing apart and shaking your booty instead of holding hands and swinging around. Still, somehow, I incorporated the dirty bop into the new style. By the late sixties and early seventies, we were doing what my friends called "hippie dancing," which meant communal. We might start dancing as couples but eventually we were holding hands or embracing in a group hug, linked together and moving all around the room to Derek and the Dominos' "Layla" in a cloud of marijuana smoke. Variations on jitterbugging and shake-your-booty dancing continued throughout the seventies, eighties, and nineties, and my generation is still doing something like it today.

Drinking and Dancing

By the time I got to college, dancing and drinking were inextricably intertwined—to go native on a Saturday night we still thought we needed alcohol. This connection had something to do with my church telling me that both activities were sinful. As I've said, in Texas in the fifties Church of Christ and Baptist kids dressed up in formal wear and went to a movie instead of having a senior prom. Dancing was sexual and therefore a sin, but what if I was just dancing to records in my bedroom? Was that sinful? Was moving to the music by myself on the sidelines at junior and high school dances a sin? I stood on the sidelines too many times, picked out a likely girl but never had the courage to make a move, so I danced standing in place, as much as I could without drawing attention, or later in college, having enough drinks to not care about drawing attention.

Dancing a slow dance *with* a girl was definitely a sin for me and other Church of Christ kids. I found that out for sure at a high school dance in 1957 when a girl pressed her entire body tightly against mine for the first time. I don't remember her name, but I remember how she felt and how I felt. I was used to slow dancing with girls who kept their bodies at a distance. I'll never forget that feeling—the template for slow dancing for the rest of my life. Once you cross that line, the first "sin" demands more.

I didn't drink in high school, so dancing and drinking remained separate sins. I went back to my hometown of Beaumont for college, and I was still going to the same church that I had been baptized in. But I had started breaking church rules by drinking with buddies in the dorm and on trips to the beach. Drinking was outlawed but widespread in the men's dorm at Lamar Tech in 1959. One night during my freshman year, I came in drunk and fell into bed. I woke up sometime during the night when someone plopped into bed next to me. I thought it was my friend Bud, who was also out drinking that night, and I rolled over and went back to sleep. When I woke up the next morning, he was still there. I started to crawl over him to go to the bathroom and realized that I'd never seen this guy before. I jumped out of bed and woke him up, and he mumbled, "What are you doing in my room?" "You're in the wrong room, you dope." We figured out he lived in the identical dorm down the street, and he staggered out. I walked through the study area on the way to the bathroom and realized he had gotten confused about directions and instead of turning left to the bathroom, went the other way and pissed on my desk.

One year, my roommate Bill Stuessy and I sneaked what was left of a beer keg into our dorm room and invited all our friends to an after-party party. The RAs usually looked the other way when we brought booze into the dorm, but we were so rowdy that the RA came in and told us to be a little quieter. Bo Diddley's song "Say Man" was popular then, and we were all spouting insult lines from the song, which was basically the African American game of "Playing the Dozens" set to a Bo Diddley beat. "Why you're so ugly the stork that brought you into the world oughta be arrested." "Hey, since you told me about my girl, I'm gonna tell you about yours. . . . That chick looked so ugly, she had to sneak up on a glass to get a drink of water." "You look like you been whupped with an ugly stick." We were pretty good friends with the RA, so Stuessy's response to his request to hold it down was to pick up a baseball bat and chase him out of the room shouting, "I'm gonna whup you with my ugly stick." Music and drinking were so closely connected that they became part of the fabric of our everyday lives.

We would drive the thirty-five miles to the beach to drink beer, try to pick up girls, lay out in the sun listening to music on a portable radio, and swim—in that order. Sometimes we would play the car radio with the volume turned up as loud as it would go. If we were with girls, we would even dance on the sand. This was the same stretch of Gulf Coast beach along the Bolivar Peninsula where my parents took us when we were kids. Daddy drank beer, and they both drank highballs, usually bourbon and 7-Up, at their Saturday-night poker parties with other couples, but I only remember Daddy driving a little tipsy one time, and that was coming home from the beach. Our college gang was not so discrete. At the beach, we drank a lot of beer, turned the car radio up full volume, opened all the car doors, and listened to current hit music. In 1962, that would be songs like Little Eva's "The Loco-Motion," Chubby Checker's "The Twist," and Dee Dee Sharp's "Mashed Potato Song." You can imagine what it was like doing the twist barefoot in the sand. We kept the radio blasting while we drove back to the dorm "three sheets to the wind," as my parents would say, or "bombed out of our minds," as we said in college in the early sixties.

One time my buddies and I started back from the beach drunk and were stopped at the drawbridge across the intercoastal canal as a line of barges went slowly through. When I was little and we were caught by the bridge and the season was right, the whole family would get out of the car and pick dewberries growing alongside the road. Not us college boys: we knew we were going to be late picking up our dates and sat cursing and drinking more beer. When the bridge finally opened, we took off like a ruptured duck, an expression my parents were fond of using. I was driving my grandfather Big Daddy's beige '55 Ford Fairlane sedan, which I had inherited and painted a '48 Mercury maroon. The paint job was to make it cool and not so grand-fatherly looking (although he didn't drink at all, he too drove like a bat out of hell sometimes).

I must have thought it was cool to pass long lines of cars at ninety miles per hour, ducking back into a narrow space when a pickup came along from the other direction, with the radio blasting rock 'n' roll all the way home. We somehow made it back alive and even on time to pick up our dates, but I had one bad scare that night. Almost back to campus I wasn't going ninety but was still speeding when a car pulled right out in front of me; I barely slammed on the brakes in time. I pondered how the slightest wrong move by me or someone else going ninety miles per hour would have caused a terrible "wreck on the highway" (I was already familiar with that old Roy Acuff song). I've done dumb things driving since then but never anything that dangerous. The invulnerable feeling of being young mixed with the uninhibited feeling of being drunk: I was lucky to be scared straight, at least while driving, if not while dancing or partying.

In college, there were dances at the student union, and I started drinking before going to a dance. I was shy, hesitant, and repressed, so my thinking was, "Let loose, get drunk and let loose." I knew the music and beer or bourbon would take me outside my inhibited self, but I wasn't sure if my dancing partners would take the trip with me. Despite attempts to get them as drunk as I was, alcohol didn't always work on girls. Not that I gave up on alcohol; I must have thought that it might eventually work. As good as I felt, she might feel the same and be more willing to make out.

One band that played at the Lamar Student Union more than once was led by two brothers with albinism—they played hard rock 'n' roll and R&B, great to drink and dance to even if we couldn't do both in the same place. They called themselves Johnny and the Jammers. They were local boys, Johnny and Edgar Winter, who both went on to fame as rock and blues performers. Johnny was enrolled at Lamar Tech for a while but dropped out. They were my favorite band at the union dances; I think I would have remembered them even if they hadn't gone on to be rock stars. For one thing, the fact that they were albinos fascinated my girlfriend Mary Lou (not her real name) and her friends who wanted to fix Johnny or Edgar up with their albino girlfriend in the dorm. An early sixties example of a white exotic other, I guess. (Johnny Winter died on July 17, 2014, while I was writing this book. He was definitely one of the greatest blues/rock guitarists I ever heard.)

"Black exotic other" music was represented by Big Sambo and the House Wreckers, an African American R&B band that played at fraternity parties. (Their name was their own, not one white boys had made up.) They were the preferred choice of me and my fraternity brothers because they played great dance music and did covers of all the black music we already loved—Bobby Blue Bland, B. B. King, and Little Junior Parker. The band was all black and the fraternity was all white, something we didn't give much thought to. In fact, we thought of ourselves as pretty liberal on race since we didn't have a written clause forbidding black members or use the Confederate flag as our emblem the way another fraternity on campus did. Those fraternity parties were well fueled by alcohol because we held them at private party houses to avoid problems with the law, although I did get arrested my senior year for buying alcohol for a frat brother who was a minor.

I was dumb enough to hand him the bottle of bourbon on the liquor-store steps, and the Liquor Control Board agents were parked right across the street. With siren and flashing lights, they swooped in to hand me my citation and court date. Thinking I'd probably lose my graduate teaching assistantship for the next year, I couldn't enjoy myself at the party; I didn't even dance. Class privilege saved me: one of our adult fraternity brothers heard about my dilemma at the party and told me not to worry. He set up a meeting with a judge who was also a fraternity brother, and he got the case dismissed. I had never met a judge before, much less visited one in his courthouse chambers, but I was grateful for having a connection to save my ass.

As freshmen and sophomores if we wanted to dance and drink in public, we had to drive thirty miles or so to Louisiana, where you could drink at eighteen. Across the Sabine River, right after you got out of the swampy river bottom on old Highway 90, sat the legendary Big Oak club with live music and all the beer and liquor an eighteen-year-old Texas boy could want. The bands at the Big Oak played wild rock 'n' roll with a strong dose of R&B, even horns in some cases. I remember two Cajun rock bands in particular, Jay Richard and the Blues Kings, who played "Band Doll" (see chapter 3), and Jerry "Count" Jackson and the Dominos. Jerry Jackson was actually Jerry LeCroix, who later teamed up with Edgar Winter in the group White Trash. LeCroix had a great R&B voice and his was our favorite of all the bands we heard in "The Golden Triangle" (Beaumont, Port Arthur, and Orange, Texas) and across the river near Vinton, Louisiana.

The Blues Kings had lots of Lamar Tech fans, including one girl who became legendary because they wrote a song about her. "The Band Doll" was Sharon Lake (not her real name); she seemed to be at the Big Oak every time I went, and she was one of the best dancers I'd ever seen. I knew her from Lamar and had been trying to get up enough nerve to ask her to dance for months. Finally, I must have had enough to drink, not enough to be "pig falling down drunk," but enough to ask her to dance—one of the great moments of my dancing/drinking youth.

When we left the Big Oak, we always had to walk around the drunken guys fighting in the parking lot. I didn't realize until fairly recently how much the Big Oak and other sixties rock and R&B clubs in Texas and Louisiana were like the southern country honky-tonks of the previous generation with heavy drinking and fighting expressing a distinct cultural form of male bonding (see chapter 3 for a more detailed description of the Big Oak).

"Brown Bottle Blues"

I didn't start drinking until I was in college, but I was around drinking as I was growing up. As I noted earlier, Mama drank highballs at their Saturday-night poker parties with other Braun couples (Braun was the construction company my father worked for), and Daddy drank highballs at the poker games or beer when he was out hunting or fishing with his friends. There's a picture of me in knee pants with Daddy, Aunt Mildred, and a friend named Herschel sitting on a log bench at Daddy's fishing camp on Taylor's Bayou south of Beaumont. The adults all have beer bottles in their hands. Mama must have taken the picture; she was the family photographer with her fold-up Kodak.

Since they were drinking in the mid-forties when I was still in knee pants, they were probably drinking when they were dating in the late thirties. They didn't talk about drinking or dancing at country music bars, but I imagine them dancing to Bob Wills and the Texas Playboys and Moon Mullican. They probably heard Bob Wills on the radio and jukeboxes but Moon Mullican in person since he played in Beaumont so often that my mother got phone calls in the middle of the night from drunken guys at bars who confused the honky-tonk piano player with my father, whose nickname was also Moon: "Come on down here and listen to Moon play the piano." Or it might have been his friends teasing her, which made more sense to me later when my own drunken friends called me late at night.

Mama and Daddy continued listening to country music on the car radio in the forties, and they liked country music the rest of their lives. After Daddy retired and they went back to Beaumont to live, they had an eight-track tape player in their Cadillac. Their favorite tape was by Willie Nelson—Mama's favorite anyway; Daddy didn't usually express his musical tastes.

I wrote about my older sister, Carol (Sissy when I was growing up), in the first chapter; she's the one who was a big Hank Williams fan in the late forties and a dedicated country music fan for the rest of her life. She and her husband, Bob, loved Willie Nelson, Ricky Skaggs, George Strait, and lots of other country singers. Bob grew up on a cattle ranch in Saskatchewan, worked cattle in Montana for many years, and always wore cowboy shirts and boots even when he was driving a logging truck, which was his main job until he was in a bad wreck. After he recovered, he operated a combine. His favorite George Strait songs were "The Cowboy Rides Away" and "Amarillo by Morning" (about a lonesome rodeo rider trying to make it to the next town). One of my favorite songs by George is "All My Ex's Live in Texas." Even though I have only one ex-wife, she does live in Texas.

Carol and our younger sister, Linda, went to a George Strait concert in Beaumont in the late eighties. Caught up in the hysteria among his women fans (some of whom traditionally throw their panties on the stage during his performance), they followed his bus back to the Holiday Inn, hoping to meet him, only to learn that the bus was a decoy and he had sneaked into the hotel through a back entrance. My mother was also a George Strait and Willie Nelson fan—something that linked the women in our family together. My brother, David, and I are also big fans, and I saw George Strait at a concert at Veterans Memorial Auditorium in Columbus in the early nineties. It was a great show, and I thought about my sisters when I saw women fans throwing their panties on the stage.

Some of my best musical memories are those of being with Carol and Bob at bars in Montana or Texas listening to live music or a jukebox. They lived many years in the valley of the North Fork of the Blackfoot River in western Montana near the small town of Ovando. Their favorite bar there was Trixie's Antler Saloon, which had a jukebox that featured country music with lots of favorites about cowboys. The owner was a former rodeo trick rider. Hanging over the bar was a picture of her standing on the saddle of a galloping horse while twirling a rope. Many stories come to mind when I recall the saloon. One in particular about my sister stands out. Carol was six feet tall and a pretty imposing woman. She walked up to the bar at Trixie's one night, and a stranger looked up at her and said, "You're the biggest woman I've ever seen!" She responded, "You're the ugliest son-of-a-bitch I've ever seen." The story doesn't mention his reaction.

You can't find a more authentic western atmosphere than Trixie's Antler Saloon offered, and Carol and Bob fit right in—Bob in his cowboy clothes and boots and Carol with her sense of belonging in bars and honky-tonks whether in Texas or in Montana, or for that matter, in Denver (where they changed planes flying back and forth between Missoula and Houston), Bakersfield, California (where they lived for several years), or Ohio (where Carol came to visit Roseanne and me). This impressive range of places that played country music indicates how country had expanded beyond its original southern audience. Bob and Carol are gone now, but whenever I visit my brother, David, in Houston, he takes me to one of the local country dance halls. He's a great dancer to boot-scootin' music, and at the place we visit, lots of people know him; I have to lean on the bar with my drink and watch as dozens of women come up and ask him to dance. David met his second wife at one of those dance halls (it might have been Gilley's in Pasadena), and, yes, all his exes live in Texas too.

Drinking continues to be part of the dancing experience. Bob and Carol always drank Jim Beam, and David now drinks Jim Beam Black label. At some point I switched to Jack Daniels, probably pop culture influence, something about image that also means advertising, but I do like its taste. All this awareness of the connection between drinking and music prompted me to make a cassette in the early eighties that I labeled "The Drinking Tape." It was country, blues, R&B, and a little rock 'n' roll, more country than any other genre, with good reason—country music just has more songs on that subject. The following is the original play list except for one addition, Suzanne Thomas's "You're Doing Me Wrong, Jim Beam," too perfect a fit not to include later on my CD version:

DRINKING TAPE A: HEY BARTENDER

1. Floyd Dixon/"Hey Bartender"
2. John Lee Hooker/"One Bourbon, One Scotch, One Beer"
3. Johnnie Johnson/"Tanqueray"
4. Vern Gosdin/"Tanqueray"
5. John Anderson/"Honky Tonk Saturday Night"

6. Merle Haggard/"The Bottle Let Me Down"
7. Ted Hawkins/"There Stands the Glass"
8. Squeeze/"When the Hangover Comes"
9. Jerry Jeff Walker/"Sangria Wine"
10. Gary Stewart/"Backslider's Wine"
11. Keith Whitley/"Tennessee Courage"
12. Suzanne Thomas/"You're Doing Me Wrong, Jim Beam"
13. George Jones and Willie Nelson/"I Gotta Get Drunk"
14. Albert Collins/"I Ain't Drunk"
15. UB40/"Red Red Wine"

DRINKING TAPE B: LET'S GO GET STONED

1. Tex Ritter/"Rye Whiskey"
2. Slim Harbert and His Boys/"Brown Bottle Blues"
3. The Clovers/"One Mint Julep"
4. Ray Charles/"One Mint Julep"
5. Lil' Bob and the Lollipops/"I Got Loaded"
6. Stick McGhee/"Drinkin' Wine Spo-Dee-O-Dee"
7. The Rock 'n' Roll Trio/"Drinkin' Wine Spo-Dee-O-Dee"
8. George Jones/"Relief Is Just a Swallow Away"
9. Gary Stewart/"She's Acting Single, I'm Drinking Doubles"
10. Seldom Scene/"Bottom of the Glass"
11. Willie Nelson/"Bloody Mary Morning"
12. Dwight Yoakum/"Since I Started Drinking Again"
13. Jerry Lee Lewis/"What Made Milwaukee Famous"
14. Johnny B. Moore/"Whiskey Drinkin' Woman"
15. Delbert McClinton/"Two More Bottles of Wine"
16. Hank Williams Jr./"Stoned at the Jukebox"
17. George Jones/"Tennessee Whiskey"
18. Ian and Sylvia/"Smiling Wine"
19. Ray Charles/"Let's Go Get Stoned"

These songs represent a wide range of attitudes and emotions about alcohol, and they're all good dance tunes, and fairly obviously they also reveal something about me and my identity, both cultural and personal.

The first tape starts off with some R&B and blues from the forties, fifties, and sixties, and the mood is mellow and celebratory. Floyd Dixon sounds like he's having a good time as he sings "Hey bartender, give me one, two, three more glasses of beer," but John Lee Hooker then comes in with his more menacing vocal and guitar on "One Bourbon, One Scotch, One Beer." His reason for drinking is to forget: "My baby's gone, been gone two nights. . . . I wanna get drunk, get her off my mind," but eventually his drinking seems to work when he sings, "Getting high, mellow, knocked out, feelin' good." Both Dixon and Hooker have a sense of humor about drinking what to others might seem to be excessive amounts.

Next Johnnie Johnson, the piano player in Chuck Berry's band, and Keith Richards of Rolling Stones fame play around with "Tanqueray," not going anywhere, just expressing the anticipation and immediate pleasure of having a drink of gin, repeating "Drink of Tanqueray" several times with great piano and guitar interludes—capturing a certain attitude as they're about to go out and have a drink. They must have been too lazy to write any more lyrics, but, wow, what a solid blues groove. And then Vern Gosdin's lazy-sounding, escapist Caribbean country music about drinking "Tanqueray." After that, John Anderson takes us back to the authentic historical country setting of a "Honky Tonk Saturday Night" while giving us some of the reasons that men and women drink. What were they listening to at the honky-tonk? Had to be Merle Haggard singing "The Bottle Let Me Down," the next song on the drinking tape.

That will give you some idea of the mix of music on the tape—back and forth from celebration to alcoholic depression—a full range of emotions including laugh-out-loud funny. One of the funniest is Tex Ritter's vocal on "Rye Whiskey," in which he sounds drunker as the song progresses. Another comic favorite of mine is Houston blues guitarist Albert Collins's denial in "I Ain't Drunk": "I ain't drunk, I'm just drinkin'." The saddest song among many sad ones is Ted Hawkins's cover of Webb Pierce's surrender to alcoholism, "There Stands the Glass." Hawkins was a street musician who performed along the boardwalk at Venice Beach for years; I was lucky enough to hear him there during a West Coast visit. The next saddest song has to be Keith Whitley's emotional "Tennessee Courage" because his death was related to alcoholism.

Not surprisingly, the most represented singer on the discs is the legendary country singer George Jones. He sings "Relief Is Just a Swallow Away," "Tennessee Whiskey," and a duet with Willie Nelson, "I Gotta Get Drunk." There are only two women lead singers on the CD, Sylvia Fricker, who sings "Smiling Wine" with Ian Tyson, and Suzanne Thomas, who sings her own composition "You're Doing Me Wrong, Jim Beam." I guess women don't drink as much, or maybe they don't talk and sing about it as much as men. The only other song about a drinking woman is Johnny B. Moore's "Whiskey Drinkin' Woman," which is a sad and funny blues complaint. It's mostly American music on the tape, but I really like the two songs by British bands, Squeeze's "When the Hangover Comes" and UB40's reggae version of Neil Diamond's "Red Red Wine."

"Hyperbolicsyllabicsesquedalymistic"

In the summer of 1969, right before I started teaching at Ohio State, I taught in a summer institute at the University of Wisconsin, Milwaukee. One of my fellow teachers at the institute also taught at Ohio State, and we became great friends that summer and still are forty-four years later. Darnell and I partied intensely that summer and continued when we got back to our regular jobs at OSU in the fall. He is a black man originally from Marshall in northeast Texas, and our friendship is at least partially based on that common cultural origin. We liked each other immediately and went out nearly every night drinking and dancing and talking about East Texas and how much our traditions overlapped. Darnell is gay and totally out, even back in the less-tolerant late sixties. The difference in our sexual orientation did not interfere with the deep bonding that took place between us. We still see each other when he comes back to Columbus, and we still talk on the phone, at somewhat irregular intervals now, but the affection is always there.

The participants in the institute were teachers of English as a second language and adult basic education; they were an ethnically and racially mixed group of whites, blacks, and Mexican Americans. Maybe it was late-sixties political and cultural liberal ideals being lived out; I've never been with such an easygoing bunch of people in my life. We partied together and went to bars in black neighborhoods, homes in the section of town where many Hispanics lived, and restaurants in old Hungarian and Polish enclaves of the city. It was also a wonderful summer for music.

We heard lots of different kinds of music: a group of us went to hear Johnny Cash at the Wisconsin State Fair; we heard hippies playing rock music in Lake Park near the campus; and we heard the big R&B hits of that summer at black bars and parties in the houses and apartments of the institute participants. I especially remember a record by Lou Rawls, "Your Good Thing (Is About to End)" and the Isaac Hayes album *Hot Buttered Soul* (Enterprise, ENS-1001) because both were ubiquitous in the summer of 1969. Isaac Hayes's LP was firmly grounded in the soul music tradition of the late sixties, but there was something new in terms of the sound and the songs.

Hot Buttered Soul featured not just soul music but a mix of musical genres—funk ("Hyperbolicsyllabicsesquedalymistic"), pop ("Walk on By"), and country ("By the Time I Get to Phoenix") all held together by Hayes's smoky, sexy vocals. The unusual length of the four numbers on the album, 12:00, 9:55, 5:00, and a whopping 18:40, made it great as a soundtrack for parties—lots of people talking, drinking, getting high, dancing to the slow and up-tempo parts of the album—it felt as if you were in a party scene in a movie with wonderful background music. I bought the album as soon as I got back to Columbus but discovered that it didn't sound as good when I listened to it alone at home. In that context it sounded over produced and bombastic, the slower songs too lugubrious, and the long cuts way too long. You had to be at a party during the summer it was released to appreciate it.

It must have been *the* summer of Isaac Hayes since he also wrote another big hit, "Your Good Thing," a smoldering slow song with Lou Rawls taking on the traditional role of a man standing up to his woman with the threat to leave her if she continues to take him for granted. He tells her that he doesn't have to beg her "'cause somebody else will" take her place. He then warns her,

> Look out, your good thing
> Is about to come to an end.
> Your real good thing
> Is about to come to an end.
> (Transcribed by the author)

The singing is especially effective when Rawls slowly draws out, "Your . . . real . . . good . . . thing." Couples dancing would always react to that line, both men and women, straight and gay. That summer I was dating a woman who also taught at the institute, and the lyrics had meaning for both of us. It was a rocky relationship, and at various points we each could sing, "Your good thing is about to come to an end," and eventually it did. Unlike the Isaac Hayes album, Lou Rawls's song held up outside the party context.

Although we smoked a little weed at the spontaneous hippie celebrations in Lake Park, it was mainly alcohol that summer. But after I got back to Columbus, a marijuana-alcohol mix was the norm. Drinking beer and bourbon had been part of my experience with music since I started college in Beaumont in 1959, and ten years later, at the end of the sixties, drinking wine and smoking pot was added. In some ways, I missed the sixties during the sixties, when I was more an observer, but by the turn of the new decade, I was a full-fledged part of it.

"Don't You Know We're Riding on the Marrakesh Express": Marijuana and Music

From my freshman year in college on, drinking was part of the context of music, and eventually other drugs were too. Before that time, I wasn't even aware of drugs except hearing my mother say she was going to blow opium in our faces when we were acting up. It must have been a reference to some thirties movie. Years later, Daddy told me about the cops in Beaumont selling confiscated marijuana to teenagers when he was in high school, but he didn't say anything about buying or smoking it himself. My first toke was in the dorm at Lamar; it must have been 1960. We had suitemates from the Middle East who came to southeast Texas because of the reputation of Lamar's College of Engineering. Our attitude toward them was typical of our provincial background: everyone referred to them as "camel jockeys" when they weren't around. I might have been more sophisticated and accepting of difference than most of my friends because I had lived on the East and the West Coast and in Canada, and they were mainly small town Texas boys. I was friendly with these slightly older, seemingly serious Arab guys, and at some point they offered me my first joint.

It didn't do anything for me, and it wasn't until 1967, when I was in graduate school in Austin, that I had my second toke. Again, I felt nothing, but it did provide my first connection between marijuana and music. At a party given by undergraduate friends, someone brought in freshly picked home-grown marijuana, they put it in the oven on low to dry it out a little, and of course the smoke started filling up the kitchen for a pre-high. I smoked a little (I didn't smoke cigarettes and was not very good at inhaling) but didn't feel anything but drunk from the booze. We were dancing to the Beatles and the Doors, so there was already that cultural atmosphere bringing music and drugs together.

We were, of course, part of something larger—the whole counterculture movement of the sixties. I was already too old to be part of the avant-garde. I didn't always fit in with a younger hippie crowd, and I didn't become a regular pothead until 1969 when I came to Columbus as a new assistant professor in the English department at Ohio State. I looked like a hippie by then even though I was not doing any drugs. My long, straggly hair, raggedy blue jeans, and tie-dyed T-shirts must have been a signal to kindred spirits of my generation because it didn't take long for me to connect with other young profs who were smoking marijuana and trying other drugs. I was late to the revolution but jumped in enthusiastically, protesting the Vietnam War on the Oval (large green space in the middle of campus) and joining student marches after Kent State.

My African American friend Darnell and I were talking in his office on the third floor of Denney Hall one afternoon when we heard students protesting as they walked down Seventeenth Avenue in the heart of the OSU campus. We stuck our heads out the window and yelled encouragement; the crowd looked up as Darnell grabbed my hand in his as we gave them a clinched fist salute. They all started cheering, and we ran down to the street and joined the protest march. I took part in other marches and sit-ins, but that was the emotional peak of my political engagement of the late sixties–early seventies.

Music and dancing were always part of the experience. In fact, this was a period of my life when music was pervasive—preparing food, eating, hanging around the house, driving the car, sitting on the OSU Oval with friends with a portable radio; that cliché "soundtrack of my life" was true. The music was an extension of what I had been listening to all my life: lots of rock 'n' roll, jazz, blues, R&B, country, bluegrass, and something new, reggae.

Reggae was like religion. Well, it was religion. I never thought about becoming a Rastafarian, but I shared many beliefs and attitudes with followers of this religious movement. What Zap Pow sings on the LP *This Is Reggae Music* (Mango, 7501, 1973) is true, "Once reggae gets in your soul, there will be no more war." Not enough people heard and understood, but I was grabbed by it when I first heard those quirky-sounding sprung rhythms in the late sixties. Having listened to soul music on Stax/Volt records all those years and interacted with black people extensively around the same time, I and many white American reggae fans were already in love with exotic others, and to those of us who romanticized otherness, Jamaicans were even more exotic than American black people.

Being swept up in reggae made us part of a movement that was bigger than we were. Toots and the Maytals sang, "Funky Kingston is all over America," and they were right—North and South, East and West, reggae in Columbus, reggae in Chicago, reggae in the Jamaica of our minds. I heard

Bob Marley and the Wailers at Veterans Memorial Auditorium in Columbus, Toots and the Maytals at the Agora on High Street across from the OSU campus, and other great bands whose names I can't remember at clubs on the north side of Chicago, with pot being passed around every time. I also listened to lots of reggae on records, usually while smoking marijuana. How could we have a more sixties consciousness in the seventies than we did in the sixties? By listening to music that sounded like R&B and soul but expanded our horizons to the Caribbean. Even now, every year in the warming days of early spring, I get the urge to hear reggae and have to get out my old LPs and put on the music that carries me back to that era.

Listening and dancing to reggae in the early seventies, I was smoking more marijuana than I had before, which meant I had to replenish my stash more often, and that led me to some exotic experiences right here in Columbus. I had a friend who was recently divorced and living with two other guys in the student-housing neighborhood near campus. One of his roommates was a dope dealer and through my professor friend, my source at the time. The first and only time I went to their house to pick up an ounce, they invited me and another friend in, told us their roommate was bringing the stuff in from the airport, and offered us a beer and a few tokes while we waited. This was my first time meeting a dealer in person, and when he came in the back door, walked over to me, waved a knife in my face, and said, "Who the fuck is this?" it scared the shit out of me. He laughed and said, "Only joking."

They brought in a large plastic garbage bag full of marijuana, dropped it in the middle of the living-room floor, and started to weigh and put it in sandwich-size baggies. They were all paranoid, for good reason, and when someone knocked at the front door, we all freaked out. Word of the delivery was already out on the street, and the visitor was someone wanting to buy a bag. We smoked and drank a little more, and then my friend and I left. I decided never to pick it up at their house again but have my colleague deliver it to me at my office in Denney Hall. I don't think the chair of the Department of English or any of the senior professors realized that we exchanged drugs in the halls of academe, but they must have smelled it coming out of the bathrooms at various department parties in private homes.

It wasn't always wonderful high times. I had another friend who lived with a dope dealer, and he smoked and drank all the time. Larry (not his real name) had been recently divorced and seemed depressed and somewhat paranoid. He came to a Department of English meeting one night drunk and stoned with a bleeding wound on his forehead; he told us that as he walked to the meeting he saw the guy who had stolen money from his apartment and confronted him. They fought, and the alleged thief roughed up my drunken friend pretty badly. Larry insisted on staying at the meeting even though he was almost incoherent. Later he was driving on a freeway near campus, crossed the median, and crashed into another car. He was injured but survived. We all wondered if it was a suicide attempt. Not too long after this incident, a relative found him hanging in his bedroom closet.

Someone with such serious psychological and emotional problems obviously should not have been doing drugs, and the potential for harming ourselves was always there. We were lucky and usually careful about sources, and my experiences were mainly positive as were those of most of my friends.

Our marijuana use was portable; we even took it with us to academic conferences, where you often caught a whiff of that familiar aroma coming out of hotel rooms. At American Folklore Society meetings, the preferred drug was alcohol, for me Jack Daniels on the rocks. But occasionally someone would bring a small amount of marijuana and share it with friends. I only brought it once, and that was at an AFS meeting in New Orleans in the late seventies. I never did it again because airport security in New Orleans caught me taking it back home. Several planes had been hijacked recently, and security had just become tighter.

I made it through security in Columbus in spite of a nervous friend joking about bombs on planes and drawing unwanted attention to our group. My briefcase was searched, but the security guards didn't look under the papers and books, so on the way home I put the dope in a shirt pocket since they hadn't searched my person the first time. But going home the guard asked me to empty my pockets. The baggie was inside a rolled-up paper lunch bag. "Open it up and empty it," she said. She took the baggie and opened it, smelled it, shook her head, and handed it back to me. "Go on," she said in a tone that said, "You stupid bastard." My heart was somewhere near my shoes; I was convinced that I was headed for a Louisiana jail and would be there a long, long time.

One of the reasons I had brought weed in the first place was to get stoned listening to New Orleans music, and that part worked out fine. Wandering around the French Quarter and going in bars at random, we did hear some great New Orleans R&B, funk, and jazz. I remember hearing Al Hirt, who was big at the time, and some very good local R&B singers whose names I can't remember—too much drinking and toking I guess.

Many years later, the AFS meeting was again in Louisiana, but this time in Lafayette, a town that could be considered the capitol of Cajun music. I didn't bring marijuana with me this time, but a friend did. A group of us were drinking at the hotel late Saturday afternoon, getting liquored up for the conference banquet and dance that night. Steve Riley and the Mamou Playboys were playing at the dance, which was at an outdoor pavilion in a park on the outskirts of Lafayette. I had been collecting Cajun records for years, and the Mamou Playboys became one of my favorites, blending a good dose of R&B saxophone, rock 'n' roll rhythms, and accordion and fiddle that could sound traditionally Cajun and zydeco bluesy, a perfect mix of all the ingredients.

We had been successful in liquoring up for the first stage of the evening, and as soon as we got to the outdoor pavilion, we ate some fantastic Cajun food. Then several of us took a stroll along the bayou while waiting for the band to set up. We ran into an old friend I hadn't seen in several years, and he offered us a joint. After one toke, I realized it was some of the best stuff I'd ever had. The band started to play as we walked back to the pavilion, and I started dancing with a friend. She was as stoned and drunk as I was, and the music took us higher: Cajun two-steps, waltzes, up-tempo zydeco, jitterbugging, dancing on the edge but never falling off. I had never taken Cajun dancing lessons to learn particular steps, so I'm sure our improvised dancing looked ragged, but it felt right. As we were leaving, a good friend who did field research in Louisiana laughed and said, "I've never seen Cajun dancing like that before."

Some of the music that Steve Riley and the Mamou Playboys played that night is on their CD *La Toussaint* (Rounder CD 6068, 1995); even though it's a studio album, it captures the spirit of a live performance with dancers bringing the musicians' energy level even higher. A few years ago, I heard the great Cajun band Beausoleil in Columbus, but this particular performance lacked that excitement because they were playing at the Lincoln Theatre, up on a stage removed from the audience who were politely sitting in rows and not dancing. The playing was technically perfect, but the concert was almost academic, a display of a vital tradition without the vitality of a dance hall. If you can't make it to Lafayette or someplace "Between Eunice and Opelousas" (one of the songs on *La Toussaint*), the next best thing is to have a few drinks, put the CD on your stereo, and dance. "Je M'en Fous Pas Mal," "La Toussaint," and "La Danse de Mardi Gras" will pull you in (for more on Cajun music, see chapter 8).

Lafayette was in 1994, and I was still smoking marijuana. Back in the late sixties and early seventies, when I first started smoking grass, I was also experimenting with psychedelic drugs, and here again music was all around. Whenever we got stoned on marijuana or tripped on LSD, mescaline, or psilocybin (I had to look up the spelling) mushrooms, we always had to spend some of our high time listening to music, and not surprisingly, the music itself often referred to the very drugs we were taking. The music at least partially determined the way the drugs affected us. The first time I took mescaline, I was at home with friends, and we listened to a lot of music, everything from Leo Kottke's *Ice Water* to Bob Dylan's *Nashville Skyline* to Charlie Mingus's *Changes*, and the whole feeling was "mellow," as we used to say.

But the second time was a very different experience. The music and the movie in which it figured and problems with an ex-girlfriend undermined any mellowness I might have felt. The movie was *Fantasia*, and the music was "Night on Bald Mountain." The rerelease of the old Disney movie in 1969 became something potheads and druggies had to see high. I took a girl I had just started dating. Judi was an undergraduate at OSU, but I had met her in Milwaukee when she came to visit a friend who worked as the secretary at the summer institute where I was teaching. We met, started dating, and the relationship continued back in Columbus.

The trouble was that I had been dating another woman in Columbus before I left for the summer, and I neglected to tell Ellie about Judi (not their real names). The relationship with Ellie was passionate; I was in love with her but afraid to make a commitment to her and her three children. Having an affair with another woman was dishonest, cowardly behavior, and I have no excuses. At twenty-nine, freshly divorced and in the midst of sowing my wild oats, I hadn't learned yet to take responsibility for my actions or even to think about the consequences of what I was doing.

At first, watching *Fantasia* high on mescaline was fantastic—the music and animation reimagined through the lens of psychedelic drugs, funny and flying to somewhere else. But when the "Night on Bald Mountain" sequence started, ominous and dark, it was, in the lingo, a real downer. I can joke about it now, but then and there I became more terrified as the music went on. I didn't even realize that I was chewing on my knuckles in anxiety and fear until I started to feel as if I was swallowing my fist. I jerked my knuckles out of my mouth, but the fear remained. Part of me knew this was a hallucination, but that didn't keep me from feeling that I was losing my mind, that the feeling of dread would never go away, that I was altered for life. The dread stayed with me as Judi and I walked out of the theater and ran into Ellie. She looked directly into my eyes, and her anger penetrated my body and soul.

Judi and I went back to my house, and if anything, my fear of being insane for the rest of my life was even stronger. As we walked up the front steps, a car pulled up in front of the building, and I was convinced it was Ellie with a gun. She never had a gun and wasn't a violent person, but I had seen her in the past so angry that it scared me, the feeling now horribly exaggerated by guilt and mescaline. The car pulled away, but I couldn't go in the house. Judi drove me around Columbus the rest of the night. All night I was convinced that I was going to be insane forever. We were sitting in the car at a park on the east side when the sun came up and I finally started to come down.

Once the drug reaction started, I didn't think about the irony of music as the cause of my fear—music was the love of my life; music always made me feel joyful; music had saved me when I fell away from my religion as a teenager. I didn't analyze it then; I didn't think about Modest Mussorgsky making me feel terribly anxious, something Chuck Berry never did no matter what drug I was on. I grew up with very little exposure to classical music, just the Houston Symphony concert for kids in the sixth grade, *Peter and the Wolf*, the 1812 *Overture*, and such. I could listen to blues recordings that were about fear, death, depression, and still feel uplifted. But "Night on Bald Mountain," Disney animation, and mescaline made me go out of my mind.

Forty years later as I was writing this, I looked at the animated "Bald Mountain" sequence from the movie online, and the images seemed pretty silly—sinners in the hands of an angry devil burning in eternal flames, and all of it rendered in clichéd Halloween images. Doesn't do much for me now, but for years I couldn't put my knuckles between my front teeth without conjuring up that feeling of dread. Just now while watching and listening to the original film, I tried it and nothing happened. The explanation is all too obvious: the film and the music and mescaline turned a twenty-nine-year-old man into a thirteen-year-old boy fearful that his sins were condemning him to burn in hell. Those Church of Christ preachers were good at what they did, and their lesson was still in me and pretty damn strong on a subconscious level—the guilt brought to the surface by my betrayal of Ellie.

Other psychedelic experiences also involved Ellie but under happier circumstances. My first acid trip was with her at her house listening mainly to the Beatles. She had been a fan longer than I had, and her record collection had albums I still hadn't bought. It was wonderful to become belatedly familiar with *Rubber Soul* and *Revolver* while high on LSD with her. At one point, I was lying on my back on the bed, looking up at my outstretched arm. It began to get bigger and stronger, more muscular, but then it started to shrivel up and look thin and weak. None of this scared me at all; I was always aware that it was hallucination and, unlike the mescaline experience, would only last a while and then go away. At one point, I went in the bathroom, stood at the sink, and looked down at the toothpaste tube and toothbrush. The purple script letters on the side of the toothbrush, Py-co-pay, started to run off the handle and down the sink like purple ink. It was more like something on a Beatles album cover than anything real.

I heard the Beatles for the first time in a more innocent era when the strongest drug for me was alcohol. It was in 1964 when I was twenty-four and working on my MA at North Texas. My apartment mates and I decided to drive to Southern California on spring break. We drove my Corvair Monza (yes, the car that Ralph Nader said was "unsafe at any speed"), left Denton in the afternoon, and drove straight through to San Diego, stopping only to pee or buy gas. We made tuna sandwiches for the trip and ate them for dinner, breakfast, and lunch. We were crossing the Rocky Mountains that night near Cloud Croft, New Mexico, when one of the cylinders gave out. We drove the rest of the way through the deserts of New Mexico, Arizona, and California on three cylinders.

It was on that trip that Tom, Jim, and I first heard the Beatles singing "I Want to Hold Your Hand" on the radio. I have to say I wasn't blown away, although by the time we got to San Diego, we were all singing along. I could hear echoes of Buddy Holly, and for years I thought of the Beatles as fun rock 'n' roll. But from my perspective as a pretentious twenty-four-year-old graduate student into Thelonious Monk and Miles Davis, the Beatles were too adolescent for my taste.

Several years later when I was in the PhD program in Austin, I bought my first Beatles album. I first heard *Sgt. Pepper's Lonely Hearts Club Band* (Capitol Records, SLEM 081, 1967) being played at the University of Texas Student Co-Op on the drag and bought it before I left the store. Once I was hooked on *Sgt. Pepper*, I realized how much I had underestimated the Beatles, and I eventually bought the earlier albums. I especially remember what I thought of as the "trippy" quality of *Sgt. Pepper*. Even though I wasn't smoking marijuana or taking other drugs at the time, part of the appeal was the psychedelic music and lyrics like "I'd love to tuuuuuuurn yoooouuuu ooooooaaaaaaon" in "Lucy in the Sky with Diamonds," and in "A Day in the Life," "Picture yourself in a boat on a river / With tangerine trees and marmalade skies / Somebody calls you, you answer quite slowly / A girl with kaleidoscope eyes." Later in the early seventies, when I started smoking marijuana regularly and listening to music stoned, I had a throwback sense of experiencing the sixties for the first time.

Except for that one terrible, frightening "Night on Bald Mountain" mescaline trip, my musical/drug experiences were all pretty positive, sometimes euphoric when music and dance and being high came together in just the right way. The hallucinogenic drug experiments continued for about a year, and then I was back to the usual routine of alcohol and marijuana and music and dancing, which continued at more moderate levels until fairly recently when I gave up alcohol, marijuana, and drugs completely because I was having memory problems—relatively mild effects but still worth abstinence.

CHAPTER 5

Blues and the Abstract Truth

From Blues to Jazz

Blues is essential to every kind of music I've written about so far. Blues is obviously the root of rhythm and blues but also in rock 'n' roll, jazz, Broadway show tunes, George Gershwin's *Rhapsody in Blue*, TV commercials, and so on and so on. Blues was crucial to my own teenage engagement in rock 'n' roll, and I continued to learn more about blues as I completed high school and started college in 1959—the end of the fifties and the beginning of the sixties, an era that became associated with the blues revival.

The personal and cultural context for my introduction to the blues was when I finished high school in Ontario in 1959, and we moved to Hammond, Indiana, for yet another refinery construction job in nearby East Chicago. It was here that I started to prepare for going away to college in the fall. Mama and Daddy encouraged me to look for a job to help pay tuition and room and board. I made a half-assed attempt but didn't find anything. I remember having only one interview, for a job as a shoe salesman at a discount store. I did not get it as I must have looked exactly like what I was: inexperienced at anything, someone who had never had a job.

Relieved, I spent the summer reading books from the library, playing tennis with my brother, David, and listening to Top 40 music on the radio. Several of the songs that appealed to me expressed how much I was missing Shirley, the girl I had a couple of dates with back in Oakville. I wallowed in my misery listening to "Since I Don't Have You" by the Skyliners and "There Goes My Baby" by the Drifters, but I must have had some hope of meeting another girl as I fantasized to Dee Clark's "Hey Little Girl in the High School Sweater," "Gee I'd like to know you better." My teenage years were filled with music that matched my volatile emotions—from sheer unbridled joy to abject loneliness.

That summer I was listening to long-playing records for the first time on my new record player, a gift from my parents when I finished the twelfth grade. The first LPs I bought were a mix of jazz (*Ahmad Jamal at the Pershing*; Duke Ellington, *Hi-Fi Ellington Uptown*; Dave Brubeck Quartet, *Time Out*, Columbia, CS 8192, 1959) and rock 'n' roll and R&B (Ray Charles, *What'd I Say*, Atlantic, 2031, 1959; Buddy Holly, *That'll Be the Day*, Decca DL 8707, 1958; Chuck Berry, *After School Session*, Chess, LP 1426, 1957). I was buying records that reflected the blues roots of R&B and rock with some recognition of jazz history in the choice of Duke Ellington. The most recent albums I had bought at the time were *Time Out*, *At the Pershing*, and *What'd I Say*. All these records remain favorites that I still play today, both the original LPs and the CD versions. I took the records and the portable record player with me when I flew for the first time in my life from Midway Airport in Chicago to the Jefferson County Airport, just outside Beaumont, to begin my freshman year at Lamar State College of Technology. It was in southeast Texas that my lessons in blues really started to take off.

It was inevitable that I would go back to my roots in Texas for college. As we moved all over the United States and Canada, Daddy maintained his legal residence in Texas so that David, Linda, and I could attend Lamar on in-state tuition, which was ninety dollars a semester in the fall of 1959. We all ended up getting our BA degrees there, and even though we all lived in the dorm, we felt as if we were home because the Lamar Tech campus was between the smelly refineries we had grown up with and our old neighborhood, South Park, where most of our extended family still lived. Back in Beaumont, I started listening to the same radio stations I had listened to in high school, rock 'n' roll on KTRM in Beaumont and KPAC in Port Arthur.

At Lamar a guy in one of my classes introduced me to R&B music that was unlike any I had heard before. Billy Parrott drove a '56 Chevy, the ultimate cool car that appealed to young men our age because it appealed to young women our age (and younger). The radio in Billy's car was always tuned to the local black radio station, KJET. I wondered why a working-class white kid from deep East Texas had become such a fan of black blues music and singers like B. B. King, Bobby Bland, Little Junior Parker, and Jimmy Reed. I think it was part of his coolness, although I didn't know until much later that we were part of a broader pattern of white teenagers being attracted to African American culture, especially music. We were in some ways like the white hipsters of the previous generation such as Jack Kerouac and his fictional creations Sal Paradise and Dean Moriarty, who made black music and style the essence of cool. In many ways I was ready for this kind of R&B because I had already listened to Big Joe Turner and Fats Domino during my junior high and high school days.

From that moment on, B. B. King was one of my favorite singers and guitarists. I loved the song "Sweet Sixteen" so much that if it was on my car radio when I parked, I wouldn't turn it off until the song was over. Never mind that I was late or one of my friends wanted to get out of the car and go inside. "Sweet Sixteen" was twice as long as any other song on the radio (two sides of a standard 45), and the deejays always played it all the way through. In the early sixties, black blues singers like B. B. King and Bobby Bland were selling records and performing concerts for a mainly black audience. Billy and I were part of a young white audience composed of fans of R&B then, but it would be years before B. B. King made a crossover record that reached a much wider white audience, especially with the popularity of "The Thrill Is Gone" on the LP *Completely Well* (Bluesway, BLS-6037, 1969).

Even though I had been a huge fan of African American R&B for a long time, there was something different about the music on KJET. Ethnomusicologist Charles Keil later called it "urban blues" in his book of the same name. I met Charlie in the late sixties when I was teaching at Buffalo State College and he was at SUNY Buffalo. We met at a twenty-mile walk around Buffalo to raise money for the starving people of Biafra. After that we would occasionally go out for a beer and talk about blues. In his book he defined urban blues by the audience who listened to it, "urban lower-class people . . . who live in big cities and have very little money."

I knew from living in Beaumont that many of the black people who listened to B. B. King, Bobby "Blue" Bland, Little Junior Parker, and the other singers on KJET were poor because they were living in run-down neighborhoods on both sides of South Park. Not all black people were living in poverty, of course; there was an upscale black neighborhood on the southwest side of Beaumont, and the professional people there also listened to R&B.

All the cooks, dishwashers, and servers in the college dorm dining hall at Lamar were black. The cafeteria workers played B. B. King and Bobby Bland over the sound system even though (or because) the dorms were entirely white. Lamar was first integrated in 1958, the year before I started as a freshman, and the dorms weren't integrated until sometime after I graduated. Most of the white kids liked the R&B played in the cafeteria even if they weren't listening to KJET and buying urban blues records.

What was the appeal of working-class black music for young, upwardly mobile white college students? What role did socioeconomic class and gender play within the larger consideration of the exotic other and cross-racial "desire" (see chapters 2 and 8)? Why did white guys like music sung by black guys even after white kids had assumed command of rock 'n' roll as "our" music? These are still significant questions for twenty-first-century popular music with so many white singers emulating black rap and hip-hop.

"Paying the Cost to Be the Boss"

We white blues fans maintained other stereotypes about black blues musicians: they were heavy drinkers, they attracted women with their powerful sexuality, they spent money irresponsibly, and they drove big, flashy Cadillacs (the cover of Little Junior Parker's LP *Driving Wheel* has a photo of him stepping out of a long white Caddy). These images were part of the blues lyrics they sang and part of their performing personas, but white fans and writers alike saw these representations not as racial images but as basic facts. The underlying stereotypes were also part of the perception of black pimps, criminals, and lower-class black men in general. Hardworking, churchgoing, family-supporting black men who would counter the stereotype were left out of the representation.

Since I was a student interested in African American culture, some of the appeal of blues for me was the assumption that the lyrics depicted the reality of lower-socioeconomic African American life. I wasn't conscious that this was a stereotype in my teens and twenties, and only became cognizant of it in my thirties when I started reading more widely in articles and books on African American culture. The lyrics take on new meanings when you consider what they probably meant to black listeners and how these meanings contradicted interpretations filtered through the racial imagination of white critics and fans. A good example is the opening lines of B. B. King's "Sweet Sixteen" (1960).

> When I first met you baby, baby you were just sweet sixteen
> (repeat)
> You left your home then woman, oh the sweetest thing I'd
> ever seen
> But you wouldn't do nothing for me baby;
> You wouldn't do anything I asked you to (repeat)

You know you ran away from your home baby
And now you wanna run away from old me (or B) too.
(Transcribed by the author)

His girlfriend's age of "sweet sixteen" might reinforce the white image of poor blacks as more sexual and promiscuous than whites, an image that was even depicted in the scholarship.

For instance, folk song scholar Alan Lomax, a white southerner and a Texan like myself, depicted black female sexuality as beginning at an early age: "Sexually active at ten or eleven, with marriage maybe only a couple of years off, a [black Mississippi] Delta country girl needed to know how to sort through the males, and how to move between marriage partners." According to Lomax, African American sexuality was maintained and expressed through music and dance as he revealed in his description of black dancers: "The couples, glued together in a belly-to-belly, loin-to-loin embrace, approximated sexual intercourse as closely as their vertical posture, their clothing, and the crowd around them would allow." He doesn't seem to realize that young white dancers in the fifties were also dancing this way; at least I have not been able to find any examples in his writings. He probably would have interpreted B. B. King's "Sweet Sixteen" as a continuation of the sexual functions of African American folk song and dance. He saw such behavior as culturally based, but unfortunately his descriptions reinforced a widely held white stereotype of black people.

Bobby Bland's "Your Friends" (1962) conjured up other kinds of stereotypes in the minds of some white listeners in the early sixties.

Don't let your friends turn you against me, baby,
'Cause they ain't giving you one red cent (repeat)
I said, when I leave you this time baby,
I just want to know who's gonna pay your house rent?
(Transcribed by the author)

Her friends say that he hunts "women like a dog hunt(s) a bone," but he reminds her, "Every week I bring my paycheck home." My sense of what the song means was based on a white middle-class perception of black lower-class economic life. I imagined the relationship to be what used to be called a "common law" marriage; the couple is not married, just living together, and the only thing keeping them together is the man's paycheck. From the man's perspective, his own promiscuous sexual behavior, "hunting women like a dog hunt a bone," has to be excused because he is the breadwinner in the family. Money establishes his rights and his power over the woman. He is so full of his own sense of power that he thinks her girlfriends are trying to break them up because they want to have sex with him. I didn't perceive white middle-class marriages in this way because in my mind the couples were legally and religiously joined in matrimony, ignoring the fact of infidelity and common-law marriage among white couples as well.

This theme continued in urban blues for quite a while. B. B. King's 1968 song "Paying the Cost to Be the Boss" paints a similar picture of a married relationship, and I took it as more evidence of my interpretation of African American lower-class married life.

> You act like you don't wanna listen, when I'm talking to you.
> You think you outta be my baby, anything you wanna do.
> You must be crazy, baby, you just gotta be out of your mind
> As long as I'm payin' the bills, woman, I'm payin' the cost to be
>   the boss.
> (Transcribed by the author)

He's even more emphatic than Bobby Bland, and he offers a more detailed rationale for his power over the woman.

I heard B. B. King sing "Paying the Cost to be the Boss" in person in the late sixties, and the mostly black audience responded with loud approval, even many of the women in the crowd. I went backstage after the show and used my acquaintance with Charlie Keil, who had traveled with B.B. while doing research for *Urban Blues*, to gain access to his dressing room. It seemed that a small party was going on, with several people drinking and talking. B.B. graciously invited me in as soon as I mentioned Keil's name, and I sat down with his other guests and joined the conversation. B.B. was expressing a little nervousness about being on Merv Griffin's network television talk show the next day, and his friends were assuring him that he was going to be a hit. People then started chatting in smaller groups, and I began talking with the woman sitting next to me. She was complaining about her boyfriend ordering her around too much. I took a chance and said, "Paying the cost to be the boss?" She laughed and agreed that he was supporting her but still thought he was too controlling.

We had somehow avoided a potential cultural gender clash, and later I figured out it was because certain attitudes about gender are shared across racial/cultural lines. The song expressed certain attitudes of the black record-buying and concert-going public, but these inclinations are probably more socioeconomic than racial; white working-class couples had similar gender-role expectations. Even if the wife worked outside the home, when the man made more money, he expected to exercise more power. And, in fact, the same pattern probably existed in middle- and upper-class behavior.

The Blues Revival

B. B. King, Bobby Bland, and the other urban blues singers had jazz-influenced bands with pianos, saxophones, trumpets, trombones, and electric guitars, but some black musicians performing and recording in the late fifties and early sixties were still playing an earlier acoustic style of blues that reached a wider audience of young white college students than urban blues did. These performers were considered part of the blues revival, which was more directly linked to the acoustic music of the broader folk music revival. The country blues performers included singers and guitarists like Mississippi John Hurt and Furry Lewis, who had originally recorded in the 1930s but usually weren't recorded again until the blues revival. Once I became aware of country blues, I started buying more records by both the old and the new singers and guitarists.

As noted in chapter 1, the first record I bought by an early blues performer was the Robert Johnson LP *King of the Delta Blues*. In the same way I had discovered B. B. King, I became aware of Robert Johnson through a college friend, not Billy Parrott this time, but another friend, Brady Parker, who was living with his parents in Port Arthur, fourteen miles away. One afternoon he drove up to the Lamar campus and burst into my dorm room with an LP in his hand. "You have to hear this!" I put it on the turntable, and the first sounds of Robert Johnson's "Crossroad Blues" came tearing out of the speakers. I had never heard anything quite like his singing and guitar playing before. The album introduced me to an older form of blues, in this case from the 1930s, and it taught me where everything else in that genre had come from. After listening to that first cut, Brady and I jumped up and ran outside screaming. People were used to this kind of behavior in the dorms, and we didn't find anybody else to listen to the record with us. We went back to my room and listened to the rest of it in awe and wonder, and almost fifty years later I was still teaching a song from the album in my folk music classes.

"Terraplane Blues" is alternately despairing, ironically funny, and triumphant (Terraplane was a model of Hudson automobiles).

> I feel so lonesome, you hear me when I moan
> When I feel so lonesome, you hear me when I moan
> Who's been drivin' my Terraplane, for you since I been gone?
>
> I flash your lights, Mama, your horn won't even blow
> (Spoken: Somebody's been runnin' my batteries down on
>   this machine)
> I flash my lights, Mama, this horn won't even blow
> There sure is a missed connection, woo now baby, way
>   down below.
> (Transcribed by the author)

He continues the car/sex metaphor throughout the song: "I'm gonna heist your hood, Mama, I'm bound to check your oil," "When a woman in a bad condition, you gotta get the battery charged," "I'm gonna get deep down in this connection, keep on tanglin' with your wires," "when I mash down on your starter, and your spark plug will give me fire."

One of the amazing things about this song is how the narrator starts out deeply depressed because his lover won't respond to him sexually the way she did previously. He suspects another man has "been kicking in his stall," as Muddy Waters expressed it years later, but here instead of a barnyard metaphor, his girlfriend's lack of response is compared to a slick, new car that won't start. The metaphor seems comically effective in describing his sexual frustration and his feelings of betrayal, "black" comedy in terms of blending humor and despair. Finally, though, after all his weeping and moaning, he seems determined and convinced that when he mashes down on her starter, her sparkplug *will* give him fire. Great poetry, but as with most blues, folk, rock, and pop lyrics, the full artistic power is lost to a certain degree on the printed page. Hearing the emotion in Robert Johnson's voice and from his bottleneck guitar gives you the full effect of his art.

Brady Parker first led me to Robert Johnson, and he was also a link to other facets of the blues revival. His hometown, Port Arthur, was also the home of Janis Joplin, who was a student at Lamar for a couple of semesters while I was there. I saw her perform twice in Austin (more on this later) before she made her first Columbia record and became nationally famous. She was a student at Lamar off and on in 1963 and '64. I never met her, but

I knew her reputation because two of her friends from Port Arthur, Jim Langdon and Wally Stover, were also students at Lamar. Although they were in my English classes, I didn't know either of them very well, but somehow through the grapevine I heard about this friend of theirs who sang blues.

I and my closest English-major friends, Terry Brown and Madeleine Bloch, who were from Nederland between Beaumont and Port Arthur, thought of Jim and Wally as the resident Lamar beatniks. Wally's hair and attire were like a hippie before there was such a term, and Jim looked more like a beatnik from the late forties and early fifties. They and their friends had a regular table at the student union, and so did Terry, Madeleine, Brady, and I. We lovers of literature would talk about e. e. cummings's poems and Faulkner's *Light in August*, which we were reading in the modern American novel class, but we also talked about the latest Ray Charles or Cannonball Adderly albums, our English profs, or the beatniks at their nearby table.

Langdon was the closest to Janis Joplin; he is mentioned and quoted numerous times in the two biographies I have read about her. In the biographies, Langdon also refers to his frequent weekend trips with Janis to the Big Oak, where I and my friends also went to hear live blues and rock (see chapter 3). Langdon was a jazz musician and had a goatee, which counted a lot on the beatnik meter. We probably had more in common with him and Janis than any of us realized, but we looked more conventional than they did at the time. Langdon and I were in the same creative writing class. I think the teacher, Miss Scurlock, gave everybody As, but Jim Langdon deserved his and I didn't. I wrote bad modern poetry imitating e. e. cummings: "Small in the immense presence of night's sky."

Because Jim Langdon, Wally Stover, Brady Parker, and Janis Joplin were from Port Arthur, I thought of it as a hip town for music. Then again, my hometown, Beaumont, wasn't bad either since Johnny and Edgar Winter were both from there. Brady, Janis, and I and all our friends were deeply into blues. Southeast Texas had left its musical mark on all of us. Looking back, I think the atmosphere in our corner of the world was just right for white kids to be blues fans.

Janis Joplin was part of the same culture and in the same age cohort as we were, but she had a talent as a singer and interpreter of blues into rock 'n' roll that transcended the rest of us. I heard her twice while I was in graduate school in Austin. I don't remember the exact dates, probably in 1965, when she sang at a club near the UT campus called the Eleventh Door. It was on the second floor of a ramshackle wood building, and you entered by an outdoor stairway—not very big inside, a fairly intimate setting for hearing her sing and play the guitar. She was already singing in her boisterous, loud, and emotionally charged way, and I loved the show. At this time, she was also singing regularly at Threadgill's, a place that was becoming legendary during that period.

I also heard her in an even more intimate setting, and I know the exact date, April 17, 1965, at the annual meeting of the Texas Folklore Society. My mother was visiting me in Austin, and she was excited about going to an academic meeting with me. Neither of us knew Janis Joplin was going to be there, although I wasn't surprised since I knew she had been in a folklore class at Lamar taught by Francis Abernethy, better known as Ab to some of his students. I had taken a class with him too (see below); he liked the paper I wrote for his class on blues and jazz, and he asked me to read it at the 1964 TFS meeting. I became a member of the society and started attending their annual meetings, not knowing that at next year's meeting, Janis Joplin would be performing at the Thursday night "beer-and-barbecue hootenanny," as Ab called it in a book he wrote on the history of the society. Here's his description of Janis at this event:

> That was the night Janis Joplin showed up. She had briefly sat in on one of my folklore classes at Lamar and regularly stopped by my office to play my guitar when she was on that campus. She had since, however, moved to the University of Texas campus and had become a regular performer at Threadgill's. She was always looking for an audience, so she called me and asked to sing at the hoot. I was a little leery of what she might come up with, so I suggested to Hermes (Nye, the song leader that night) that she be held to the end of the first round of singing. . . . She was at that time getting into hard blues and blues-rock sounds that later became her style and was completely involved in her delivery of the song. . . . That night she sang "Sal's Got a Meatskin" and some blues. She was great, really strong and vital, and a true part of what she was singing, and everybody there was impressed by her.

My mother certainly was. There was no stage, and we happened to be sitting a couple of feet from where Janis was singing. I told Mama who she was and that she was from Port Arthur and had gone to Lamar. Being from Beaumont, my mother immediately liked her as almost a hometown girl, and she liked her even more after she sang. After several numbers, Mama reached over and touched her arm and told her how much she liked her singing, and Janis smiled and thanked her. Two Texas women, one quite a bit older than the other, but their Texas drawls were the same, and their outgoing attitude was similar despite the difference in age. This little incident remains one of the most pleasant and satisfying musical moments of my life.

My mother did something else that night that tickled me. There was an older man sitting near us who was talking a lot and seemed to be trying to impress everybody. "Who's that old coot?" Mama asked me in her usual loud voice. "Shh," I whispered, "that's my boss, the chair of the English department." I was a teaching assistant at the time, and it occurred to me that Mama's remark wouldn't be the best thing for my career.

Janis Joplin's performance affected us all. I think Ab's description of her is one of the most insightful I've read. As he said, she did sing a lot of blues that night, giving us some sense of the delivery that later made her famous. I don't remember her singing any Robert Johnson songs that night, but knowing about her deep interest in blues, and the fact that my Port Arthur friend Brady had introduced me to Robert Johnson's music, I'm sure Janis Joplin was a fan too. Robert Johnson was the start of my deep interest in rural acoustic blues, and as a fan of urban blues, rock 'n' roll, jazz, and country music, I began to see connections between all these different genres.

Pretty soon I started to analyze and write about the various forms of American vernacular music. In 1963, when I was a senior at Lamar and taking an intro to folklore class that Ab taught, I wrote a term paper titled "Folk Elements in Modern Jazz: The Soul Movement." As mentioned earlier, Ab asked me to read the paper at a meeting of the Texas Folklore Society at the Shamrock Hotel in Houston in 1964, the year before we heard Janis in Austin. I still have the 1964 program, a memorable souvenir since on the back John Lomax Jr. had written the phone number of the great Texas blues singer Lightnin' Hopkins, CA 5-6847.

John Lomax Sr. was the father of American folk music field research. His younger son, Alan, became a major international folk song scholar, and John Jr. worked in construction like my father, but he was also a collector and singer of folk songs. At the Texas Folklore Society meeting in Houston, John Jr. came up to me after I finished my paper and asked if I was a Lightnin' Hopkins fan. When I said yes, he asked if I'd like to meet him. Wow, it was a possibility beyond a young blues fan's wildest imaginings. He said I could call Lightnin' and invite him to the hotel to play for us. All I had to do was offer him a bottle of gin. So many songs by blues musicians are about drinking that blues scholars assume that the musicians themselves are heavy drinkers. I called and sure enough Lightnin' answered and said he would like to play for us but was booked at a club in Arcola, south of Houston, that night. I was disappointed but still thrilled to talk to him on the phone.

I met him a few years later when I was in graduate school in Austin and he was playing at a campus music joint, the Matchbox. He was sitting at the bar having a drink, and I sat down and we talked for a little while. I think mentioning John Lomax Jr.'s name helped, and he seemed open to my questions. The only other time I saw him was when I was visiting my friends Kyle and Nancy in Los Angeles in the late sixties, and we went to hear him at the Ash Grove. Again, he was friendly and pretended to remember me.

Discovering Lightnin' Hopkins in the early sixties indicated that I was already influenced by the blues revival, although I wasn't aware of it as a popular culture movement or that different generations of musicians were involved. Robert Johnson was one of those singer/guitarists who recorded in the twenties and thirties and were long dead by the early sixties, but there were also old bluesmen like Bukka White, Fred McDowell, Mississippi John Hurt, and Furry Lewis who were still alive. They were rediscovered and recorded by white researchers in the late fifties and early sixties, and their records along with their white imitators like Dave Van Ronk (*Van Ronk Sings Ballads, Blues, and a Spiritual*, Folkways, FS 3818, 1959) and Koerner, Ray and Glover (*Blues, Rags and Hollers*, Elektra, EKL 240, 1963) were expressions of the blues revival.

Finally, there were people like Lightnin' Hopkins. Originally from rural, small-town East Texas, he started out playing acoustic country blues, but after he moved to Houston he began playing amplified blues for an urban black audience while maintaining a connection to the earlier country blues tradition of Blind Lemon Jefferson and Texas Alexander. Once the white market was established for country blues, record producers started recording singer/guitarists like Lightnin' Hopkins who were playing the acoustic folk blues that was popular among college students. I bought both his earlier records of amplified music and his more recently recorded acoustic country blues. Listening to those albums prompted me to write the paper about the connections between folk music and jazz and I was lucky enough to meet him and hear him live in Austin and Los Angeles.

I tended to be attracted to Texas blues performers because they were close at hand—Lightnin' Hopkins in Houston and another favorite, Mance Lipscomb, from the small town of Navasota, north of Houston, whom I heard at the University of Texas Student Union when I was a graduate student. He appeared to be a kind, gentle man onstage, unassuming and honored to be at the university; at the same time we students were honored to be able to hear such an authentic performer in person, someone who represented an earlier period of history. For me, that was the era when my grandmother Nanny had grown up on a tenant farm in North Texas, but I also knew that was a time when the races were even farther apart than during my childhood in Beaumont. Still I felt nostalgic, although now I know how ironic it is to romanticize a period of widespread racism.

Mance Lipscomb was an incredible guitar player and singer, not in the urban blues style I was used to, not a shouter or a moaner, but still deeply emotional. His first album, *Mance Lipscomb: Texas Sharecropper and Songster*, was recorded in Navasota in 1960 by fieldworker/producer Mack McCormick and Chris Strachwitz, owner of Arhoolie records. The *sharecropper* tag was typical of blues revival albums, a way of establishing the authenticity of the performer. The term *songster* was Mack McCormick's way of indicating that Mance's tradition was more than blues since it contained "ballads, breakdowns, reels, shouts, drags, jubilees, *and blues*," McCormick's way to emphasize that the African American music tradition was more varied and complex than blues revival writers had realized. This was news to me because I and most fans had focused mostly on just one kind of black traditional music.

The first Mance Lipscomb album expressed that variety, and even though the second Arhoolie album recorded by Strachwitz in California in 1964 (*Texas Songster, Volume 2*, Arhoolie Records, F1023) was supposed to have an "emphasis . . . on the blues," ("Come Back Baby," "Key to the Highway," "Boogie in A"), it also contained songs like the country dance piece "Alabama Jubilee," the gospel song "God Moves on the Water (The Titanic)," and "Spanish Flang Dang," an instrumental that was played by "many songsters all through the South and Mance says he heard it from a bunch of Mexican field hands." I love finding such information on album liner notes; it reinforces my sense of the tremendous blending across racial and ethnic lines in American vernacular music. I bought the second album first, right after I heard Mance in person, and it remains my favorite. I've listened to it many times over the years, and I know every song and every guitar note, like an old friend telling stories I've heard a hundred times before.

"Blues around the Corner" (in Italy)

Mance Lipscomb was one of those black musicians who were discovered during the early years of the blues revival in the United States. The revival had also spread to England during the early sixties when white British performers like Eric Clapton, Mick Jagger, Keith Richards, John Mayall, Jimmy Page, and Jeff Beck first heard African American blues and began to develop it into blues rock. They were members of some of the most popular rock bands of that era—the Rolling Stones, Led Zeppelin, Cream, the Yardbirds, and the Bluesbreakers. I bought records by most of the British blues rockers, but I didn't realize until 1983, when I heard Italian blues, that the blues revival had also spread to the rest of Europe.

I was in Italy on a Fulbright scholarship teaching American folklore and literature at the University of Rome. One of my Italian colleagues at the Magistero (College of Education in American terms) asked me to read not one paper but three at a seminar on American literature at the Centro di Studi Americani, which was right around the corner from my apartment. Being the "innocent abroad," I agreed to the overload. The papers were titled "Folklore in *Adventures of Huckleberry Finn*," "Folklore and Feminism in *Their Eyes Were Watching God*," and "Rockabilly Music and the Beat Generation" (see chapter 3). They were all well received, but the rockabilly paper caused the most discussion. I was still talking to a member of the audience about American music after most people had left. She suggested we continue our discussion at a nearby coffee bar. Her name was Cinzia Biagiotti, and we became good friends through our love of American folk music.

Not that our tastes were exactly the same; I was more into rock 'n' roll, while Cinzia loved acoustic folk music and was a huge fan of Joan Baez. She played guitar and sang in the Baez style. She was a teacher in Pisa, and she invited me to visit her. A few weeks later, I took the train to Grosetto, where she was staying with her mother while Cinzia was working at a nearby camp for the summer. While she was working, I took a side trip to Siena but got back in time to go to a concert that evening where two of Cinzia's friends were playing. To my pleasant surprise, they were in a very good blues band that sang traditional and original songs in both Italian and English. Her friends were Luciano Federighi, who played piano, sax, and sang, and Fabio Ragghianti, who played guitar, dobro, and sang. The traditional songs they played that night were "How Long," "C. C. Rider," and others I forget. Some of their own compositions were "Fabio's Fables," "Gregory Corso" (Beat poet of the late forties and early fifties), "Blues around the Corner," and "Se noi volessimo e o non volessimo essere." We went out for drinks with them after the concert, and I hung out with them the next day.

Luciano did most of the singing; he had a gravelly voice unlike his ordinary speaking voice, and it nicely evoked some black blues singers of the forties especially in his version of "Cherry Red." They were mainly playing in an older acoustic-blues style, although when Fabio played electric guitar, it definitely showed the influence of the amplified sounds of T-Bone Walker and other blues guitarists from the forties and fifties. They gave me a copy of their album *Loose As a Goose* (1979), which was produced by a collective they belonged to called UXA Musical Workshop.

The album contained most of the songs they played that night, including an acoustic guitar number written and played by Fabio that had blues elements in it but also ventured into jazz and folk guitar improvisations. They were both as educated in American blues as any musician or fan I had ever known in the United States. I still have their *Loose As a Goose* album, which is now available online (http://www.discogs.com/Uxa-Musical-Workshop-Loose-As-A Goose/ release/4449607). Luciano is also a blues scholar, and he gave me a copy of his book, *Blues nel mio animo: Temi e poesia del blues.* He graciously signed it "To Pat, With friendship & admiration."

"Make My Home Where I Hang My Hat": Texas Blues in Ohio

I took my love of Texas blues with me when I moved to Ohio, and it was in Ohio that I became a fan of the Houston bluesman Johnny Copeland. I had several of his albums, and I could hear the connection between his urban style and B. B. King's. Copeland came to Columbus in 1982, and I couldn't wait to hear him. I was so struck by his performance that night that I wrote a review right after I got home. It wasn't published until after Copeland died in 1997, when I submitted it to the *Columbus Blues Alliance Newsletter* as a tribute. Here it is as it appeared in a subsequent (undated) issue of the newsletter:

> On Wednesday night, May 16, Johnny Copeland's blues band played before a small but enthusiastic crowd at Stache's, a campus bar near Ohio State. The music was tough and electric, an amazing synthesis of blues,

soul, funk, and jazz, proof of the continuing vitality of contemporary blues. And it was definitely blues; at the core postwar southwestern blues which paid homage to T-Bone Walker, Clarence "Gatemouth" Brown, and B. B. King, but it was also blues which had absorbed the sounds of Muddy Waters, James Brown, Otis Redding, and John Coltrane. Blues which was finally what blues has always been—a personal statement of the performer. Johnny Copeland managed to incorporate all of these influences and keep a distinctive voice.

During the intermission Copeland sat at the bar drinking coffee and talking to a couple of eager blues fans (me and my brother-in-law Vic). I mentioned my Texas background, and he seized on it immediately.

"I always say that my blues is Texas blues. If I can make people aware of it, it will help those coming up back home."

He told us that there will be a Texas Blues Night at the Chicago Fest this summer which will feature Copeland, Albert Collins, and "Gatemouth" Brown. Copeland repeatedly referred to the importance of "links" in blues, and as if to illustrate he played a T-Bone Walker number in the second set and quoted from other great bluesmen throughout both sets.

Johnny Copeland currently lives in New York, but he still performs frequently in his hometown of Houston. From the age of thirteen he lived in Houston's Third Ward where he heard Lightnin' Hopkins' early country-becoming-urban blues.

The other end of the spectrum of influences is represented by the New York musicians who backed him on his first Rounder album *Copeland Special*—noted jazz sax players George Adams, Arthur Blythe, and Bayard Lancaster. The album is a remarkable combination of blues tradition and current jazz.

The second Rounder album, appropriately entitled *Make My Home Where I Hang My Hat* has back-up by the band that appeared with Copeland in Columbus—Ken Vangel, piano; Mitchell Merritt, bass; Julian Vaughan, drums; John Pratt, trumpet; and Joe Rigby, saxophone—a polished and exciting contemporary blues band, all dedicated to making powerful music. They were equally adept at the fast jump blues tunes such as "Boogie Woogie Nighthawk" and "Claim Jumper," slow blues such as "Devil's Hand" and "Well Well Baby-La," and funk influenced numbers such as "Love Utopia."

Johnny Copeland was always at the center, intensely singing and playing every song, putting everything into his performance despite the small crowd. Dressed in a dark grey double-breasted suit, with a white shirt opened to reveal numerous gold chains, he played soaring guitar solos as his voice moved easily from growling bass depths to falsetto screams.

The blues are alive and well in Columbus, Ohio, and thanks to performers like Johnny Copeland, the blues are alive and well in the rest of the world. To find out just how alive, go out and buy a Johnny Copeland album.

Genius + Soul = Jazz: Blues into Jazz

I became a jazz fan in high school in Ontario when I met Scott Cushnie. He was two years older and out of school. That was enough for him to seem cool to me, but he also played piano and had a jazz record collection, even cooler. We met through a high school fraternity I was asked to join. I never figured out why they asked me; I wasn't that cool. Only one thing made me stand out: I was the only teenage Texas boy in Oakville. Scott would invite another friend and me over to his house to listen to records when his parents weren't home. This was significant to me because his father was my physics, chemistry, and homeroom teacher, a stern and intimidating figure. This image of Mr. Cushnie was reinforced on the first day of school my last year at Blakelock High School.

I had been out in Montana that summer baling hay on my brother-in-law's father's ranch. Mama took Linda, David, and me with her on the long drive out there from Ontario to visit Sissy and Bob and their six kids, my mother's only grandchildren at the time. Some college guys were working for Elmer, and I expressed an interest in working with them, which I did for about two weeks. It was a good experience and I expected my first paycheck ever, but Elmer must have thought I had worked for the experience—no paycheck. It was still a great experience; I liked the other guys and hung out with them at their bunkhouse a few times. Two of them were growing beards, and I thought what a great idea and started to grow one. It was a thick beard by the time we went back home except my mustache was kind of scraggly, and I shaved it off and kept the beard. At the Canadian border at Detroit/Windsor, we stopped and went into the customs office. Some Amish people noticed my beard and smiled and nodded at me as I walked by. That gave me pause; I thought I looked cool, like a hipster or a jazz musician, but being mistaken for an Amish teenager didn't seem very cool.

I kept the beard and went to school with it the first day. I was a little late, and everybody was already assembled in the gym/auditorium for the principal's welcome speech. He had already started, and when I walked in (remember this was 1958), the other kids started pointing and whispering, which got louder and louder until Mr. Pew had to stop talking and demand that people quiet down. I hadn't expected anything like this and was embarrassed, but I also liked the attention. As I walked to class, I was enjoying the sudden notoriety, but my homeroom and science teacher, Mr. Cushnie, ignored me when I came in. He gave us the standard first-day instructions, and when the bell rang, we all walked out. As I passed his desk, he stopped me and said, "Don't come back with that." I was too intimidated to say anything and just left. I had a fleeting thought of going to the principal's office to appeal, but quickly realized the futility of that since I had disrupted Mr. Pew's speech.

I went to my classes, talked to friends, and basked in all the attention, especially from girls. I was thinking about keeping the beard and coming back with it the next day as a form of protest. Later in the sixties, I realized what a great teenage act of rebellion this would have been, but I couldn't work up enough courage to do it in 1958. For one thing I was on the football team, and I knew I would be kicked off the team if I was suspended from school. I shaved that night and meekly returned to Mr. Cushnie's class the next morning.

You can see why I wasn't eager to run into him when I dropped by the Cushnies' house. Somehow I never saw either of his parents there. Scott would sometimes have a drink, and I would say, "No, thanks," still feeling my Church of Christ background combined with fear of being caught. I think perhaps his drinking was the reason he made sure his parents were never home when he asked us over. The music he played was my introduction to jazz, and what I heard was the foundation for my jazz record collection, the same albums I mentioned at the beginning of this chapter: *Ahmad Jamal at the Pershing* and *Hi-Fi Ellington Uptown*.

Scott's great taste in jazz must have come from playing jazz piano. I heard him in person a few times; he performed with two other guys in the fraternity who played bass and drums. There was a nonalcoholic jazz club in Oakville, making it possible for an underage fan like me to get in. It was another cool thing I experienced for the first time, and I was impressed by the place, the hip older crowd, the music, and myself for being there. I looked up Scott Cushnie on the internet recently, and it turns out he has had a successful career as a musician and is still well known in Toronto. He's been in several pop/rock groups whose records have sold well in Canada, and he has recorded with a number of American singers and bands.

I've had a copy of one of the American recordings that he plays on since it first came out in 1970. It was recorded in Muscle Shoals, the legendary recording studio in Alabama. The album features Ronnie Hawkins, the Arkansas singer who was playing in Canada in the late fifties and early sixties when he put together a backup band with musicians who later became the Band. The musicians on the 1970 *Ronnie Hawkins* LP (Roulette SR 25078) are described on the album notes: "The personnel is: King Biscuit Boy, harmonica; Barry Beckett & Scotty Cushnie, keyboard; Duane Allman, Eddie Hinton & Jimmy Johnson, guitars; David Hood, bass; Roger Hawkins, drums"—pretty impressive musical company for my high school friend.

Scott made his name in rock 'n' roll and pop, but he also had a strong background in jazz, and his knowledge of jazz determined my early jazz aesthetic. He made me aware of the jazz magazine *Downbeat*, which was my introduction to jazz criticism. I learned a lot about the music from the critics, but I wasn't too fond of their jazz snobbery. Because of my love of R&B and rock 'n' roll, I could never see popular music as inferior to jazz. The critics always acknowledged a relationship between jazz and other genres, but too many considered jazz superior. To me the connection between jazz, blues, pop, country, bluegrass, gospel, and other genres of vernacular music was extensive.

This musical interaction seemed so apparent that it was the basis for the college paper I mentioned earlier, "Folk Elements in Modern Jazz: The Soul Movement." "Folk" in the title mainly meant blues, and it's obvious to anyone who knows anything about jazz that its roots are in African American folk music, especially the blues. I could not understand why musical genres had to be hierarchical in terms of aesthetics; there can be great transcendent art in jazz and in blues just as there is in classical and folk music. None of these categories is uniformly great art, but the best of all of them can be. I would say the same about rock, country, bluegrass, folk, conjunto, Cajun, and zydeco. I deal with these genres in other chapters, but here I want to concentrate on some of the connections between blues and jazz and my own experiences with them.

One of the major common elements of blues and jazz is improvisation; both depend on making it up as you go along, not just playing a tune the same way every time but changing it while keeping the basic structure in place (although even this can be altered in avant-garde jazz). Both blues and jazz musicians improvise in singing and instrument playing. One traditional blues song structure is made up of three lines with the second repeating the first, and a new third line. One idea behind this form is that the singer can think of a new line while repeating the first. Also, different performances by the same singer of the same song might have the verses in a different order—all improvised as she sings. A guitar solo in blues can also vary every time it is played.

Jazz took the improvising of blues and extended it. One key pattern in jazz is to state the melody fairly briefly and then go off into extended improvisations in which each instrument takes a turn before returning to the melody for a short time at the end. It can be more complicated than this, but the sense of surprise and sometimes delight for the listener, not knowing what might come next, is part of the excitement of listening to blues and jazz. Some singers and musicians are better at improvisation than others, more original, clever, or funny, but the essence of the music depends on improvising.

The jazz albums I bought at first—Dave Brubeck, Duke Ellington, Ahmad Jamal—weren't especially defined by blues, but they all incorporated elements of it. At the 1958 Newport Jazz Festival, one of the Ellington numbers that Dave Brubeck chose to play to honor the Duke was "C Jam Blues," just one example to indicate their common grounding in the blues. Ahmad Jamal on his album *Jamal at the Penthouse* (Argo, LP-646S, 1959) plays his own composition "Jamal's Blues." The direct connection of blues and jazz didn't sink in completely until I heard the first jazz recordings of Ray Charles. As I mentioned in chapter 2, Ray Charles was one of my very first discoveries when I started listening to R&B and rock 'n' roll in 1954. I had been buying his R&B 45s for years before I discovered his jazz side.

In 1959 I bought his first album *Ray Charles* (Atlantic, 8006, 1957), which featured his hit R&B singles. Later I bought *Ray Charles at Newport* (Atlanta, 1289, 1958), which mixed R&B and jazz. I liked all the jazz performances— "In a Little Spanish Town," "Blues Waltz," "Hot Rod," "Sherry"—which were alternated with the R&B songs—"The Right Time," "I Got a Woman," "Talkin' 'bout You," "A Fool for You." To me they fit perfectly together; nothing was jarring when switching back and forth between an R&B vocal and a jazz instrumental—all were connected by the band's emphasis on blues and gospel throughout.

The conscious blending of blues and gospel in jazz of the late fifties and early sixties came to be called soul jazz, what I called the "Soul Movement" in the title of my 1963 paper on folk music and jazz. I loved soul jazz, but many jazz critics dismissed it as a crass appeal to commercialism. Some commercialized albums were bland, but some works have stood the test of time. I was in Philadelphia in 1961 when I bought a jazz compilation album titled *Riverside: The Soul of Jazz—1961* (Riverside, S-5, 1961), which helped define the music for me. It was after my sophomore year in college; spring semester was over, and I drove my '55 Ford Fairlane from Beaumont to Woodbury, New Jersey, to join my family. Daddy was working at a Shell Oil chemical plant on the Delaware River a few miles away from the house they rented. He had arranged a job for me in the labor gang.

This was my second summer working in construction; the year before we lived in Southern California, and I worked at a Union Oil refinery between Long Beach and Palos Verdes. I worked that first summer as a "swamper" on the dump truck that drove around the work site picking up construction trash and taking it to the dump. The other swamper was another college kid who had just finished his freshman year at Stanford. We got to be friends and played tennis together several times that summer. One of the things we learned from working construction was about unions. We were in the Hod Carriers and Laborers Union, and the truck driver was in the Teamsters Union. His job was driving the truck and nothing else. Our jobs were picking up the trash and loading it on the truck and nothing else. He never lifted a piece of trash; neither of us ever drove the truck. We also learned about goldbricking from him. The place where we dumped the trash was in an isolated part of the refinery where no one could see us sit and shoot the shit and listen to rock music on the radio for fifteen to twenty minutes before returning to work.

The next year in New Jersey, I was still in the laborers union, but my work was different; it involved scraping dried concrete off steel-framed wooden forms with an iron brush, then oiling and stacking them to be used again, repeating the same process all day long—dirty, boring work. What made it interesting was that I was working with a middle-aged black laborer named Spike who lived in nearby Camden. He taught me how to do the job; then we worked and talked all day every day the rest of the summer. He asked about my college experiences, and we talked about that for a while. At first I didn't know what to ask him about. He made it easy for me by volunteering information about his life starting with work experiences but shifting to his private life after a few days. He told me about his relationship with his wife and kids, both good things and bad, and that opened me up to talk about girlfriends and my limited sex life at the time.

Spike was the first black person I really got to know on a personal level, and that helped me have a fuller understanding of African American culture than I had from just reading about it in books and imagining it from the music I listened to. (What did Huck know about black people until he floated down the Mississippi with Jim?) Spike encouraged me to stay in school, told me my sex life would get better, and generally was a supportive and good friend. We never saw each other outside work, but you can get to know someone pretty well when you work with him and talk all day long.

We talked about music too; he liked urban blues and jazz, but we never got into any extended conversations about music. I managed to buy some LPs that summer, mainly jazz. On several weekends, David and I drove from Woodbury up to Camden and crossed the Delaware River into downtown Philadelphia. We would browse in a record store, eat dinner (grilled steak and baked potato at a cafeteria-style steak house), and see a movie. As an English major, I got caught up in foreign art films that were finding an American audience then. How could I resist the symbolism and imagery of Bergman or Fellini? That summer I dragged David to see *La Dolce Vita* and *The Virgin Spring*. He was okay with the selections but would have preferred an American movie. Our differences were indicated by our majors, English and chemical engineering. We both liked country music, but he wasn't a big fan of jazz like I was, although he was patient as I browsed through the jazz bins at the record store.

One of the LPs I bought in Philadelphia that summer was the one I mentioned earlier, *Riverside: The Soul of Jazz—1961*. What a lineup: Thelonious Monk, Cannonball Adderley, Wes Montgomery (with Tommy Flanagan), Bill Evans, Nat Adderley, Bobby Timmons, Blue Mitchell, Johnny Griffin, Jimmy Heath, the Jazz Brothers. The soul and roots elements were emphasized in the name of one of the bands, Johnny Griffin's Big Soul Band, and by a couple of song titles, "Wade in the Water" (an old gospel song) and "Blue Soul," but no matter what the song was, the music hung together as representative of jazz of that period, what I already knew as hard bop. The term *soul jazz* was nebulous though, and some of the cuts on the album didn't really fit the genre. Bill Evans and Wes Montgomery were more on the "cool" jazz side, and Thelonious Monk was so unique as to defy any categories.

The late forties and early fifties bebop revolution of Charlie Parker, Dizzy Gillespie, Bud Powell, and the rest had evolved into two broad "schools"— the cool jazz of Miles Davis, Gerry Mulligan, and Chet Baker, and the hard bop of Thelonious Monk, Cannonball Adderley, and Art Blakey and the Jazz Messengers. Like any dichotomy, this is oversimplified; there was a lot of overlap but with enough differences for fans and critics to make a distinction. Some of the musicians associated with hard bop started to look back beyond the invention of bebop for their musical roots, not to swing music of the thirties and forties, but all the way back to the roots in works songs, field hollers, spirituals, and gospel, in other words in African American folk music. So you started hearing gospel call-and-response and improvisations based on early blues songs in otherwise cutting-edge hard bop—soul jazz.

All the music on *The Soul of Jazz* did not fit this description, and finally the compilation is a gimmick to take advantage of the popularity of soul jazz. The album starts with Thelonious Monk and one of his quintets playing the popular song "I'm Getting Sentimental over You," which was first recorded in 1935, associated with Tommy Dorsey's orchestra, and later sung by Frank Sinatra. Not exactly African American folk roots, but that's my point—the album isn't really about cultural roots; it's about jazz on the Riverside label recorded in 1960 and 1961, compiled to promote the label's current jazz albums.

It's still a fine album that says a lot about the state of jazz at the beginning of the sixties. The music is fresh and innovative, played by some great artists, and even the not-as-great were at the top of their form. For me it was the right time and the right place for music fitting my age and my tastes and my experiences—jazz and soul, not just takeoffs on gospel and blues, but some cool jazz as well, rooted in bop and hard bop. In fact, the soul was always there in jazz going back to Buddy Bolden, King Oliver's Creole Jazz Band, and Louis Armstrong; it just hadn't been labeled as such.

I bought the album in Philadelphia, listened to it for the first time in Woodbury, New Jersey, then in my dorm room in Beaumont, Texas, after which I took it with me to my next job the following summer at a paper mill in Port Townsend, Washington, on the Olympic Peninsula across Puget Sound from Seattle. Daddy and I drove from Beaumont to the little town of Quilcene, where he had rented a small house at the foot of the Olympic Mountains. The music felt right in all those places from coast to coast to coast, and it still sounds good in Columbus, Ohio, far from any coast. Take your music with you, even easier now with iPods and MP3s (and probably some other electronic devices by the time this book is published).

Another album that came out the same year better fits the pattern of jazz musicians looking for their roots, Oliver Nelson's *The Blues and the Abstract Truth* (Impulse, LP-5, 1961). It is my favorite example of the use of an album to consciously pay tribute to the vernacular sources of jazz. Nelson composed and arranged all the numbers on the LP, and in the liner notes he explains that they are all based in the blues. This is true, but a song he calls "Hoe-Down" is unmistakably a blending of blues and gospel because of the call-and-response pattern of the horns in the chorus. The title "Hoe-Down" sounds more like an Aaron Copland composition based on a traditional fiddle tune, and maybe this was Nelson's nod to the influence of Copland on his music. To me, though, the number conjures up an African American church. Nelson's compositions on the LP are steeped in traditional blues and gospel with innovative arrangements and a fine group of cutting-edge soloists including Eric Dolphy, Freddie Hubbard, Bill Evans, and Oliver Nelson himself. This is another album that I still have in the original LP record version and on CD, and I play both regularly. (Another good example of soul jazz of the period is Gigi Gryce, *The Rat Race Blues*, Prestige, NJLP, 1960.)

Nelson's album was considered avant-garde at the time, but many of the jazz albums I bought at first would be considered mainstream or popular jazz, meaning that they sold well. I continued to buy mainstream albums, but my tastes were expanding to more esoteric and cutting-edge jazz, including Miles Davis, Thelonious Monk, John Coltrane, and Sonny Rollins, all of whom were gradually increasing in popularity. A cover story in *Time* magazine boosted Monk's record sales, and Davis's fan base grew partially because he was a cult figure. My introduction to these artists was usually through reading about them in magazines or hearing them on FM radio. Sometimes I would buy a record because it had gained notoriety, and when I played it for the first time, it sounded too avant-garde for me.

I didn't really understand what Miles Davis and Thelonious Monk were doing when I first heard them, but I continued to listen and gradually got it. Not that I could explain it in musicological terms, but I understood the music enough to like it. I would buy a Miles Davis album and discover that I didn't like it because I couldn't understand it, but I'd listen to the album occasionally anyway and a year or so later would begin to get it. I was always two or three albums behind in terms of understanding what he was doing. My favorite Miles Davis albums remain the ones I heard early such as *Kind of Blue* (Columbia, CL 1355, 1959), and I love his playing on Cannonball Adderley's *Somethin' Else* (Blue Note, BST 1595, 1958). Cannonball Adderley plays alto sax on both LPs, and they were recorded about a year apart, which explains their similar appeal to me.

I liked and understood Monk more quickly. I started to think of Thelonious's solo improvisations as being like a short story—I was making connections and hearing a development of an idea that made sense, or maybe a better explanation was that I *felt* a coherence in it. I was emotionally involved in Monk's music even though the angularity of it, the way it seems fragmented, put a lot of people off. The first LP of his that I bought was one put together by Columbia records and features Monk on one side and Miles Davis on the other, ironically, my first album by him too. It's titled *Miles & Monk at Newport* (Columbia, CS 8978, 1963) and features Miles with John Coltrane and Cannonball Adderley at the 1958 Jazz Festival, and from the 1963 Festival, Thelonious with Pee Wee Russell, who was a clarinet player from an older generation. I don't know why they put Monk and Russell together, but somehow it worked.

I played the Monk side a lot more since I hadn't caught up with Davis and company yet. I didn't understand Monk's piano improvisations, but the compositions, "Nutty" and "Blue Monk," sounded down-home and funky to me (his soul side?), and I was intrigued by his piano playing. He grew on me, and I kept buying his albums over the years and getting more deeply involved in his music. Now I probably have more LPs and CDs by Monk than any other jazz artist except maybe Sonny Rollins. I should check.

I bought *Miles & Monk at Newport* at a locally owned record store in Denton, Texas; it was across the street from the North Texas State University campus, where I was a graduate student. The store was small but had a large selection of jazz records, and the owner was knowledgeable about jazz and would talk at length with his customers. He told me, "Chico Hamilton is a tasty drummer," so I bought *Man from Two Worlds* (Impulse, AS-59, 1964) and later read in the album liner notes, "Chico is always a tasty drummer." They were both right, and I loved this album, which introduced me to Charles Lloyd on tenor sax and flute and Gabor Szabo on guitar, and I bought their albums too. I liked the combination of sax or flute with guitar and the original compositions, seven of the eight by Charles Lloyd. The highlight for me was his "Forest Flower," which was divided into two parts,

"Sunrise" and "Sunset," beautiful melodies and, to quote the liner notes again, "provocative and fresh" improvisations (*Forest Flower*, Atlantic, SD 1473, 19670. I bought a later CD by him recently, *Lift Every Voice* (ECM, 1832/33, 2002), which shows that he has continued to develop and is still deeply soulful.

There's a reason why a small Texas town like Denton had such a good record store: the campus was home to the NTSU Jazz Lab Band, one of the best-known college jazz programs in the country. What a lucky break for me that I was working on my master's degree in English there, and spent two years taking classes and writing my thesis (on e. e. cummings) and listening to live jazz. They had several different bands, and the best group rehearsed in the student union at one in the afternoon and was called the One O'clock Lab Band. I regularly ate lunch at the union so I could listen to the band, and I went to most of their evening concerts as well—an education within an education. The star student musician was a saxophone player, Billy Harper from Houston. He was featured on several numbers; everyone thought he had the potential to be a major player, and we were right. He went on to have a successful career on the national and international stage and made several critically acclaimed albums: *Capra Black* (Strata-East, SES-19739, 1973), *Black Saint* (Black Saint, BSR 0001, 1975), *Billy Harper Quintet in Europe* (Soul Note, SN 1001,1979), *Somalia* (Evidence, ECD 22133-2, 1995).

My jazz luck continued when I went on to the University of Texas. Austin had an annual Longhorn Jazz Festival in the mid-sixties, and its producer, Rod Kennedy, brought in some of the top names in jazz, including Duke Ellington, Ella Fitzgerald, Miles Davis, Dave Brubeck, and Cannonball Adderley. What a treat to hear all these great musicians in person after listening to them only on recordings. I have vivid memories of them on stage: Miles turning his back on the audience while playing (which those of us who read *Downbeat* magazine expected and would have been disappointed if he hadn't); Duke saying repeatedly, "Love you madly" (again, meeting our expectations); Ella gracious, generous, and singing brilliantly (as we had expected). The concerts were at the same Austin Municipal Auditorium where I first heard Bob Dylan and the Band in 1965 (see chapter 6).

Through the years, I've been lucky enough to hear some of my favorite jazz artists in person. All gave me a thrill at finally seeing them live, and most lived up to my highest expectations. They include, to name a few, Stan Getz at the Village Vanguard, when I made a trip to New York City in the mid-sixties; Sonny Rollins at the Riffe Theatre in Columbus in the nineties;

Tito Puente at the Latino Festival outdoors in downtown Columbus not too long before he died; Dexter Gordon at Mershon Auditorium on the OSU campus; the Modern Jazz Quartet also at Mershon; Teddy Wilson at the Ohio Theatre in downtown Columbus; David "Fathead" Newman at the King Arts Complex in Columbus. If I had to pick one that meant the most to me, it would be Sonny Rollins. At the time he was getting up there in years, and as far as I knew he didn't tour widely, or at least Columbus wasn't on his schedule. When he finally did come here, I bought tickets when they first went on sale, and Roseanne and I sat in the front row. He was magnificent—great improvising, intelligent, playful, serious, joyful, and mournful, with plenty of his unique West Indian rhythmic excursions thrown in.

I could go on writing about the jazz music that I love, but that would make this a hundred-page chapter, and I think I've already made the most relevant points about my personal perspective on jazz. I'm not a professional jazz critic or a jazz musician, but I think a fan's take on the music is significant as a lived experience from the 1960s to the present.

I typed in "present" and thought, "What am I listening to in the present?" It occurred to me that I could give an answer simply by looking around my study to see which jazz CDs were lying around. Here they are.

Charles Mingus, *Blues & Roots* (Atlantic, SD 1305, 1960), one of my all-time favorite jazz LPs. Mingus intentionally does a soul jazz album, the song titles indicate as much—"Wednesday Night Prayer Meeting," "Moanin,'" "My Jelly Roll Soul"—and he also shows what a great sense of humor he has, especially with "E's Flat Ah's Flat Too."

Horace Silver, *The HardBop Grandpop* (Impulse, IMPD 192, 1996). Horace Silver died on June 18, 2014, and this CD has been next to my CD player since I heard about his passing. I think he was one of the best soul jazz pianists, and he always had other great musicians in his band: Joe Henderson on tenor sax, Art Farmer on trumpet, Percy Heath on bass, Art Blakey on drums, Stanley Turrentine on tenor sax, J. J. Johnson on trombone, to name a few.

Count Basie, *Basie in London* (Verve, MG V-8199, 1957). I bought the LP in the early 1960s, and it's still a roaring, romping recording of big band jazz including some of his greatest hits: "Jumpin' at the Woodside," "One O'Clock Jump,'" "Corner Pocket," and some knock-out Kansas City Jazz vocals by Joe Williams, "Alright, Okay, You Win" and "Roll 'Em Pete" especially.

Rhino Presents the Rhino/Atlantic Jazz Gallery (Rhino/Atlantic 8122-

71282-2, 1993). This album features the greatest Atlantic-label jazz recordings from 1957 to 1970, most of it from the sixties, including John Coltrane, Charles Mingus, Ray Charles, David "Fathead" Newman, the Modern Jazz Quartet, Rahsaan Roland Kirk (from Columbus, Ohio), Ornette Coleman, and so on and so on.

Gerry Mulligan All-Star Tribute Band, *Thank You, Gerry* (Arkadia Jazz CD 71191, 1998). I picked up this CD because Mulligan's *What Is There to Say?* (Columbia, CL 1307, 1959) was probably the first modern jazz LP I bought; it defined cool jazz for me and introduced me to the terrific sound of the baritone sax. I'm sure this CD is a sincere tribute, but it didn't intoxicate me like the original.

Finally, Charles Lloyd's *Lift Every Voice* (ECM 1832/1833, 2002). As I mentioned earlier in this chapter, I've been a Charles Lloyd fan since I bought the LP *Forest Flower* (Atlantic SD 1473, 1967), and *Lift Every Voice* is even more emotional and spiritual as some of the song titles indicate—"Hymn to the Mother," "Amazing Grace," "Lift Every Voice and Sing." I will always be excited by Charles Lloyd's music.

These CDs contain a wonderful range of jazz styles from the 1960s to the twenty-first century. What (else) is there to say?

CHAPTER 6

I Was So Much Older Then

Folk Revival into Rock 'n' Roll

The emergence of the folk music revival and the invention of rock 'n' roll overlapped in the late forties and early fifties, and both had elements of revival because of the need for a new identity among American teenagers rebelling against everything their parents' generation stood for. Identifying with folk and rock music was a way of rejecting middle-class white values and romanticizing white and black working-class folk. Although I liked the folk songs I heard in the late 1940s and early 1960s, I was too young for them to have any effect on my identity; that came later with the emerging rock 'n' roll of the mid-1950s and later. The appeal of rock 'n' roll was directly racial because it was derived from black rhythm and blues, and it was also a way to romanticize African Americans as naturally primitive and rhythmic (see chapter 2). But the folk revival had more to do with finding a new identity in an idealized pastoral past. The folk have been imagined as simple rural people since the eighteenth century, when European intellectuals invented the notion of folk (see chapter 1), and folk still had that meaning when the folk music revival captivated teenagers in the fifties and early sixties.

The American folk were imagined by middle- and upper-middle-class people as being rural, uneducated, and backward to some extent but also in touch with nature in a way that "civilized" educated urban and suburban people had lost. This is part of the meaning of "going native" within the underlying civilized/native dichotomy of American popular music in general. There was an elite "we" that both looked down on and romanticized a folk, "they," and other dichotomies followed: educated/uneducated, urban/rural, civilized/primitive, complex/simple. The folk were conceived as simple, but the *idea* of folk in the popular imagination is a complex mixture of romantic and pathological traits.

For instance, Appalachian folk were stereotyped as ignorant, superstitious hillbillies but also as people who were close to nature and had knowledge of herbs and roots that were perceived as folk medicine that really worked. Their music might be thought of as simple, but it communicated emotional depth and timeless homespun truths. At a time after the Second World War when high school kids and college students were becoming disenchanted with their middle-class surroundings, the folk offered an intriguing alternative to bland conformity. Folk music was familiar and exotic at the same time; it represented a simpler and more authentic past since the folk were considered isolated from modernity, uncontaminated by technological change and industrialization—a pure source of tradition.

And you could tap into that source fairly easily by wearing blue jeans and work clothes, playing the guitar or banjo, and singing in a nasal mountain or bluesy Mississippi Delta style. By imitating the folk, you could become one. You might still be living in the suburbs or in an urban college dorm, but you could take on a new identity by playing and listening to a different kind of music. The folk music movement revived an imaginary rural past that was preferable to the stultified urban/suburban present. Individually a person could create a new identity that was the antithesis of his or her previous one. We did so as part of a communal revival of the old and isolated that was antithetical to the new and threatening present of local suburban conformity, global cold war, and nuclear threat. No wonder we preferred the idealized pastoral American past.

As a rock 'n' roll fan, I was never caught up in the folk music revival as much as the folkies were, but as a child, folk music did appeal to me. In 1950, when I was nine and lived with my family in Bay City, Texas, we often went to eat at Etie's Café on the courthouse square. That was where I first heard the Weavers' "Goodnight Irene" on the jukebox, and I loved it. The Weavers learned the song from the black singer Leadbelly, so white people's fascination with African American folk was already part of the process. The song made me want to sing along, and I still remember most of the words, especially the chorus, "Irene, good night; Irene, good night / Good night, Irene, good night, Irene. I'll see you in my dreams." The narrative part begins

> Last Saturday night I got married.
> Me and my wife settled down.
> Now me and my wife are parted.
> Let's take another stroll downtown.
> (Transcribed by the author)

There was something sad but somehow comforting in taking another stroll downtown, especially in my nine-year-old imagination, as we strolled along the sidewalk on the courthouse square in Bay City. "Goodnight Irene" was considered a folk song because of the stereotyped perception of the folk as uneducated, which in this song is reinforced by the ungrammatical expression "me and my wife settled down" (imagine how stilted "my wife and I settled down" would sound).

The Weavers' song was a huge hit as part of the urban folk song revival of the 1940s. This was the first of two folk song revivals; the second was in the late 1950s and early 1960s, and I will focus on it later in this chapter. The forties revival was grounded in the leftist Popular Front of the 1930s, which became more widespread in the 1940s with the political and artistic endeavors in New York City of Woody Guthrie, Pete Seeger, Bess Lomax Hawes, the rest of the Almanac Singers, and other seminal figures such as Josh White and Alan Lomax. The urban folk song revival spawned other hits like "On Top of Old Smokey" and "Wimoweh," and pop covers of folk songs by Mitch Miller, Jo Stafford, and other popular/folk artists.

But the urban revival was soon to recede because of anti-Communist witch hunts and blacklists of the late forties and early fifties. That first urban folk song revival almost died out completely when Pete Seeger was blacklisted and Alan Lomax and others left the country. Then in an amazing turnaround, the folk music revival was itself revived because of the popularity of the Kingston Trio, which opened the door for Joan Baez, Bob Dylan, Odetta, Phil Ochs, and others. As I indicated in chapter 2, the Kingston Trio and other revival groups from the mid-fifties were not politically leftist but firmly based in the fifties middle-class status quo, not a threat but a nostalgic reassurance of traditional American pastoral values. However, many of the performers and songwriters who followed the apolitical Kingston Trio, Brothers Four, and New Christy Minstrels of the fifties were more politically inspired by the leftist musical movement of Woody Guthrie and Pete Seeger from the thirties and forties.

There were complex political and social reasons for this shift; chief among them was the influence of the civil rights movement on the folk music revival in the late fifties and early sixties. We can use the two most popular figures of the sixties folk revival, Joan Baez and Bob Dylan, to trace its political development and eventual transformation through Dylan into a new kind of rock 'n' roll. Baez achieved popularity first and helped Dylan find his folk music audience.

"Wildwood Flower"

I lived in a dorm at Lamar Tech in Beaumont, and during my sophomore year (1960–61) I had a roommate from Boston. What Dennis (not his real name) was doing at a state college in southeast Texas, I don't know, but he brought his Joan Baez albums with him, and I listened. Joan Baez is another of those singers that I liked okay but not enough to buy the records. I enjoyed the traditional ballads she sang and the purity of her voice, but I knew even then that it was not pure in the sense of what I thought of as authentic folk music. Remember that *authentic* is a slippery concept; authenticity is a relative concept and depends on different contexts. As I've noted earlier, we have to ask the question, authentic to whom and for what reasons? One reason, in this case, was that I was influenced by my working-class background and my suspicion of anything that smelled "high class" or pretentious. I thought my Boston roommate was a little snooty and looked down on the music that I and our other roommate, Bill Stuessy, liked. Stuessy was from Bay City, where we had lived when I was in the fourth grade, and we shared the same tastes in rock 'n' roll and R&B.

We used to play a game in which one of us would choose a record, not let the other see the label, start to play it, and lift the needle after only one or two notes. One or the other of us would shout out, "Fats Domino, 'Blue Monday'" or whatever. It was amazing how often we were right. But Dennis wouldn't condescend to play the game with us. He preferred Joan Baez, and he was from Boston, which we had already stereotyped as an elite bastion of snobs, and we expressed our disdain for him and his music in no uncertain terms. We were not alone in this prejudice; the early sixties folk singers were satirized widely as privileged and pretentious. Al Capp, the creator of the comic strip "Li'l Abner," had a character he called Joanie Phoanie, and I remember hearing him mock Baez's politics on late-night television talk shows. I disagreed with his conservative politics, and after I heard about Baez's liberal political views on civil rights, I agreed with her, but I still had this gut response based on class suspicion of privilege.

There were definitely things I liked about Joan Baez's music. Her voice seemed to dramatically evoke the mournfulness of some of the old mountain ballads, and I had never heard any other singers like her. To my untrained ear, she sounded like an opera singer, and that quality suggested high art. I imagined people in suits and evening dresses sitting quietly, attentively, in a wood-paneled room. I thought of it as some kind of "chamber music," a term that I had read someplace. As steeped in folk tradition as the words and melodies of her songs were, my stereotyped view of the upper class was triggered by the sound of her voice and the arrangements of the songs. Her voice was so different from what I knew and liked that I was not able to be entirely open to it; I was not educated enough in her tradition to accept it. Someone like me who was used to listening to raucous women singers like Ruth Brown, LaVern Baker, Wanda Jackson, and Big Mama Thornton couldn't relate to a voice that seemed so tame and contemplative. It wasn't something you could dance to when you went native on a Saturday night— folk revival music was too civilized for me and most of my friends.

My likes and dislikes in music were determined not by some abstract musical aesthetic but by concrete cultural, social, and political experiences all dynamically interacting to influence my responses to music. I have described many of the experiences that formed my musical tastes in the first four chapters including growing up with a class bias, the regional influence of childhood and adolescence in southeast Texas, hearing black rhythm and blues at the right age for maximum effect, and listening to southern hymns sung in traditional harmonies in church. Before hearing Joan Baez for the first time in 1961, I had a lifetime of listening to Sissy's country music on the car radio and at home, including songs by Red Foley, Hank Williams, Curly Fox, and Miss Texas Ruby.

For me country music fit comfortably with my love of rock 'n' roll and rhythm and blues because I heard echoes of country in those other kinds of music, especially rock. I knew there was a strong, direct country-music influence on the early rockers simply by listening to Elvis Presley, Chuck Berry, Jerry Lee Lewis, Carl Perkins, and the Everly Brothers. Ray Charles had been influenced by country, as he demonstrated when he covered Hank Snow's "I'm Movin' On" on his 1961 album *The Genius Sings the Blues* (Atlantic, 8052) and later with an entire album, *Modern Sounds in Country and Western Music* (ABC-Paramount ABC 410, 1962). Even though rock and R&B were my favorites, I was still a C&W fan in college, especially of the crossover hits—Stonewall Jackson's "Waterloo" (1959), Johnny Horton's "Battle of New Orleans" (1959), and Marty Robbins's "El Paso" (1959). Equally important to hearing popular country songs in developing my aesthetic response to Baez and other folkies was hearing old-time country music live in college.

One effect of the folk music revival of the late fifties and early sixties was that older forms of country music started to be played on college campuses.

I took an American folklore class with Francis Abernethy at Lamar Tech (see chapter 5). He was a literary scholar, folklorist, musician, and singer, and we used to go hear him sing at a beer joint down the Port Arthur Road from campus. He was laid back in behavior but rigorous in his teaching standards—an influence on my teaching style later—and we started calling him Ab. We were taken with his music, lots of songs he had grown up with in West Texas. One day he announced that a group was coming to play in class that day, the Stoneman Family. I had never heard of them and didn't know what to expect. They were a little late, and I was looking out the window and saw them as they walked across the quadrangle, an old man, three young men, and two young women carrying their instruments, a stand-up bass, fiddle, guitar, mandolin, and banjo. Ab yelled out the window to let them know where the classroom was. He introduced them: Ernest "Pop" Stoneman and his children, Scott on fiddle, Donna on mandolin, Jim on bass, Van on guitar, and Roni on banjo.

They seemed as laidback and at home as Ab in front of the class. They were funny, joking with Ab and the students as they set up, and they continued to keep us laughing throughout the performance. They started playing, and I was immediately emotionally enthralled. It was sort of like the first time I heard the thirties Delta blues singer Robert Johnson on record—I suddenly knew where the music I was hearing on records and on radio had come from. They played old-time country from the twenties and thirties and some of the nineteenth-century folk music that influenced country music, and they mixed it with newer but still traditional-sounding bluegrass. It was like hearing the music I imagined my parents and grandparents had grown up with in rural North Texas, Oklahoma, and the Ozark Mountains of Arkansas.

I had to fight back the tears in my eyes; a young man from southern protestant working-class culture didn't "blubber" in front of people, to use my mother's term. And it was all a surprise; I had not expected to hear music that made me react so emotionally in an English class. The sound of the banjo and the mandolin were especially intriguing; commercial Nashville did not have much of that in the early sixties, and the sounds of the voices, instrumental solos, and especially the harmonies evoked feelings of church services and my imagined rural American past. The folk revival finally got to me.

This must have been what I was looking for but did not find when I heard Burl Ives singing "The Big Rock Candy Mountain" in 1949, the Kingston Trio singing "Tom Dooley" in 1957, and Joan Baez singing "Wildwood Flower" in 1961. Because of my cultural and class background, those particular "pop" versions of folk songs didn't quite do it for me. Years later I figured out why my quest for authenticity was not satisfied by the early folk revival, but at the time I didn't even know what my basis for "genuine" folk music was. Reading the history of country music in graduate school, I learned that Ernest Stoneman was one of the original musicians recorded by Ralph Peer at the famous Bristol Sessions in 1927, along with Jimmie Rodgers and the Carter Family, recordings that Johnny Cash called "the single most important event in the history of country music" (from the liner notes of *The Bristol Sessions* LP, Country Music Foundation, CMF-011-L, 1987). Pop Stoneman was an important part of country's transition from a music played locally in the rural South to one that came to be heard nationally and internationally on radio, phonograph records, and television.

Calling it a transition from folk to popular music is not too far off if you recognize an ongoing overlap and not a defining line. In the early seventies, I recognized Roni Stoneman as one of the regulars on the television show *Hee Haw* doing what I thought of as a more commercial act but still with that traditional sound in it. I didn't react to the Kingston Trio, Joan Baez, or early Bob Dylan in such a personal and emotional way, but I did share with folk revivalists a romantic involvement in the source music. By the early seventies, I was a professional folklorist with a whole set of ideas about what constituted authentic folk music, but back in 1961, when I first heard Joan Baez, I had no intellectual basis for my judgment of what was genuine, just an unarticulated emotional response.

Baez sang a nice version of "Wildwood Flower" on her first album, but she didn't sing like Sara or Maybelle Carter of the Carter Family. I formed this opinion before I had taken a folklore class, but as someone who had grown up with country music, I could hear the difference between her singing style and that of the women country singers I had heard, like Miss Texas Ruby, whom my family watched every week on television with her partner, Curly Fox, in Houston in 1950.

I remember Joan Baez saying at some point early in her career that she was not a folk singer but a singer of folk songs. That always made sense to me; she was simply pointing out differences in social and cultural contexts. She was the daughter of a Mexican American physics professor and a Scottish teacher of drama. The family lived in Ithaca, New York; Palo Alto and Redlands, California; and Boston, where she attended Boston University.

Her learning to play and sing took place within an educated, intellectual family and social setting. She has a wonderful voice and she is an accomplished guitarist, so this discussion is not about who is a better singer, a person who grew up poor in the Appalachian Mountains or someone from a fairly privileged suburban/urban environment. It is about different singing styles that originate in different cultural contexts. Those different contexts produce different aesthetics, different ways of deciding what is good and bad, and there are many different kinds of musical contexts and aesthetics—folk, pop, classical, to name a few of the broadest and best known categories, and of course they overlap to a certain extent.

The other thing Baez brought to the folk revival that I did not realize in the early sixties was a leftist political perspective. The album *Joan Baez* (Vanguard, VSD 2077, 1960) was not overtly political, but it implied a cultural meaning that is clearer within the context of the folk music revival as a movement. That is, the revivalists, both musicians and audience, were seeking emotional truths in the traditional songs of ordinary people, whom we call the folk. According to Maynard Solomon, the writer of the erudite album liner notes on *Joan Baez*, one song on the LP contains a "haunting and mysterious" verse, another an "outcry against pain" and an "assertion of faith," while "Little Moses" has a "tender and child-like quality."

These qualities all fit preconceived notions about the folk as simple, emotional, religious, sometimes oppressed, and possessing certain spiritual attributes that "civilized," educated people have lost. This conception overlapped with my own romantic sense of the folk, but there was a difference. Since Baez was not from the folk, Solomon saw these qualities residing in the lyrics and tunes and then praised her interpretations that came from her unique talent as an artist. I, on the other hand, placed more importance on the inherent qualities of the people who had originated and carried on the tradition; I thought of their performances as more emotionally intense, as better because they were more authentic.

Solomon articulates what folklorist Ellen Stekert calls a "new aesthetic" for many of the educated people who listened to and wrote about folk music. In his notes, Solomon says:

> Joan is representative of the "new wave" among the younger folksingers, who are disenchanted by the commercial, over-arranged-and-orchestrated trends in folk music performance, where the individuality of the singer is sacrificed to the arranger's conception. . . . On the other hand, she does not

follow those singers who painstakingly imitate the rich ethnic heritage, often thereby submerging their own personalities and more often draining the tradition of its essentially dynamic, creative qualities.

By "commercial" he is referring to the elaborate choral folk song arrangements of Mitch Miller and others who attempted to popularize folk music, and "on the other hand," the attempts by such groups as the New Lost City Ramblers to closely replicate the sound of twenties and thirties recordings of old-time string bands. Solomon does not like these imitations, but years later New Lost City Rambler Mike Seeger responded to such criticisms with the assertion, "Some have called this 'slavish imitation,' but we prefer to call it creative fidelity to tradition" (in the liner notes to New Lost City Ramblers, *There Ain't No Way Out*, Smithsonian Folkways CD 40098, 1997). For Solomon, Joan Baez's music is better than both the commercial and the imitation folk revival styles because of her "sense of stylistic authenticity" in which she reinterprets each song through her individual vision and talent.

To me there is room for both imitators and reinterpreters; for one thing, they are not as dichotomous as the critics think—both have elements of imitation and reinterpretation. That is what folk tradition has always been, a dynamic process that takes in outside influences and technological change, although some lines of tradition are more conservative while others are more innovative. The invention of the radio, phonograph records, and television did not end folk music, but media obviously accelerated the speed and nature of change in vernacular music. Where does folk end and popular begin? Not with the advent of radio and records, that's for sure. In fact, no one can mark an exact place to demarcate the line; it is as nebulous as the concept of authenticity, as arbitrary as the idea of folk. So, again, we have to consider the music and these issues in the context of their time. Joan Baez is as genuine as Sara Carter of the Appalachian singing group the Carter Family in different although overlapping universes.

These were underlying issues, and they have their political dimension in terms of unspoken ideas about socioeconomic class, especially the educated elite's attitude toward working-class folk, but at some point in the early sixties folk revival, direct political statements emerged, and Joan Baez and Bob Dylan were key figures in bringing this about.

"I'm Younger than That Now"

Like those of most early sixties folk revivalists, Dylan's politics were rooted in the urban folk revival of the forties and the Popular Front of the thirties; he was especially influenced politically and musically by Woody Guthrie, who also provided him with his initial performing persona, the wandering working-class poet of the people. Dylan's first album, *Bob Dylan* (Columbia CL 1779, 1962), contains a tribute called "Song to Woody" and another, "Talkin' New York," that mimics Guthrie's "talkin' blues" style. During this period, Dylan dressed like the scruffy, rural working man as Woody himself had in the thirties. The young Dylan arrived in New York spinning elaborate tales of his made-up life as a hobo who had traveled all over the West, trying to match Woody's own exaggerated 1943 autobiography, *Bound for Glory*.

Anglo-American folk revival influences were apparent in Dylan's repertoire in the early sixties, but he had also been listening to African American blues music, and that too is reflected on his first album, especially in his cover of Mississippi bluesman Bukka White's "Fixin' to Die." Dylan changes the lyrics and does not try to sound like Bukka White in vocal or guitar style; rather he emulates the blues of white folk revival performers like Dave Van Ronk. Dylan was definitely not one of the precise imitators of traditional style like the New Lost City Ramblers. Much later in his career, he more self-consciously represented his interest in the process of imitation/emulation/exploitation by naming his 2001 CD *Love and Theft* (Columbia, CK 85975) and including the song "High Water," which he dedicates to seminal Mississippi Delta blues singer/guitarist Charlie Patton. I think Dylan might also have read a book on race by Eric Lott called *Love and Theft*.

I was not aware of any of these issues when Dylan's first album was released in 1962; I didn't even hear the album until several years later. The first thing I heard by Dylan was on FM radio in the summer of 1963. The song was "Blowin' in the Wind" from his second album, *The Freewheelin' Bob Dylan* (Columbia, CL 1986, 1963). I had just started graduate school at North Texas State and was living in what my roommate Tom Cameron and I thought of as a garret, the third-floor attic of a boardinghouse in Denton, the closest I would ever come to experiencing Bohemian life in Greenwich Village, where Dylan was living in the early sixties.

I had never heard anything quite like "Blowin' in the Wind," and I didn't especially like it. Remember, in the fifties I had been a rocker, not a folkie. I recognized the folk qualities in the song, especially ones that connected

Dylan to Woody Guthrie and Pete Seeger, but his voice sounded weird, too nasal, and not in the Webb Pierce country way; in fact, in a way he seemed to be mocking that sound. Unlike Joan Baez's, Dylan's voice was not trained and beautiful, and he was not a direct imitator of southern rural singers either. I didn't come to appreciate his uniqueness until several years later. I didn't buy the second album and, in fact, didn't buy my first Dylan album until 1965's *Highway 61 Revisited* (Columbia, CL 2389), and then only because it was so obviously and proudly rock 'n' roll. Unlike the purists among the folkies, including two other heroes of mine, Pete Seeger and Alan Lomax, who according to legend tried to cut the power cord when Dylan played his first amplified rock set at the Newport Folk Festival, I was ready for and preferred the electric Bob Dylan.

The first time I heard him in person was in 1965, at the beginning of my first year at the University of Texas. The concert was a "warm-up" for the tour he did with a rock 'n' roll band, the Hawks, later the Band. I recently found an anniversary article, "Playback: Bob Dylan Goes Electric—Again!," about that concert in the *Austin Chronicle*, so I know the date was September 24 and tickets were four dollars. It was an incredible concert. The old Municipal Auditorium was packed; we were drinking beer out of giant paper cups, and I even liked Dylan's acoustic solo set, which opened the show. But the real rapture started after intermission, when he came back with the Hawks and played a blistering "Tombstone Blues," followed by "Baby Let Me Follow You Down," "It Ain't Me Babe," "Ballad of a Thin Man," and "Like a Rolling Stone," which I had been hearing all summer while traveling through Europe for the first time. I have now taught a course on Dylan a couple of times, and I tell my students I may not know as much as some of them do about Dylan, but my rock creds come from being at that concert.

I listened to *Bringing It All Back Home* (Columbia, CS 9128, 1965), *Highway 61 Revisited*, and *Blonde on Blonde* (Columbia, C2L 41, 1966) constantly in the mid-sixties while I was in graduate school. My ex-wife and I had a console hi-fi in the living room of our sixty-five-dollars-a-month house near the UT student housing on the west side of Austin, and I would stack up the LPs and play them one after the other while I worked on my dissertation and during our loud, raucous, alcohol-infused parties. We listened *and* we danced to Dylan's music. I had intellectual discussions about music with my fellow graduate students while we drank beer at Sholtz's beer garden or at our neighborhood pizza joint, but dancing was part of it too. It was not all serious listening and deciphering the lyrics. We talked about him in much the same way we talked about movies, arguing about whether it was high art.

I had an ongoing argument with a grad student friend named Mike about whether Hitchcock's *Psycho* was serious art like the films of Fellini, Bergman, or Godard, which we had been watching since we were undergraduates in the early sixties. You could not be an English major without going to see art films during that era, even at a small state college in southeast Texas. I argued for Hitchcock's and Dylan's work as complex art worthy of analysis, but I also felt the visceral appeal of both as popular entertainment. Why did there have to be a hierarchical ranking, high culture and low culture? I was ahead of my time, but then a lot of us were in the sixties.

I have to admit that I did not spend a lot of time analyzing Dylan's lyrics. I realized they were influenced by some of the poets we discussed in graduate seminars—Whitman, Eliot, cummings—but I did not really care about that angle. I spent more time listening to his songs as music, responding to the sound more than the words. Part of the appeal was recognition that the lyrics could be profound, but the overall experience of the music was more important. We danced to Dylan just like we danced to the Beatles and the Paul Butterfield Blues Band. Some critics say Dylan's recordings don't lend themselves to dancing, but my lived experience said otherwise. He wrote songs about the primacy of direct experience over abstract intellectualizing and learned responses, and somehow we lived that out as we danced to his music.

I think our generation was part of a broader cultural shift, one that Dylan could articulate better than the rest of us, but we all felt it. Dylan and I were born in the same year, 1941, and I think our experiences growing up were similar even though he was in northern Minnesota, and I was on the Gulf Coast of Texas. We shared a changing consciousness with many others who were in their twenties in the sixties. Certain traits describing our generation have been repeated so many times that they have become clichés, but that cannot deny the reality of our shared experiences. I identified with Dylan throughout my life, but I was not aware until lately how much of that was displayed in my behavior—naming a CD of Dylan covers *To Zimmie from Pat* and posting photos on my bulletin board of Bob and me as teenagers dressed in similar belted chino pants and rolled-up, short-sleeved shirts, both of us with serious looks straight at the camera lens.

Dylan and I are pre–baby boomers, who by accident of birth, were just the right age for the birth of rock 'n' roll, not as old as the originators, Elvis

Presley, Jerry Lee Lewis, Chuck Berry, and Ray Charles, but the right age to be the first wave of fans in the fifties, and for some, like Dylan, Lennon, McCartney, and Hendrix, to take rock to a new level as composers and performers in the sixties.

This generational consciousness was linked culturally to our search for a new identity in folk and rock 'n' roll in the 1950s that rejected our parents' generation, but these new ideas and attitudes could not be fully articulated until the sixties, and initially only by a few visionary songwriters, poets, fiction writers, and filmmakers. The rest of us heard the songs, saw the movies, read the poems and stories, and understood what they were about. Dylan was probably the best of those artists at touching something in us that most of us could not express in art, but we felt and expressed our sense of it by dancing, singing along, drinking, taking drugs, and protesting the Vietnam War and racial inequality.

Dylan expressed this generational attitude in his lyrics in ways I didn't completely understand at the time, and that I have only come to understand more fully in the last fifteen years by listening more closely to his songs and reading and rereading the lyrics. In some ways, I was forced to do this when I decided to teach courses on Dylan at Ohio State. New meanings opened up that I could relate to experiences and feelings I had had in the sixties when I first heard the songs. Somewhat ironically, I realized that what Dylan was saying in his songs also fit the explanation I was trying to craft of the significance of the music to my generation—the whole idea of looking for a new self in the sixties.

These ideas run through his albums from this period. You can hear them in the protest songs of *The Freewheelin' Bob Dylan* and *The Times They Are A-Changin'* (Columbia, CL 2105, 1964), but he starts to express a more complex consciousness on his fourth album, *Another Side of Bob Dylan* (Columbia, CS 8993, 1964). The songs become denser in their imagery, and the words start to hide their own meaning in songs like "Chimes of Freedom" and "My Back Pages," both of which express the change of consciousness that was taking place. Many critics and scholars have written about these songs, and I'm sure their interpretations have influenced mine, but I'm trying to do something a little different: to relate them to my feelings and thoughts at the time while also taking into account how the intervening years and all my experiences since then have influenced how I emotionally respond to and interpret the songs now. My perspective while I am writing this book is from age sixty-five to seventy-five, not twenty-five to thirty-five, when I first heard the songs.

"Chimes of Freedom" is one of the first Dylan songs to layer the imagery, alliteration, rhyme, and repetition on so thick that it almost overwhelms the listener, and all to express a moment of subjective experience that listeners could identify with as something new in the air. (You should play the song while reading these lyrics for the full experience.)

> Far between sundown's finish an' midnight's broken toll
> We ducked inside the doorway, thunder crashing
> As majestic bells of bolts struck shadows in the sounds
> Seeming to be the chimes of freedom flashing.
> (Transcribed by the author)

Dylan wrote this during a period when he had been reading French Symbolist poet Arthur Rimbaud, who was known for writing poetry expressing subjective feelings that sprang from concrete personal experience. For both Rimbaud and Dylan, poetic technique is directly related to the feelings and ideas being expressed—the images are a personal vision, not an idea that is being taught in school, not a notion received from the past, but one experienced directly in the present. The songs on *Another Side of Bob Dylan* make a definite break with the folk revival songs on his previous albums.

"Chimes of Freedom" is still a protest song, but like none of those that came before it. It is not a description by an outside observer of racial injustice, as in "The Lonesome Death of Hattie Carroll" and "Only a Pawn in Their Game"; rather, it is a personal insight from a single experience that gives him a sense of outrage toward all the injustices of the world. It is not something learned from others in "the movement," but something felt in the moment and expressed through an almost incoherent mélange of images that mix sight and sound—"shadows in the sound," "chimes . . . flashing." Instead of the triumphant tone of "When the Ship Comes In" and "The Times They Are A-Changin'," there is recognition in the last stanza of the difficulties ahead, "Tolling for the aching whose wounds cannot be nursed," conjuring up images from Walt Whitman's Civil War poems.

"My Back Pages" states this new consciousness even more strongly in its direct rejection of Dylan's former self as spokesman for the protest movement:

> Crimson flames tied through my ears
> Rollin' high and might traps
> Pounced with fire on flaming roads

Using ideas as my maps
"We'll meet on edges soon," said I
Proud 'neath heated brow
Ah but I was so much older then
I'm younger than that now.
(Transcribed by the author)

There are remnants of the folk revival here—the alternating unrhymed and rhymed lines and the now-stilted, archaic language of the traditional British ballad ("Proud 'neath heated brow")—all in ironic counterpoint to the speaker rejecting the politics of the movement associated with the folk revival. The "high and mighty traps" could be the exalted pronouncements and self-righteous indignation of leftist protest leaders, reinforced by references to "romantic facts" in the next stanza and "memorizing politics of ancient history" in the third.

He implicitly rejects the folk revival's oversimplified dichotomous thinking in the line "Lies that life is black and white." I think Dylan was rejecting not the principles of civil rights and antiwar protest but rather the way they had become a party line with lockstep acceptance by the people organized for protest. He is especially contemptuous here of the loss of individual identity when one becomes part of a movement. The song can be read as an expression of the generational divide that Dylan was feeling at the time, which helps explain his seeming contradiction of the ordinary sequential passage of time. He "was so much older then" (during his involvement in the movement) because he was following the old, worn-out politics of the previous generation. He is "younger than that now" because he has freed himself from the conformity of the movement and established his own identity, existing in the present moment and open to his own individual experience, as he also suggested in "Chimes of Freedom."

This notion relates back to the idea of self and identity in both the folk revival and the emergence of rock 'n' roll. In the fifties, during our teenage years, we rejected our parents' generation but ironically found folk music from the past and poverty-stricken black people's music in the present to identify with. Both identities were outside our selves and had histories associated with our parents' generation. Artificial and removed from our actual experience, these identities did not work for us even as we continued to love the music and emulate rural white folk and black working-class performers. Finally in the 1960s, when we were in our twenties, we started to look within for our new identities, following artists such as Dylan who were exploring possibilities and letting us know through their music, fiction, and poetry what they had found.

Dylan continued to write songs about finding oneself within by opening up to one's own consciousness. The album after *Another Side of Bob Dylan* was *Bringing It All Back Home*, followed by *Highway 61 Revisited* later the same year (1965). I was grabbed by the rock 'n' roll on these albums in ways that his acoustic folk music could not grab me. The shift from folk to rock 'n' roll did not mean the end of his writing protest songs; these songs were just different in sound, style, and intent, becoming more complex as his songwriting ability developed and his political consciousness changed. He rejected the direct moral messages and movement righteousness of "Blowin' in the Wind," "The Times They Are A-Changin'," and "The Lonesome Death of Hattie Carroll" for the obscure, indirect symbols and imagery of "Subterranean Homesick Blues" and "It's Alright, Ma (I'm Only Bleeding)." Both "Chimes of Freedom" and "My Back Pages" signaled the shift that was taking place, but the transformation was made complete with the songs on *Bringin' It All Back Home*.

As Dylan broke new ground, he ironically went back to early rock 'n' roll for his inspiration. There would be no "Subterranean Homesick Blues" as we know it without Chuck Berry's "Too Much Monkey Business," which was within the blues tradition of complaint songs but had a political edge intensified by rock guitar and rhythm. Dylan acknowledges the influence in the notes to *Biograph* (Columbia, C5X 38830, 1985): "Probably 'Too Much Monkey Business' is in here somewhere." What is the "monkey business" the narrator of the song is complaining about? He starts with

> Runnin' to-and-fro hard workin' at the mill.
> Never fail in the mail, here come a rotten bill!
> Too much monkey business, too much monkey business.
> Too much monkey business for me to be involved in!
> (Transcribed by the author)

Later in the song he adds a litany of injustices: "Pay phone, somethin' wrong, dime gone, will mail / Ought to sue the operator for tellin' me a tale." Later he complains about "Workin' in the fillin' station, too many tasks / Wipe the windows, check the tires, check the oil, dollar gas!" It's personal, but the narrator shares these complaints with an entire range of frustrated, working-class young men (and implicitly women) in America in the 1950s.

I don't think it's farfetched to say that the song is a protest against working-class conditions in a capitalist society, specifically the boring, repetitive, low-paying work in a mill, a gas station, or as a private in the army. He is at the bottom of the economic ladder so that even the monopoly power of an AT&T telephone operator can seem oppressive. He also complains about the conniving car salesman who is "tryin' to run me up a creek" with dishonest sales tricks, suckering him in with "you can pay me next week." Monotonous classroom work will not help him escape: "Same thing every day, gettin' up, goin' to school / No need for me complainin', my objection's overruled." Even his girlfriend becomes an oppressor because of her impossible demands: "Want me to marry, get a home, settle down, write a book!" The implicit tone in his list of her demands illustrates what helps him cope with his situation: his sense of humor allows him to see the comic absurdity of her wanting him to write a book, a pretentious social-climbing expectation for a young, working-class man like him.

The fast-paced singing of the song, the staccato rhythm, and the piled-on rhymes fit the humorous tone perfectly, and all these were a direct influence on Dylan's "Subterranean Homesick Blues."

> Johnny's in the basement
> Mixing up the medicine
> I'm on the pavement
> Thinking about the government
> The man in the trench coat
> Badge out, laid off
> Says he's got a bad cough
> Wants to get it paid off.
> (Transcribed by the author)

Finally the narrator gives the kid some radical advice, "Look out kid / They keep it all hid / Better jump down a manhole / Light yourself a candle." The "kid" whom the narrator addresses could be the 1960s version of Chuck Berry's working-class hero; they face many of the same problems. With school: "Hang around a ink well / Ring bell, hard to tell / If anything is goin' to sell." After school ending up in a monotonous, low-paying job: "Twenty years of schoolin' / And they put you on the day shift." The inevitability of the army: "Join the army, if you fail." Even the girlfriend who tries to control him: "Girl by the whirlpool / Lookin' for a new fool." The difference is that Dylan's narrator adds a pervasive sense of paranoia to the kid's dilemma.

Chuck Berry's hero is trapped and frustrated but doesn't resort to crime. Dylan's subterranean world is full of drugs, bugged phones, undercover cops, "users, cheaters," and "six-time losers."

Both songs give a sense of life as it is being lived but in different ways. "Monkey Business" jumps around in time—starting with an adult job and later mentioning school. "Subterranean" jumps around too but sums up the kid's life in eight lines:

> Ah get born, keep warm
> Short pants, romance, learn to dance
> Get dressed, get blessed
> Try to be a success
> Please her, please him, buy gifts
> Don't steal, don't lift
> Twenty years of schoolin'
> And they put you on the day shift

Finally ending with the advice, "Better jump down a manhole / Light yourself a candle," which evokes the underground, existential dilemma of Ralph Ellison's *Invisible Man*. But this is not the end; instead Dylan concludes the song with six lines of absurd non sequiturs in keeping with Chuck Berry's comic response to American twentieth-century monkey business.

> Don't wear sandals
> Try to avoid the scandals
> Don't wanna be a bum
> You better chew gum
> The pump don't work
> 'Cause the vandals took the handles

The political protest in folk, blues, folk revival, and popular music of the forties, fifties, and sixties continued into the seventies, eighties, nineties, and finally into the twenty-first century.

"It's Up to You Not to Heed the Call-Up (I Don't Want to Die)": Political Songs beyond the Folk Music Revival

Protest songs didn't die with the passing of the 1960s folk revival. There continued to be an ongoing political dimension in folk, rock 'n' roll, blues, R&B,

and reggae in the seventies, eighties, nineties, and now in the twenty-first century. From Woody Guthrie's "Talkin' Dust Bowl Blues" to Steve Earle's "Christmas in Washington," from Merle Haggard's "Workin' Man Blues" to Kieran Kane's "This Dirty Little Town," from Marvin Gaye's "What's Goin' On" to Bob Marley's "Concrete Jungle," from Tom Waits's "The Day after Tomorrow" to Patti Smith's "Without Chains," from the Clash's "The Call-Up" to Billy Bragg's "Rumours of War," protest songs have remained a significant element in popular music.

Ry Cooder started making political albums in the early seventies and is still making them today. His eponymous first album contained Woody Guthrie's "Do-Re-Mi" (see chapter 1) and Alfred Reed's "How Can a Poor Man Stand Such Times and Live?" By the twenty-first century, he was writing his own protest songs, especially in his politically charged trilogy of albums *Chávez Ravine* (Nonesuch CD 79877-2, 2005), *My Name Is Buddy* (Nonesuch CD 79961-2, 2007), and *I, Flathead* (Nonesuch CD 465916-2, 2008). *Chávez Ravine* is an especially good example of his concern for oppressed minorities. Rather than poor southern blacks or Okie migrants, the displaced people on this album are Mexican Americans living in the Chávez Ravine neighborhood in Los Angeles after they were driven from their homes to make way for construction of Dodger Stadium in the late 1950s. The variety of music on the album works together to reinforce the sense of injustice and loss; the range of styles and genres includes Mexican ballads ("Corrido de Boxeo"), Latin dance music from the forties ("Los Chucos Suaves"), a Lieber and Stoller fifties rock 'n' roll song ("3 Cool Cats"), Mexican conjunto ("Ejercito Militar"), and Spanish language R&B ("Onda Callejera"). Cooder's palette has broadened tremendously from the folk, rock, and protest songs of his early albums.

In 2011 he explained the political shift that had taken place: "These times call for a very different kind of protest song. 'Where Have All the Flowers Gone?' We're way down the road from that." That same year, he released *Pull Up Some Dust and Sit Down* (Nonesuch CD 527407-1), his most outspoken political protest album at that point, this time about the effects of the Great Recession on ordinary people. He seems to be trying to conjure up the ghost of Woody Guthrie in these albums, but he was already doing that in the 1970s.

I'm not sure everyone who heard his second album, *Into the Purple Valley* (Reprise Records, MS 2052), when it first came out in 1972 realized how political it was. It seems to be a belated folk revival record covering old blues and gospel, early rock 'n' roll and country songs, an outlaw ballad, a Trinidadian folk song, and of course a Woody Guthrie song. The album cover shows Ry and a beautiful woman riding in an open convertible looking anxious under a dark sky as rain is starting to fall. On the back is a photo of them in the car smiling and laughing under a clear blue sky. Inside the double album is a bigger picture of them in dressy retro clothing smiling while standing next to the car in front of a flat backdrop of an urban Southern California scene. All the photographs intentionally communicate that they were shot in a studio. This remains one of my favorite album covers among many great ones from the seventies; I just retrieved my original copy from the shelf. It's coming apart, but I still enjoy looking at it and thinking about the connection between the cover and the songs inside. It doesn't look like a political protest album, but in some ways it is, most often directly but in a few cases by implication.

The album starts with "How Can You Keep on Moving," a song from the perspective of a displaced farmer: "I can't go back to the homestead, the shack no longer stands / They said I was unneeded, had no claim to the land." Wherever he travels, the authorities won't allow him to stay.

> Now if you pitch your little tent along the broad highway
> The Board of Sanitation says, "Sorry, you can't stay"
> Come on, come on, get movin', it's their everlasting cry
> Can't stay, can't go back, and can't migrate, so where in the
>   hell am I.
> (Transcribed by the author)

The song was written by Sis Cunningham, who for a while in the forties was part of the Almanac Singers with Woody Guthrie, Pete Seeger, Bess Lomax Hawes, and others. Even though at the time the album was recorded Cooder wasn't aware that Cunningham wrote the song, it does provide an appropriate connection to Woody Guthrie and the thirties and forties leftist political concern for displaced people and the unemployed.

Into the Purple Valley begins with "How Can You Keep on Moving" and ends with Woody Guthrie's "Vigilante Man," a figure who was a constant threat to migrant workers in the 1930s. (Years later Bruce Springsteen also recorded the song.)

> Oh, why does a vigilante man?
> Why does a vigilante man

Carry that sawed-off shotgun in his hand?
Would he shoot his brother and sister down?
(Transcribed by the author)

There is also a song on the album written by one of Guthrie's contemporaries, Leadbelly. "On a Monday" begins with the narrator being thrown in jail and continues with his lament:

Take these stripes, stripes from around my shoulder
Take these chains, these chains from around my legs
Lord, these stripes, it sure don't worry me
But these chains, these chain's gonna kill me dead.
(Transcribed by the author)

Huddie Ledbetter was in prison himself when he was "discovered" by John and Alan Lomax, and the song reminds us that the enslavement of young African American men is still part of the black experience in the twentieth and twenty-first centuries, just as there are still "Vigilante Men" to hassle migrant workers and unemployed people looking for jobs.

Leadbelly's lament is ironically followed by Johnny Cash's "Hey Porter," a song about a southerner whose desire to get back home is so strong that he can't wait for the train to cross the Mason-Dixon line.

Hey porter! Hey porter! Please open up the door.
When they stop the train I'm gonna get off first 'cause I can't
wait no more.
Tell that engineer I said thanks a lot, and I didn't mind the fare.
I'm gonna set my feet on southern soil and breathe that
southern air.
(Transcribed by the author)

The song isn't directly political. At the time the original was recorded in 1954, it did not necessarily have racial implications even though most southerners would recognize that the porter was black and the southern passenger was white. However, in 1972, following a song about a black man in prison, it does suggest racial and political meanings. I don't think Ry Cooder was being critical of Johnny Cash, but he does seem to recognize the irony of placing two great southern songwriters, one black and one white, next to each other to contrast their views of the South.

The album also contains a traditional outlaw ballad, "Billy the Kid," which imagines a different hero than the more common Jesse James or Pretty Boy Floyd, who rob from the rich and give to the poor. Instead, "Billy the Kid" is a cautionary tale of a young man caught up in the circumstances of a violent place and dangerous time—the 1878 Lincoln County, New Mexico, range wars.

> I'll sing you a true song of Billy the Kid
> I'll sing the record of deeds that he did
> Way out in New Mexico a long time ago
> When a man's only friend was his own forty-four.
>
> Now when Billy the Kid was a very young lad
> In old Silver City he went to the bad
> Way out west with a knife in his hand
> At the age of twelve years he killed his first man.
> . . . .
> Well, this is how Billy the Kid met his fate
> A big moon was shining and the hour was late
> Shot down by Pat Garrett, Silver City's best friend
> The poor outlaw's life had reached its sad end.
> (Transcribed by the author)

The historical record supports the fact that William McCarty killed numerous men including two guards when he was escaping jail. The song presents him as a killer, but while not justifying his actions, it does attempt to provide the social and cultural context to explain his behavior. This was a time and a place "when a man's only friend was his own .44." "He went to the bad" when he was only twelve years old, and it seems inevitable that "the poor outlaw's life" would reach "its sad end." The ballad's description of "Mexican maidens" celebrating his life through music and song and referring to him as "their boy bandit king" are supported by the fact that Mexicanos in the region protected him and gave him shelter when he was on the run from Anglo lawmen, who were their oppressors. According to my friend Bob Jones, who lives in West Texas close to the New Mexico border, Mexican Americans there still see him as legendary hero. In *Into the Purple Valley* Ry Cooder again suggests a relationship between two songs: "Billy the Kid" and the jailed narrator of "On a Monday" are linked together as men who have done wrong but who are sympathetic figures because of what society has done to them.

"Billy the Kid" was collected by John Lomax and published in 1934 in a book he wrote with his son, Alan, *American Ballads and Folk Songs*, and again in 1938 in *Cowboy Songs and Other Frontier Ballads*. Alan recorded Woody Guthrie singing it in 1940 for the Library of Congress, and Marty Robbins sang a version on his album *Gunfighter Ballads & Trail Songs Volume 3* (Columbia 1349, 1962). I don't remember hearing "Billy the Kid" as a kid; I didn't hear it until I first listened to *Into the Purple Valley* in 1972, but then it resonated with me because of a childhood memory.

In 1948, when I was seven and we were living in Levelland, Texas (see chapter 1), the whole family drove 134 miles across the Llano Estacado to Fort Sumner, New Mexico, to see Billy the Kid's grave. I still have a photograph my mother took of me sitting in front of the chain-link fence that surrounded the grave site, a shy smile on my face and my blue jeans rolled up to keep me from tripping. I dug out the picture a little while ago and made out the faint words on the bottom of the grave stone:

> THE BOY
> BANDIT KING
> HE DIED AS
> HE HAD LIVED

The song was first published in 1934, the gravestone was placed there in 1940, and I saw it in 1948. Until looking at the photo after all these years, I had not realized that the words I read on the stone that day were taken from the song, but I do remember being fascinated by a *boy* bandit who had died so young. Already a cowboy fan, I became interested in outlaws and songs about them from that moment on. I even taught a folklore and literature course once titled American Outsiders and Outlaw Heroes. What a pleasant surprise that so many strands came together while I was doing research for this book, and that Ry Cooder's *Into the Purple Valley* was one of the links.

One of the things I like about Ry Cooder's music is the way he draws on a range of world music—Anglo-American, African American, Latin American, African, and different genres—Mississippi Delta blues, 1950s rock 'n' roll, country, Cuban, Hawaiian, and more. He often sang African American songs in what seemed to be a conscious style of a white man singing blackface minstrelsy. This used to bother me because I was afraid it suggested racism, but when you look at his recording career to this point and all the songs that posit political messages against racism and oppression of minorities, you can't help but hear his singing style as recognition of the musical tradition of racial imitation and emulation and as a satire of himself and all other white singers who attempt to sing in an African American cultural style. He is like an international ethnomusicologist in the way he draws on so many musical traditions, but he adds his own purpose to them while acknowledging the process of borrowing and adaptation—"love and theft" with noble intentions.

The same decade when I first listened to Ry Cooder, I also heard the Clash for the first time. The Clash kept the protest tradition alive in rock music during the late 1970s and into the 1980s. Unlike Ry Cooder and Bob Dylan, they didn't cover versions of Woody Guthrie or other political folk songs, unless you consider Junior Murvin's reggae song "Police and Thieves" and the Bobby Fuller Four's rock 'n' roll "I Fought the Law" as political folk songs, as I do. In the 1970s, the British punk rock band the Clash developed an aggressive mix of rock, reggae, funk, jazz, and rap that was electrifyingly effective for the group's leftist, antiestablishment political message. I didn't hear them until their third album, *London Calling* (Epic E2 36328, 1980), was released in the United States in 1980, and it was a revelation. I was thirty-eight when I first heard *London Calling*, and I had been thinking for several years that "real" rock was dying. I was mainly listening to the outlaw country music of Willie and Waylon and the boys in the seventies (see chapter 7) when the Clash came along and revived my passion for hard-core rock. The record contained more protest songs than any album I had heard in years. The political tone is established on the first cut; "London Calling" ironically describes the world as a wasteland on the verge of disaster.

> The ice age is coming, the sun's zooming in
> Engines stop running, the wheat is growing thin
> A nuclear error, but I have no fear
> 'Cause London is drowning, and I live by the river.
> (Transcribed by the author)

Followed by "Spanish Bombs," "Clampdown," "The Guns of Brixton," "Death or Glory," and other great songs, the album roars out of the speakers raging against drugs, chronic unemployment, and racism.

The Clash's onslaught continued with even more force on the next album, *Sandinista!* (Epic E3X 37037 FSLN1, 1980), whose title announced the group's support of the socialist movement in Nicaragua. There are other political songs on the album—for example, "Something about England," "Police on My Back," "Washington Bullets," "Career Opportunities"—but two especially stand out in my mind. I wish there had been a rock song against war and the draft during the sixties as powerful as "The Call Up."

> It's up to you not to heed the call-up
> 'N' you must not act the way you were brought up
> Who knows the reasons why you have grown up
> Who knows the plans and why they were drawn up.
> (Transcribed by the author)

The next stanza moves from second to first person, making it even more directly personal: "It's up to you not to heed the call-up / I don't wanna die." It ends with another reason for not heeding the call-up: "For he who will die is he who will kill."

The Clash express their political opinions and emotions about war in 1980 in ways that made me relive my feelings about the Vietnam War in the 1960s. I had a student deferment through most of the 1960s, safe at home while others took my place, went to jail, or moved to Canada. I was against the war through the last half of the decade but didn't publicly protest until 1969. Guilt, relief, regret, and finally resistance were warring inside me at the time. I didn't want to die; I didn't want to kill. But nothing else said it as directly and with as much understanding of the contradictory emotions until the Clash's "The Call Up."

As far as I know, Woody Guthrie didn't write any antiwar songs, but he did make an effort to avoid the draft during the Second World War. He was not drafted at the beginning of the war because he had a family, but by 1943 he had received his notice to report for a physical. Under the urging of his friend and fellow folk singer Cisco Houston, he was already considering joining the merchant marines and did so after he received the notice. He had been involved in the antifascist movement since the 1930s, and for years before the war started, he thought of himself as resisting Hitler and the Nazis through his songwriting and singing. I suspect he felt some of that "I don't want to die, I don't want to kill" resistance to the draft although eventually he was drafted into the army. After his discharge, he returned to writing songs that became essential to the tradition of political protest songs in the folk music revival.

Woody Guthrie's influence continues to the present as new generations of singers keep rediscovering him. One of my favorite singer/songwriters in the Guthrie tradition is John Prine; his first album, *John Prine* (Atlantic, SD 8296, 1971), was a revelation—it was country, it was folk, it had social awareness and political protest, and it was whimsical, sad, and funny, sometimes all in the same song. The first song on the first side, "Illegal Smile," grabbed my attention right away since it described one of my favorite activities at the time, smoking marijuana. In the first stanza, he describes waking up one morning feeling so depressed that "a bowl of oatmeal tried to stare [him] down, and won." But he has a way "to escape reality."

> And you may see me tonight with an illegal smile
> It don't cost very much, but it lasts a long while
> Won't you please tell the man I didn't kill anyone
> No, I'm just trying to have me some fun.
> (Transcribed by the author)

"Illegal Smile" manages to express both the feeling of ennui and the way to escape it. Since I was smoking marijuana regularly at the time, the song made perfect sense to me, including expressing the paranoia that we dopers felt because of police crackdowns on our illegal activity: "Well I sat down in my closet with all my overalls / Trying to get away from all the ears inside my walls / I dreamed the police heard everything I thought / What then? / Well I went to court and the judge's name was / Hoffman" (repeat chorus). At the time, everyone knew the reference was to Julius Hoffman, the notorious reactionary conservative judge in the 1969–70 trial of leftist protesters known as the "Chicago Eight," which included Bobby Seale and Abbie Hoffman. Prine had managed to write a song that points out the negative side of drug use as well as its saving graces while also making a leftist political commentary that is both funny and depressing.

Prine was born and raised in Maywood, Illinois, a suburb of Chicago, but his parents were from western Kentucky, where he had strong family ties. The most direct protest song on the album, "Paradise," reflects his concern about strip-mining there.

> When I was a child, my family would travel
> Down to Western Kentucky where my parents were born
> And there's a backwards old town that's often remembered
> So many times that my memories are worn
>
> Chorus: And daddy won't you take me back to
> Muhlenberg County

Down by the Green River where Paradise lay
Well, I'm sorry my son, but you're too late in asking
Mr. Peabody's coal train has hauled it away.
(Transcribed by the author)

"Paradise" is one of the most effective environmental songs I know of, and I think the emotional personal point of view makes it so.

One of his antiwar songs is more indirect; in "Sam Stone" he sings about a wounded veteran who came back home to his wife and kids after fighting in "the conflict overseas." "And the time that he served / Had shattered all his nerves / And left a little shrapnel in his knee / But the morphine eased the pain / And the grass grew round his brain / And gave him all the confidence he lacked / With a Purple Heart and a monkey on his back."

Chorus: There's a hole in Daddy's arm where all the money goes
And Jesus Christ died for nothin' I suppose
Little pitchers have big ears
Don't stop to count the tears
Sweet songs never last too long on broken radios.

. . . .

But life had lost its fun
And there was nothing to be done
But trade his house that he bought on the GI Bill
For a flag draped casket on a local heroes' hill.
(Transcribed by the author)

It grieves me when I hear this song now in the twenty-first century and realize how relevant it still is after the wars in Iraq and Afghanistan.

In another Prine antiwar song, the first line of the chorus is also the title:

Your flag decal won't get you into heaven anymore
They're already overcrowded from your dirty little war
And Jesus don't like killin' no matter what the reason's for
And your flag decal won't get you into heaven anymore

John Prine's political songs must have influenced a later political songwriter, Steve Earle. At the beginning of Earle's career, he was writing and singing mainly nonpolitical country music, but by the 1990s he had started writing protest songs. One indication of the musical connection between Prine and Earle is that they did a duet of the song "Loretta" at a tribute to singer/

songwriter Townes Van Zandt at the old Ryman Auditorium in Nashville on October 27, 2013. Steve Earle is a prolific writer whose songs have been recorded by Vince Gill, Johnny Lee, Patty Loveless, Carl Perkins, and Connie Smith in the 1970s and 1980s. His own performing career did not take off until his first album, *Guitar Town* (MCA-5713, 1986), appeared in 1986. The songs on the album are a blend of country and rock; they are not directly political, but a tough working-class attitude comes through that served him well when he started directly expressing his political opinions in songs.

Steve Earle has a liberal/leftist position similar to Woody Guthrie's, and it is reflected in many of his compositions. An excellent example is "Christmas in Washington" from the album *El Corazón* (Warner Bros. Records CD 9 46789-2, 1997). It is set in 1996 after Bill Clinton was elected president for his second term and addresses the political situation at the time. The song pays a direct tribute to Woody Guthrie and other historical figures who fought for justice and liberal causes.

> It's Christmastime in Washington
> The Democrats rehearsed
> Gettin' into gear for four more years
> Things not gettin' worse
> The Republicans drink whiskey neat
> And thanked their lucky stars
> They said, "He cannot seek another term
> They'll be no more FDRs."
> . . . .
> Chorus: So come back Woody Guthrie
> Come back to us now
> Tear your eyes from paradise
> And rise again somehow
> If you run into Jesus
> Maybe he can help you out
> Come back Woody Guthrie to us now.
> (Transcribed by the author)

Later in the song Earle provides a list of some of the greatest protest leaders of the twentieth century, asking them to come back to us now: Emma Goldman, Joe Hill, Malcolm X, and Martin Luther King.

The feeling of despair at the beginning is just as strong as in the Clash's "London Calling," but the memory of all the brave men and women who protested and marched against injustice in the past provides a more hopeful note at the end. The list of ideological inspiration includes some of my own personal heroes, and Steve Earle also suggests my regret that I have not done enough for the struggle: "So I sold my soul for wheels that roll / Now I'm stuck here in this town." I think he captures a shared feeling of guilt among people on the Left. Seven heroes are named from Jesus to FDR and Martin Luther King, but the chorus concentrates on Woody Guthrie, the one closest to Steve Earle's own role as troubadour for the downtrodden and disenfranchised, and an inspiration for other singer/songwriters who followed.

There are other musicians today who are linked to Woody Guthrie through the protest songs of the folk revival of the late 1950s and early 1960s. Contemporary singers and songwriters might not have been aware of Woody except for the songs of Pete Seeger, Joan Baez, and Bob Dylan that connected them to the past. Revivals of various kinds of vernacular music did not die out in the sixties; they continued in different forms in the 1970s, 1980s, 1990s, and into the twenty-first century. There have been numerous blues revivals, string band revivals, rockabilly revivals, swing revivals, and so on for the last forty-five years. Such revivals have become part of the history of American music; we seem to be always looking back for something that is missing in today's popular music, and we keep finding vital sources in our own history.

CHAPTER 7

The Night They Drove Old Dixie Down

Bluegrass, Folk Rock, and Outlaw Country

"Don't Give Up Your Day Job"

It's Tuesday, May 8, 2012, and I'm home from a trip to Cincinnati, where I met up with some old friends from California, Lynne and Keith Matheny. They're great travelers and took a train from Northern California to Cincinnati to catch a riverboat down the Ohio and Mississippi Rivers to Memphis. They had a layover in Cincinnati, and I drove down to spend the weekend with them. They're bluegrass fans, and I knew Cincinnati was a good bluegrass town. One of my former students, Larry Nager, used to write about music for the *Cincinnati Enquirer*, and he told me the best bluegrass bar in town was the Comet. Sure enough, that weekend the bar was having its regular Sunday-night concert with the Comet Bluegrass All-Stars (Jeff Roberts, banjo; Tim Strong, guitar; Missy Werner, vocals; Ed Cunningham, fiddle, vocals; Brad Meinerding, mandolin; Artie Werner, bass; John Cole, dobro).

The show started at 7:30, and we got there about an hour ahead of time. The place was already crowded and all the tables taken. We picked up some folding chairs and started looking for a table with room for us. Lynne asked at one table, and the guy said yes, but his girlfriend said they were waiting for other friends. Because I'd already had a couple of shots of Jack Daniels, I overcame my usual shyness and asked at another table with as much insistent charm as I could muster: "Hi, would y'all be willing to share your table with us? We're really nice people and won't block your view of the stage. My friends came all the way from California to hear the show." The couple, who looked to be in their thirties, smiled and said, "Sure, go ahead and sit down." "I'm Pat, this is Lynne and Keith; we sure appreciate it." Somehow in such social circumstances, I slip into my Texas drawl and southern politeness, and it usually works.

I said, "Where are y'all from?" He said, "Columbus," and I asked, "What neighborhood?" "Bexley." "I'm from Clintonville," I replied, and we started talking about Columbus and its distinctive neighborhoods. Bexley is on the east side and is one of the wealthiest neighborhoods in the city. Knowing that many Appalachian migrants had settled in a lower-income area on the south end of town and that the best bluegrass bars had historically been there on South Parsons Avenue, I said, "I didn't think Bexley was much of a bluegrass neighborhood."

He laughed and tacitly agreed, "I didn't really fit in at Bexley High School."

"What do y'all do for a livin'?"

"Electronics," he said.

"I'm a teacher," she said.

"What subject?"

"English."

"Me too."

Keith said he was a teacher too, so we had something else in common besides bluegrass. After several minutes in this vein, they asked Lynne and Keith, "What part of California are you from?" And we were well into an easygoing conversation.

The woman turned out to be from Kentucky, "just on the other side of the river in Covington."

"So you grew up with bluegrass?"

"Sure did."

And we proceeded to talk about her growing up in a bluegrass family. She said her boyfriend kidded her about being from Kentucky, which is a joking tradition in Ohio—ignorant hillbilly jokes and so on. Buckeyes call people from the mountains "briar hoppers" and other condescending names. Later she told me that a girlfriend of hers had a comeback for the insults, and she whispered in my ear, "It's better to wipe your ass with a buckeye than with a briar." I think all this camaraderie had something to do with the bonding power of bluegrass music.

After the show, Keith and I talked briefly with some members of the band. Their playing was excellent that night: high, ringing banjo played with great dexterity as was the fiddle playing; beautiful guitar solos, and twangy dobro, which always makes me think of the mountains of eastern Kentucky; solid rhythm from the bass; expert mandolin picking, which is an important element in the bluegrass sound and all of it tightly played together. The group sang high harmony with the voices blending into one. Missy Werner sang the high tenor part, which is usually sung by a male voice, and she sang in that high, lonesome way that makes bluegrass harmony so special, and for me so emotional. Sunday night in Cincinnati, they played several of my old favorites like "Long Black Veil."

> Ten years ago on a cold dark night,
> Someone was killed 'neath the town hall light.
> There were few at the scene, but they all agreed,
> That the slayer who ran looked a lot like me.
>
> She walks these hills, in a long black veil.
> She visits my grave, when the night winds wail.
> Nobody knows, nobody sees, nobody knows, but me.
> The judge said, "Son, what is your alibi?
> If you were somewhere else, then you won't have to die."
> (Transcribed by the author)

The narrator responds, "I spoke not a word, though it meant my life / For I'd been in the arms of my best friend's wife." After listening to the song, I said, "That has to be the best mournful death song" to the woman from Kentucky, and she agreed. For years I thought the song was a nineteenth-century folk ballad from the Appalachian Mountains, but the folklorist was wrong. It was a published and copyrighted song written by Danny Dill and Marijohn Wilkin and was a big country hit for Lefty Frizzell in 1959. I was listening to country radio in '59 and didn't really think about where it came from until a few years later, when I did more research on traditional ballads. This song fit the ballad style and form exactly.

The Anglo-American traditional ballad goes back to the British Isles and took hold in the Appalachian Mountains and other areas in the nineteenth century, then became one of the models for commercial country music in the 1920s and '30s, and continues to be a source in the twenty-first century. "Long Black Veil" may have started out as a country song, but it makes a perfect bluegrass song too because of the common background of both kinds of music.

The Comet All-Stars played another song that sounded old but was new. "The Night They Drove Old Dixie Down" (1969) was written by a Canadian, but it was first sung by an Arkansas hillbilly who had the authentic voice to convey the emotional and historical depth of the song. Both men were members of the Band, the innovative rock 'n' roll group from the 1960s and '70s. Robbie Robertson wrote the song, but Levon Helm sang it and claimed at least partial credit for helping write it. It is set during and after the Civil War.

> Virgil Caine is the name, and I served on the Danville train
> 'Til Stoneman's cavalry came and tore up the tracks again
> In the winter of '65, we were hungry, just barely alive
> By May the tenth, Richmond had fell
> It's a time I remember, oh so well
>
> The night they drove old Dixie down
> And the bells were ringing
> The night they drove old Dixie down
> And the people were singing
> They went, "Na, na, na, na, na, na, na."
> (www.elyrics.net/read/b/band-lyrics/the-night-they
> -drove-old-dixie-down-lyrics.html)

The first-person narrator proudly states his heritage, the strong link to his father and his commitment to "work the land," as well as to his brother "who took a rebel stand." He was "proud and brave," but "a Yankee laid him in his grave." The lyrics have the sound of a nineteenth-century song, and the melody and Levon Helm's vocal suggest a similar archaic source. I had to hide a few tears as the Comet Bluegrass All-Stars sang harmony on the chorus. A moving song anyway, but the Sunday concert took place just two weeks and three days after Levon Helm died at age seventy-one, giving the song even more immediate emotional power for a seventy-year-old longtime fan of the Band.

"The Night They Drove Old Dixie Down" is a sixties folk/rock song that sounds as if it was written for bluegrass, which was invented in the 1940s. Because of its tradition of mostly acoustic instruments and emphasis on nostalgic themes, bluegrass music has an emotional meaning for longtime fans and the general public alike. Traditional acoustic bluegrass *seems* older than country music with its electrified guitars and studio production sound, but bluegrass actually came later. This older feeling was reinforced in 1967 by the movie *Bonnie and Clyde*, which had a Flatt and Scruggs bluegrass soundtrack. The story was set in the 1930s in rural and small-town Texas locations, and the music conjured up a premodern world especially during the rapidly changing times of the sixties, when the movie was popular. The film introduced bluegrass to a wider audience and prompted a corresponding surge in record sales and popularity.

The Comet Bluegrass All-Stars played several standard bluegrass songs that night like "Rocky Top" (1969), but the songs that stuck in my mind were more contemporary and often from other genres of music. For instance, they played a country hit by the Dixie Chicks, "If I Fall You're Going Down with Me" (1999), not surprisingly sung by the only woman in the Comet band, Missy Werner.

> Was it the pull of the moon now, baby, that led you to my door?
> You say the night's got you acting crazy, I think it's
>> something more.
> I've never felt the Earth move, honey, until you shook my tree.
> Nobody runs from the law now, baby, of love and gravity,
> It pulls you so strong, baby, you gotta hold on.
> (Transcribed by the author)

When they finished, I leaned toward the Kentucky woman and said, "Wow, a real assertive woman song." She smiled and said, "Yeah." For anyone who is familiar with the Dixie Chicks, this postfeminist assertion of women's rights to the point of a threat against the man will not come as a surprise. They've been known as outspoken since their initial wave of popularity, but this attitude doesn't fit with the stereotype of bluegrass as a conservative tradition. Things are changing just as they have from the beginning.

There are other new themes in contemporary bluegrass, especially if you consider songs that originated in rock 'n' roll or pop music. "Carmelita" was written by the rock singer/songwriter Warren Zevon and released on his self-titled LP in 1976 (Asylum Records 7E-1060). I had never heard it sung as a bluegrass song until that night at the Comet. Like "The Night They Drove Old Dixie Down," the tune sounds appropriate for bluegrass, but the lyrics are not about traditional topics.

> Well, I'm sittin' here playing solitaire with my pearl-handled deck.
> The county won't give me no more methadone and they cut off
>> your welfare check.

Carmelita, hold me tighter, I think I'm sinking down
And I'm all strung out on heroin on the outskirts of town.
(Transcribed by the author)

The song became a hit for Linda Ronstadt (*Simple Dreams*, Asylum Records, 6E-104, 1977), and her version was the first I heard and liked immediately. She used the line "pawned my Smith and Wesson" instead of Zevon's original "pawned my Smith Corona," and her change is used in most versions I've heard since she introduced it, including a later recording by Warren Zevon himself. The alteration reinforces the desperation and potential violence of the heroin addict's life. It is set in urban Los Angeles and not the mountains of West Virginia or eastern Kentucky, but the sad story and pity for the desperate narrator makes it emotionally compatible with bluegrass tradition. (There is another appealing cross-genre version of the song: Texas Mexican musician Flaco Jiménez plays accordion and country star Dwight Yoakum sings "Carmelita" on a conjunto rendering of the song on Jiménez's album *Partners*, Reprise 926822-2, 1992.)

After the show, Lynne, Keith, and I left the bar beaming, satisfied at hearing such fine playing and singing. For me, the Comet Bluegrass All-Stars' show in Cincinnati on Sunday night, May 6, 2012, represents bluegrass as it is in the present—a mix of traditional rural folk music, bluegrass, and country songs, but with a contemporary attitude drawn from rock 'n' roll and all the various kinds of popular music that a new generation of bluegrass musicians grew up with whether in the mountains of Kentucky or the suburbs of Cincinnati and Los Angeles.

The Comet Bluegrass All-Stars were as good as any band I heard at the Bluegrass Palace on South Parsons Avenue, which was the best bluegrass venue in Columbus at the time. Like many bluegrass players in Columbus, their musicianship would have qualified them for national touring bands. Musicians often came from Kentucky or West Virginia, got jobs, and settled down with their wives and families in Cincinnati, Dayton, Columbus, or some other manufacturing city in Ohio. They then lived out what had become a bluegrass adage, "Don't give up your day job."

I became aware of bluegrass long before this up-close experience with it in Cincinnati. When I was doing fieldwork in Ohio for the Smithsonian American Folklife Festival, I met other folklorists who were also doing research in Ohio. One of these was singer/musician Mike Seeger, who was conducting fieldwork in southern Ohio. At one point he came to Columbus to follow some leads, and he gave me a call. We arranged to meet at the Bluegrass Palace on the south side of town. I learned a lot from him during that meeting including the name of a top-notch fiddler and mandolin player, Lake Brickey, who came to Columbus from Portsmouth, just across the Ohio River from Kentucky. His parents were from the mountains of eastern Kentucky, and like many people from that economically depressed region, they had migrated to Ohio to find work. Lake had moved to Columbus as a young man, and by the time I interviewed him in the early seventies, he was cutting hair at a barbershop on High Street in my neighborhood, Clintonville. He played in bluegrass bands on weekends at bars and festivals in central Ohio. He told me that he had grown up in a house without electricity and listened to music on a radio powered by a car battery.

I didn't get a chance to interview any of the Comet Bluegrass All-Stars, but I imagine that they or their parents had backgrounds similar to Lake's.

The New South

I was a latecomer to bluegrass, part of the new audience that came along in 1967, when we heard Lester Flatt and Earl Scruggs on the *Bonnie and Clyde* soundtrack. I knew there was such a thing as bluegrass before the movie, but I was too caught up in blues, R&B, jazz, and rock 'n' roll to pay much attention. The first bluegrass album I bought was a direct spin-off of the movie, *Foggy Mountain Breakdown and Other Music from the Bonnie and Clyde Era* (1968) by the Bluegrass Banjo Pickers. It was an all-instrumental LP in the RCA Camden budget line (CAS-2243); I probably paid anywhere from 99 cents to $1.98 for it. It sounded good to me, but little did I know at the time that the Bluegrass Banjo Pickers were actually the Osborne Brothers, one of the most popular bluegrass bands of the sixties whose big hit "Rocky Top" was released the same year as their anonymous movie-related album which turned out to be a pretty damn good intro to bluegrass for me.

My interest in bluegrass grew, and by the time I arrived at Ohio State in 1969, I was catching up by buying albums by the first generation of bluegrass pickers, Bill Monroe, Flatt and Scruggs, and the Stanley Brothers. I liked all of them of course, but I wasn't *really* excited by bluegrass until I found two albums by the Country Gentlemen, *Country Songs, Old and New* (Folkways Records, FA 2409, 1960) and *On the Road* (Folkways Records, FA 2411, 1963), while browsing through the Archives of Primitive, Ethnic, and Folk Music at Ohio State University. Fran Utley, the medievalist/folklorist who started the archives, used some of his budget to buy every album released on the Folkways label, which included these groundbreaking works. I took the albums home and kept them until a few years ago when I bought the CDs and returned the albums to the archives. Hope nobody was looking for them.

The "country songs old and new" by the Country Gentlemen that I liked best were traditional ones or sounded like they were. "Drifting Too Far" and "Have Thine Own Way" were hymns that we sang at the Highland Avenue Church of Christ as I was growing up. I remembered most of the words and could sing along with the Country Gentlemen's recording. "The Story of Charlie Lawson" was a broadside ballad from North Carolina, broadside meaning that it originated in print or a recording rather than from oral tradition. Like many broadsides, it was based on an actual historical event. The *New York Times* of December 26 and 27, 1929, gives the facts of the incident narrated in the ballad.

> Walnut Cove, N.C., Dec. 25 (AP)—Becoming suddenly insane, a Stokes county farmer today slew his wife and six children, and, after having laid them out for burial, went into a patch of woods near his home and killed himself. The body of C. D. Lawson, the 43-year-old father and husband, was found about half a mile from the home with a shotgun wound in his chest.

The words of the song contain some of the same facts but put the murders and suicide in the context of the emotional and religious response of the local community. The last line of the first stanza indicates the community's lack of understanding of such a terrible murder, "They never knew what caused him to take his family's life." His children beg to be spared, but "he would not heed their call." "He kept shooting until he killed them all," and they are buried "while the angels watch all above." The ballad continues, "Come home, come home my little ones / To the land of peace and love" and finally ends with "When we meet in another land / Our troubles will be o'er." The language and religious meaning of the song strongly reflect the values of rural and small-town southern culture of the 1920s.

Nine years after I first heard "The Story of Charlie Lawson," I went to the mountains of North Carolina as part of a team of folklorists to do field research along the Blue Ridge Parkway in Virginia and North Carolina for the American Folklife Center at the Library of Congress. Even though we were close to the place where the murders had taken place, I didn't think of that specific song until one day fellow folklorist Blanton Owen and I went to talk to someone he had heard about. Calvin Jones (not his real name) met us at the door of his house, and after we identified ourselves, he invited us in. We set up our tape recorder and microphones as he began to talk.

He acted in a way that I had begun to expect when doing fieldwork, as if he had been waiting for us and couldn't wait to tell us everything he knew. I had encountered people like him in my fieldwork along the Texas Gulf Coast and throughout Ohio. I would meet people and ask if they knew any old-timers or anyone who knew about the history and traditions of the area. They would give me a name, and sure enough the person would turn out to be a good talker, often a storyteller. Without us even asking him a question, Mr. Jones began to talk about the old windup Victrola gramophone sitting right inside the door. He told us it was originally owned by Charlie Lawson.

He got out an old 78 rpm record and put it on the gramophone; it was "The Story of Charlie Lawson" by the Morris Brothers (Blue Bird Records, ca. 1938) with lyrics similar to the version the Country Gentlemen sang. We quickly set up our equipment and recorded everything that followed. Before he put the needle in the groove, he told us to listen for a mysterious bumping sound that was made by the ghost of Charlie Lawson. As soon as it ended, he asked, "Did you hear it?" We said we thought we heard something, and he went on to tell us that as a child he knew Charlie Lawson and, in fact, had "slept with Charlie Lawson five days before the murders."

He then told us about a mysterious pine tree and gave us specific details about where it was located, down this dirt road, over some railroad tracks, up a hill to the pine tree, and when you got close to it "you just get murder in your heart." He then invited us to go with him to see the mysterious tree. We said, no, we didn't think we'd do that, and he began a long rambling tale about other ghosts and mysteries around the area. This is the closest I'd ever been to feeling the culture surrounding an old ballad or legend, and I've told the story about Calvin Jones and Charlie Lawson many times since.

The Country Gentlemen's album *Country Songs, Old and New* is like a folk history of America. The hymns give a sense of religious belief in the South, and "Charlie Lawson" a glimpse of how a community responded to sudden tragic deaths. The Country Gentlemen also sang "Jesse James," an old ballad about the American outlaw hero from the nineteenth century. I knew the song but had never heard it done bluegrass style. In that sense, it was a modern reworking of a traditional song, but to me it sounded as traditional as any song I had ever heard. They also sang "The Long Black

Veil," reinforcing my assumption that it was a nineteenth-century ballad rather than a popular country song from the fifties. But ironically, the Country Gentlemen were doing something new by bringing in a wider range of material to bluegrass—folk songs from the nineteenth century, recorded hillbilly/country music from the twenties to the fifties, and new compositions by current country and bluegrass songwriters in the sixties.

They learned about the older material not from rural oral tradition but from 78 rpm record collections, which indicates how much a part of the sixties folk revival they were. Unlike most of the previous generation of rural bluegrass musicians, they were an urban bluegrass band that was formed in Washington, D.C., and played in local clubs there in the sixties. They were an innovative influence on the development of bluegrass while still remaining connected to the roots of country music, indicating how complex the traditional cultural process of vernacular music is. Their history is another example of the shifting nature of authenticity when music is examined in cultural/historical context.

Bluegrass singer/guitar player Tony Rice's personal history shows how diverse and complex musical influences can be. He was born in Danville, Virginia, in 1951 but moved to California with his family as a child. He learned to play from his father, who was a product of southern traditional bluegrass, but in Southern California Tony came under the influence of such diverse progressive musicians as Clarence White, Ry Cooder, and folk-rock pioneers Chris Hillman of the Byrds and Desert Rose Band and Herb Pedersen also in the Desert Rose Band. In 1970 Rice moved to Kentucky, where he eventually joined J. D. Crowe's band the New South.

All these diverse influences made Tony Rice into a great, unique guitarist and one of the best singers in all bluegrass. His vocals on the album *The New South* (Rounder Records, 0044, 1975) and his solo albums are beautifully emotional. Unfortunately he doesn't sing anymore. I thought this might be because of his smoking habit; one of his solo albums, *Me and My Guitar* (Rounder CD 0201, 1987), has a photo of him on the cover looking cool with a cigarette in his hand and leaning against his guitar shipping crate with "Extremely Fragile" stamped on the side—sadly ironic in retrospect. But according to a new book by Tim Stafford and Caroline Wright, "Tony blames allergies and sinus issues for any vocal deficiencies" on his album *Tony Rice Plays and Sings Bluegrass* (Rounder CD 0253, 1993). On another album that Tony sang on, Rickie Simpkins's *Dancing on the Fingerboard* (Pinecastle, 2014), "Tony's voice was almost gone. Subdued and hoarse, his rendition of the tune was still extraordinarily beautiful." And finally the authors note "the end of his career as one of bluegrass music's most acclaimed lead singers." Whatever the explanation, it was a tragic occurrence in bluegrass history.

The New South's album *The New South* has some great examples of a perfect fit between a particular song and Tony Rice's singing. "Rock, Salt, and Nails" expresses all the hurt and anger a man feels against the woman who lied to and cheated on him. It was written by Utah Phillips, an influential folk singer/songwriter (1935–2008) who carried on the leftist labor-organizing tradition of Woody Guthrie and Pete Seeger, but this song is more about gender politics. If anything it follows in the centuries-old tradition of murdered-girl ballads such as "Pretty Polly," "The Jealous Lover," "Omie Wise," and "Banks of the Ohio." Despite its traditional roots, "Rock, Salt, and Nails" is definitely a twentieth-century take on the genre. The man sings to his former lover, referring directly to the lies that she told him and the letter that "was written in shame."

> Now the nights are so lonely, Lord, sorrow runs deep.
> Nothing is worse than a night without sleep.
> I walk out alone and look at the sky
> Too empty to sing, too lonesome to cry.
>
> Now if the ladies were blackbirds, if the ladies were thrushes
> I'd lie there for hours in the chilly cold marshes.
> If the ladies were squirrels with them high bushy tails
> I'd fill up my shotgun with rock salt and nails (repeat).
> (Transcribed by the author)

The burning resentment the singer feels toward the woman who has cheated on him and then left him alone builds slowly in the song, from images of "low moaning sounds" and "water runs cold" to the knowledge of the lies that she told. He ends up desperately unhappy: "I walk out alone and look at the sky / Too empty to sing too lonesome to cry." But even this doesn't quite prepare us for him imagining her and every other woman as hunted animals and declaring, "I'd fill up my shotgun with rock salt and nails." It's one of the most brutally honest songs about lost love in American vernacular music. He feels the anger and hurt deeply enough to want to kill her, but he absolves himself by making it all conditional and metaphoric: "*if* the ladies were blackbirds." The ending is still shockingly misogynistic.

Another song about a sensitive man on the album is "Ten Degrees," one of the many Gordon Lightfoot songs Rice has recorded (five on *Me and My Guitar* alone). Lightfoot (1938–) is a Canadian singer/songwriter whose songs have been covered by Peter, Paul, and Mary, Johnny Cash, Judy Collins, and Bob Dylan. The best known include "Early Morning Rain," "If You Could Read My Mind," and "The Wreck of the Edmund Fitzgerald." "Ten Degrees" is not among the hits, but it is one of his finest.

The main character was "just a road musician" who played at taverns "singing songs about the ramblin' / The lovin' girls and gamblin.'" He meets a girl and tells her, "I don't know when, I've had a better friend." Despite her "listening to every word that he was saying" and telling him that "she would take a ride in the morning sun," he ends up back on the road again by himself.

> Now he's traded off his Martin though his troubles aren't all over
> His feet are almost frozen and the sun is sinking low
> Won't you listen to me, brother, if you ever loved your mother
> Please pull off on the shoulder, if you're goin' Milwaukee way
> It's ten degrees and getting colder down by Boulder Dam today.
> (www.lyricsdepot.com)

Like many singer/songwriters who had to work their way up in the music business, Rice must have identified with the down-on-his-luck itinerant musician in the song. The details make the experience immediate for any listener, even one who has never written a song or sung professionally; everyone, both men and women, has felt terrible when someone we think is a friend has abandoned us.

Like the Country Gentlemen's *Country Songs, Old and New, The New South* album covers a wide range of material. Besides the contemporary "Rock, Salt, and Nails" and "Ten Degrees," it includes two traditional pieces, the fiddle tune "Sally Goodin" and an old hymn done bluegrass style, "Cryin' Holy," and one bluegrass instrumental written by Earl Scruggs, "Nashville Blues." The album also shows how bluegrass was influenced by rock 'n' roll and R&B with a cover of Fats Domino's fifties hit "I'm Walkin.'" But there are more contemporary songs than traditional ones, including "Home Sweet Home Revisited" by country singer/songwriter Rodney Crowell and "Summer Wages" by folk singer Ian Tyson.

Tyson is another Canadian songwriter who was first known as part of the duo Ian and Sylvia (Sylvia Fricker). It is worth noting that Ian and

Sylvia were one of the few "folkie" acts from the sixties I liked enough to buy their albums. I have three in my collection: their first, *Ian & Sylvia* (Vanguard, VSD 2113, 1962); their second, *Northern Journey* (Vanguard, VRS-9154, 1964); and their eponymous album as the band Great Speckled Bird (Ampex Records, A10103, 1969). Both were excellent songwriters, so I'm not surprised Tony Rice is a fan.

The protagonist in Tyson's "Summer Wages" is in the same sad situation as the men in "Rock, Salt, and Nails" and "Ten Degrees."

> Never hit seventeen when you play against the dealer
> You know that the odds won't ride with you
> And never leave your woman alone with your friends around to
> steal her
> She'll be gambled and gone like summer wages.
>
> And we'll keep rollin' on 'til we get to Vancouver
> And the woman that I love she's living there
> It's been six long months and more since I've seen her
> Years have gambled and gone like summer wages.
> (Transcribed by the author)

As in "Rock, Salt, and Nails," this guy is feeling down and desperate over a woman who left him, and as in "Ten Degrees," he's working his way across the country wondering about the woman. In this case, he's headed for Vancouver to try to get his lover back, working at jobs he hates along the way. Men in all three songs (and others like them) are the opposite of the tough, dominant man found in outlaw country music who maintains power over women and acts indifferent if he loses her. There are enough of both kinds of men in folk/country/bluegrass lyrics of this era to make them prominent masculine types, and that trend was also present in folk-rock music of the late sixties.

Sweetheart of the Rodeo: Folk Rock in the Late Sixties

In the mid- to late 1960s, rock musicians and their fans were discovering and being influenced by bluegrass and folk/country music. The confluence of performers and audience was no accident: a generation was ready to take rock music somewhere new. Many of us were born in the early forties including the Grateful Dead's Jerry Garcia in 1942 and Phil Lesh in 1940, the Byrds' Roger McGuinn and Chris Hillman in 1942, Gene Clark and David Crosby in 1941, the year I was born. The discovery of country and bluegrass by our age group was occurring all over the country, but California was especially a hot spot for musicians; the Grateful Dead formed in the San Francisco area and the Byrds in Los Angeles.

Some of these musicians started out playing in bluegrass or folk bands before taking up or returning to rock 'n' roll. Jerry Garcia began playing banjo in 1962, and by 1965 he was in a jug band that switched to electric instruments and eventually became the Grateful Dead. I first heard the Dead sometime in the late sixties and liked their music but never became a real Deadhead. I only bought one of their records, *Europe '72* (Warner Bros. Records, 3WX 2668, 1972), a live album that featured their country sound in an original song written by band members ("Cumberland Blues") and their covers of folk songs ("I Know You Rider") and country hits ("You Win Again"). I give them much of the credit for the creation and popularization of country rock in the sixties, but I'm going to concentrate on the Byrds and their various offshoots as my primary example of the history and development of folk rock or country rock. As I've said, the labels and genres for vernacular music are slippery and often overlap, sometimes to the point of meaninglessness. But there're handy when discussing cultural history, so we'll go ahead and call it folk rock.

The Byrds came together in LA in 1964, and their first hit, "Mr. Tambourine Man," was released in 1965, immediately linking them to Bob Dylan, especially to his folk music roots. The song was on Dylan's *Bringing It All Back Home* (1965) but was written around the same time he wrote "Chimes of Freedom" (1964), a period when he was making the transition from folk to rock and blending the two together. "Something is happening here," and unlike Mr. Jones, everyone knew what it was. The folk influence continued with the Byrds' next big hit, "Turn! Turn! Turn!" (1966), which was composed by folk-revival singer/songwriter Pete Seeger (see chapter 1), who used a passage from the Bible (Ecclesiastes 3:1–8) for the lyrics except for the last line. The Byrds continued to record albums such as *The Notorious Byrd Brothers* (Columbia, CS 9575, 1968), which made use of country music, but they also experimented with psychedelic music and so-called space rock. As several members of the original Byrds left the band, they were replaced by new musicians, including Gram Parsons, whose contributions helped produce their most acclaimed country folk album, *Sweetheart of the Rodeo* (Columbia, CS 9670, 1968).

The album is a nostalgic and romantic view of American folk and country music that communicates sadness at the loss of a simpler, southern rural past while at the same time implying a sense of irony because of the Byrds' previous identity as a psychedelic band. Even the album cover is both nostalgic and ironic. It's a reproduction of an illustration (copyrighted in 1933) by Joseph Jacinto "Jo" Mora (1876–1947) depicting in almost encyclopedic detail various types of western cowboys in their different outfits including "Early Spanish," "Mexican Vaquero," "Cowboy of the Plains," "South West Type," "Nevada Type," "Typical West Coast." There are pictures of cowboys roping, trick riding, bronco busting, and bull riding, and detailed views of various kinds of spurs. All the small depictions of cowboys and their paraphernalia surround a much larger illustration of a cowgirl labeled "Sweetheart of the Rodeo." She is dressed in a cowboy hat, fringed skirt, and cowboy boots and holding around her a very large yellow flower wreath in the shape of a heart.

I recognize most of these images from all the Gene Autry, Roy Rogers, Red Ryder, and Lash Larue cowboy movies my brother and I watched every Saturday morning from the ages of six to eleven in the late forties and early fifties. These illustrations are not just movie images though; on the album cover they are also historically accurate depictions brought together in such a way that the overall effect reinforces whatever romantic ideals a viewer has of the Old West, a way of life that exists now only in movies, television shows, and popular illustrations. I loved that image as a kid and still loved it when I first saw the album cover of *Sweetheart of the Rodeo*.

The music on the album reflects that same nostalgic mix. Besides Parsons, the Byrds also brought in several well-known LA country/bluegrass studio musicians for the recording; Lloyd Green, John Hartford, and Clarence White added to the "authenticity" of the sound. It was recorded in Nashville and includes a folk song popularized by Merle Travis, "I Am a Pilgrim"; an old gospel song by the Louvin Brothers, "The Christian Life"; a later country song written by the prolific and terrific Cindy Walker, "Blue Canadian Rockies," which Gene Autry sang in one of his cowboy movies; a Merle Haggard song, "Life in Prison"; country and Sun rockabilly singer/ songwriter Luke McDaniel's "You're Still on My Mind"; two Bob Dylan songs, "Nothing Was Delivered" and "You Ain't Going Nowhere" (both from *The Basement Tapes*, which was a bootleg that had not been officially released at the time); a Woody Guthrie outlaw ballad, "Pretty Boy Floyd"; and two country songs written by Gram Parsons, "Hickory Wind" and "One Hundred Years from Now."

Music critics agree that Gram Parsons was a significant influence on the country focus and sound of the album, and I think he is at the heart of romantic nostalgia and loss in the selection of songs. Part of this lies in the way the album sums up the history of country music: going back to its roots in southern folk music and gospel, to protest ballads from the thirties and cowboy songs from the forties to honky-tonk drinking songs with rockabilly rhythms from the forties and fifties, and folk rock from the sixties, and finally to newly written country folk songs by Parsons that reveal a yearning for a southern rural past in "Hickory Wind" or focus on present and future existential concerns in "One Hundred Years from Now." Only one song is not directly country, William Bell's soul song "You Don't Miss Your Water," but it fits because the Byrds turn it into a plaintive country song that demonstrates the influence of African American blues and R&B on country music.

Sweetheart of the Rodeo is by far my favorite Byrds album, but it was just the beginning of my appreciation for Gram Parsons. He and Roger McGuinn had conflicts during the making of the album, and Parsons left the group before *Sweetheart* was released. Parsons went out on his own, first forming a new band, the Flying Burrito Brothers, with Chris Hillman, who was the most country/bluegrass-oriented original member of the Byrds. They were joined by bass player Chris Ethridge, steel guitarist Sneaky Pete Klienow, and several drummers on different tracks. The album was called *The Gilded Palace of Sin* (A&M Records, SP 4175, 1969), and all the songs were cowritten by Parsons and Hillman except for "Do Right Woman," by songwriters Dan Penn and Chips Moman, and "Dark End of the Street," written by Penn and Spooner Oldham; both of these songs were soul hits for Aretha Franklin and James Carr in 1967. Throwing R&B songs done country style into the mix recalls the inclusion of the Stax hit "You Don't Miss Your Water" on *Sweetheart of the Rodeo*.

The album title, *The Gilded Palace of Sin*, suggests a more serious side of the group than the band's name, the Flying Burrito Brothers, would. This somber side becomes more obvious in "Sin City," the second track on side 1 of the LP.

This old town is filled with sin, it'll swallow you in
If you've got some money to burn take it home right away
You've got three years to pay and Satan is waiting his turn
The scientists say it'll all wash away, but we don't believe anymore
'Cause we've got our recruits in their green mohair suits
So please show your I.D. at the door.

Chorus: This old earthquake's gonna leave me in the poorhouse
It seems like this whole town's insane
On the thirty-first floor your gold-plated door
Won't keep out the Lord's burning rain.
(Transcribed by the author)

I always assumed the song was about Las Vegas, but it is general enough to apply to any city in this world of crass money changers, corrupt politicians, and crazy people seeking sinful thrills. It seems steeped in evangelical Christian beliefs in Satan and a vengeful God. I don't think it's a parody of southern Christianity because of the way it fits with "I Am a Pilgrim" and "The Christian Life" on *Sweetheart of the Rodeo* and several other songs on *The Gilded Palace of Sin*, especially "Christine's Tune," "Juanita," "Hot Burrito #1 and #2," "Do You Know How It Feels," and "Hippie Boy."

Religious themes run through all these songs, with references to Jesus Christ, Satan, the devil, and feelings of despair and the need for spiritual help. Christine is "the devil in disguise," and "she's telling dirty lies." "Hot Burrito #2" has these secular-to-spiritual lyrics:

Yes, you loved me and you sold all my clothes
I love you, baby, but that's the way that it goes, so it goes
I guess you know how I feel, so it goes, yes, it couldn't be real
And you want me home all night, you just don't want
    another fight
But you better love, find some love, love me baby, Jesus Christ.
(Transcribed by the author)

"Jesus Christ" could be taken as a profane expletive to express the singer's frustration with the woman he is addressing, fearing that her professions of love for him are lies. But Jesus is also his savior, and he could be calling out to Christ for help. The album includes several songs about his anger toward women who are mistreating him and the despair he feels because of them or *her* if they are all about the same woman. Taken together, these songs suggest a deeper anguish that is affecting his whole life, a profound depression that may require divine intervention to save his life. The need for a savior on *The Gilded Palace of Sin* may be related to the fact that Gram Parsons had been doing drugs, including heroin and cocaine, for years. He finally died of an overdose of alcohol and morphine a few years after he wrote these songs.

Parsons only made one album with the Flying Burrito Brothers before he recorded two solo albums; the first was *GP* (Reprise Records, MS 2123, 1973), and the second, his last, was *Grievous Angel* (Reprise Records, MS 2171, 1974), released after his death in 1973. Both albums contain songs about bad relationships and loss; the titles alone give a sense of despair: "Still Feeling Blue," "How Much I've Lied," "In My Hour of Darkness," all written by Parsons, and the cover songs, "We'll Sweep Out the Ashes in the Morning," "Cry One More Time," and "Love Hurts." Music critics and historians agree that his blending of country, folk, and rock had a tremendous influence on the course of all three genres after he died. Even a short list of singers, songwriters, and groups he inspired indicates how important he is in the history of rock 'n' roll: Emmylou Harris (who sang with him on the two solo albums), the Eagles, Poco, Elvis Costello, Uncle Tupelo, Steve Earle, Lucinda Williams, Waylon Jennings, Willie Nelson, and virtually anyone who played anything that could be labeled country rock.

"Good Timin' Man": Outlaw Country in the Seventies

In the late sixties and early seventies, at the same time I was becoming a devoted bluegrass and folk-rock fan, I experienced an intense revival of interest in country music mainly because of three singer/songwriters, all from Texas—Willie Nelson, Waylon Jennings, and Billy Joe Shaver. Their music at the time demonstrates the strong influence that rock 'n' roll was having on country music, especially what came to be called "outlaw country."

In 1973 Waylon made an album of Shaver songs that remains one of my all-time favorites. Nine of the ten songs on *Honky Tonk Heroes* (RCA, APL 1-0240) were written by Billy Joe (one cowritten with Waylon and one with Hillman Hall). I might have worn the record out if I hadn't been so careful and replaced the stylus often. The picture on the cover seems to capture what a good time they were having while making the music. I already imagined they were drinking a lot, and the photo on the album cover reinforced my view. It shows Waylon, Billy Joe, and the band sitting at a bar, glasses of beer in hand, laughing out loud at somebody's joke, which we'll never know. Billy Joe is sitting to Waylon's right with a cigarette in one hand and a beer glass in the other. Waylon is holding the neck of a guitar, a cigarette clamped between his teeth and a wide grin on his face.

The first cut on side A, "Honky Tonk Heroes," establishes the unifying theme of the album—every song is from that beer-drinking, bar-hopping, masculine point of view—the lyrics reveal the manly character traits and attitudes that run through the rest of the LP. The song begins as a slow, mournful country song, but when it shifts into a higher gear between the verse and the chorus, the drums and bass signal the rock 'n' roll spirit in country music.

> Low down leavin' sun, I've done did everything that needs done.
> Woe is me, why can't I see I'd best be leavin' well enough alone.
> Them neon light nights, couldn't stay out of fights
> Keep a-hauntin' me in memories.
> Well, there's one in every crowd, for cryin' out loud.
> Why was it always turnin' out to be me.

> Where does it go, the good Lord only knows.
> It seems like it was just the other day
> I was down at Green Gables, a hawkin' them tables
> And generally blowin' all my hard earned pay.
> Piano roll blues, danced holes in my shoes
> There weren't another other way to be
> For loveable losers, no-account boozers
> And honky tonk heroes like me.
> (Transcribed by the author)

For Billy Joe, this is an autobiographical song, one that resonates enough with Waylon for him to sing it with total sincerity. They both see themselves as "loveable losers and no-account boozers," but these attributes are what make them "honky tonk heroes." This seemingly contradictory image is a key to their masculine cultural identity: some regrets about their bad behavior but finally a who-gives-a-damn attitude that ties them to the rockabilly songs of the fifties—drinking and fighting to prove their masculinity and sexuality (see chapter 3). They also project pride in their limited education and working-class backgrounds when Waylon sings the ungrammatical hillbilly poetics of "I've done / Did everything that needs done" as well as the line "blowin' all my hard earned pay" and the pronunciation of "Pie-anny roll blues."

Billy Joe Shaver's life of public conflicts related to heavy drinking are well known. My friend Larry Doyle briefly summed up Billy Joe's life in an e-mail when I asked if he wanted to go to a Shaver concert: "Is from Texas. Arrested for shooting someone in a bar fight. Mentioned in a Bob Dylan song. Has a song, 'Wacko from Waco.' Divorced and remarried the same woman several times." Of course he wanted to go to the concert. His description is one fan's comic representation of Shaver's rowdy life, but it is an image that Billy Joe himself projected in his songs. It must be added that he always had a religious side, which he seems to have embraced fully later in life, and his songs now reflect that he has accepted Christ as his savior and has rejected the wild side of life.

He sang with conviction at the concert that night, both the songs about Jesus and the rowdy songs, including three of my favorites, "Black Rose," "If I Give My Soul," and "I've Been to Georgia on a Fast Train."

> I've been to Georgia on a fast train, honey.
> I wasn't born no yesterday.
> Got an eighth grade education,
> And a good Christian raisin'.
> Ain't no need in y'all a-treatin' me this way.
> (Transcribed by the author)

He expresses the same pride in his working-class roots as he did in "Honky Tonk Heroes" as well as protesting the rest of the world's treatment of him because of his poor, uneducated background.

"Black Rose" contains one of his most quoted lines: "The devil made me do it the first time / The second time I did it on my own." This resonates with a lot of his male fans, including me, and even though the song is from a man's point of view, I'm sure it resonates with lots of women too. The "it" here refers to his succumbing to a woman who has the power to bewitch men. "When the devil made that woman / Lord, it threw the pattern away / She was built for speed with the tools you need / To make a new fool every day." But the song makes clear that this fool makes a choice to sin based on his own desires and fueled by alcohol: "I was standing in the drizzling rain / With a trembling hand and a bottle of gin / And a rose of a different name."

He finally implores Jesus for help: "Lord, put a handle on a simple headed man / Help me leave that black rose alone" (http://www.genius.com).

Billy Joe's religion is embedded in many of his secular songs about sinning, but it becomes the central concern in several of his Christian songs such as "If I Give My Soul."

> Down a dangerous road, I have come to where I'm standing
> With a heavy heart, and my hat clutched in my hand
> Such a foolish fool, God ain't known no greater sinner
> I have come in search of Jesus, hoping he will understand
>
> If I give my soul, will he cleanse these clothes I'm wearin'
> If I give my soul, will he put new boots on my feet
> If I bow my head and beg God for his forgiveness
> Will he breathe new breath inside me and give back my dignity
> (www.genius.com)

The song ends with his final plea: "If I give my soul to Jesus will she take me back again." The confession of sins and need for salvation of this song sound very familiar to me because of my southern evangelical background, although, at least in the church I attended, public confession never included such specific details, and that is, of course, what gives this song its power. Also, the hymns we sang were always positive affirmations of a Jesus who could turn your life around; confessing and asking Christ to forgive you would be the beginning of a new life. What's different about Billy Joe's song is his doubt: "*If* I give my soul." And he mentions eternal life not as a desired result of salvation but as a personal goal in this life—"will she take me back again."

Hymns may not emphasize earthly rewards, but I think when many people accept Christ as their savior, they have some personal worldly desires in mind as a reward, and some preachers and televangelists have been playing on their desires for many years now. Finally, the deep shame and regret over the alcohol-induced loss of his wife and son are the most painfully wrenching emotions of the song, one that atheists and agnostics can also understand.

I think this brief consideration of Billy Joe Shaver's life and music might give you some idea of why Bob Dylan would mention him in a song he recorded in 2009, "I Feel a Change Comin' On" (on *Together through Life*, Columbia, 88697438932).

You are as porous as ever, baby, you can start a fire.
I must be losing my mind, you're the object of my desire.
I feel a change comin' on, and the fourth part of the day's
    already gone.
I'm listening to Billy Joe Shaver and I'm reading James Joyce.
Some people they tell me I got the blood of the land in my voice.
(Transcribed by the author)

This reminds me of a couplet from another Dylan song, "Tombstone Blues," when he refers to a place "where Ma Rainey and Beethoven once unwrapped their bedroll / Tuba players now rehearse around the flagpole." Dylan is still tearing down the artificial barriers between high and low art, between classical and vernacular, symphonies and blues songs, country music lyrics and literary masterpieces. Ma Rainey and Beethoven are sleeping together; Bob Dylan is listening to Billy Joe Shaver and reading James Joyce, suggesting that they all "got the blood of the land" in their voices.

Billy Joe wasn't widely known in the seventies except among fans who paid attention to songwriters. Waylon and Willie were huge stars though, the best-known performers in what was called "outlaw country" in the early seventies. Outlaw country was about more than getting drunk and raisin' hell, although there were plenty of songs in other genres that fit that mold. Part of being an "outlaw" meant taking on some of rock 'n' roll's rebellious attitude. Fans and music critics started to see it as a movement that was rebelling against conventional Nashville country music, which had become a little tired and too much of the same old thing. By 1976 the outlaw tag had become so widely known that RCA released a compilation album called *Wanted! The Outlaws* (AAL1-1321), which featured Waylon Jennings, Willie Nelson, Jessi Colter, and Tompall Glaser.

As music critic Chet Flippo says on the LP cover, "Call them outlaws, call them innovators, call them revolutionaries, call them what you will.... They *are* musical rebels, in one sense, in that they challenged the accepted way of doing things. Like all pioneers, they were criticized for that. But time has vindicated them." All four were part of the outlaw movement in that they had broken the rules of commercial country to various degrees, but Waylon and Willie were clearly recognized as the leaders, and in the sexist society of country music, men were featured more prominently as defining style and substance, and the projection of masculinity was a dominant feature of outlaw music.

On the *Outlaws* album Waylon and Willie sing a duet of a song they cowrote. The title is "Good Hearted Woman," but the song focuses on the woman's relationship with a "good timin' man."

> A long time forgotten the dreams that just fell by the way.
> The good life he promised ain't what she's livin' today.
> But she never complains of the bad times
> Or the bad things he's done, Lord.
> She just talks about the good times they've had
> And all the good times to come.
>
> She's a good hearted woman in love with a good timin' man.
> She loves him in spite of his ways she don't understand.
> With teardrops and laughter they pass through this world hand
>   in hand
> A good hearted woman, lovin' a good timin' man.
> (Transcribed by the author)

What a perfect marriage for the good timin' man: a woman who puts up with all his late-night drinking and carousing and "never complains" about "the bad things he's done." Given all the other songs about good timin' men, the bad things must include one-night stands, and yet she continues to "stand by her man." His behavior has been a part of their life since they first married, but "the good life he promised ain't what she's livin' today." Clearly the song is from the man's point of view, a projection of his fantasy about having it both ways, manipulating the image of his wife so that she tacitly approves his behavior, as Waylon improvises in one chorus: "She loves him in spite of his *wicked* ways she don't understand."

Willie cowrote "Good Hearted Woman" with Waylon, but he had a different take on masculinity than Waylon and Billy Joe, as both a singer and a songwriter. He sang many wild drinking and womanizing songs, but most of his songs reflect a more sensitive male perspective that connects him with folk/bluegrass singer/songwriters like Gordon Lightfoot, Utah Phillips, and Ian Tyson. His sensitive side can be heard in many of his own compositions, "Funny How Time Slips Away," "Crazy," "Yesterday's Wine," "Angel Flying Too Close to the Ground," "Sad Songs and Waltzes," and in his covers of other country songwriters, "Blue Eyes Crying in the Rain" (Fred Rose), "Remember Me" (T. Texas Tyler), "Hands on the Wheel" (Bill Collery), all from the album *Red Headed Stranger* (1975), and finally in his versions of songs from the Great American Songbook: "Stardust" (Hoagie Carmichael), "Don't Get Around Much Anymore" (Duke Ellington and Bob Russell), and "Someone to Watch Over Me" (George and Ira Gershwin), all from *Stardust* (Columbia, JC 35305, 1978).

His singing style was country for sure, but he was also influenced by jazz singers in the way he improvises and sings ahead or behind the tempo of a song, even to the point of sounding like one of the crooners from the thirties and forties such as Bing Crosby, Billy Eckstine, or Tony Bennett. In many ways, his song choices and style projected an image that was the opposite of the tough, hard-drinking, rowdy outlaw.

For instance, many of Willie's songs have empathy for a woman's perspective; one of my favorite examples of this is his concept album *Phases and Stages* (Atlantic, SD 7291, 1974), which depicts the woman's view of a relationship gone bad on one side of the LP and the man's point of view on the other. My wife, Roseanne, and I liked this record so much when it first came out that we discussed writing an article about it. We never got around to that, but her views are a significant part of what I have to say about the album now. In his liner notes on the back of the album (which has a photo of a red-headed, red-bearded Willie Nelson looking very intensely out at you), Willie summarizes the story through song titles and quotes.

> Side one of the album tells the woman's side of the story. Beginning with *Washing the Dishes*, "she's tired of caring for someone who don't care anymore," and "Walkin' is better than running away and crawling ain't no good at all." Finally saying to him: *Pretend I Never Happened*—"erase me from your mind; you will not want to remember any love as cold as mine." And then: *Sister's Coming Home*. "Mama's gonna let her sleep the whole day long." Then back to *the Corner Beer Joint*, "wearing jeans that fit a little tighter than they did before." The cycle is completed with *I'm Falling in Love Again*, and "if I lose or win, how will I know?"
>
> On side two, the man's side of the picture begins with *Bloody Mary Morning*. It's a long night in California and he's flying home to find there ain't *No Love Around*. His story continues with *I Still Can't Believe You're Gone* and *It's Not Supposed to Be That Way*. With *Heaven and Hell* he starts his comeback, regains his sense of humor, and the man's side of *Phases and Stages* is completed with *Pick Up the Tempo* "just a little and take it on home, the singer ain't singin' and the drummer's been draggin' too long." *Phases and Stages* "circles and cycles scenes that we've all seen before—listen I'll tell you some more." (Willie Nelson's signature is here.)

The woman and the man are presented as suffering equally as they go through their divorce. The different sides are narrated from different perspectives with some overlap. She tells her story in her own voice in "Walkin," "Pretend I Never Happened," and "(How Will I Know) I'm Falling in Love Again," and she is described by others in "Washing the Dishes," "Sister's Coming Home," and "Down at the Corner Beer Joint." He tells his story in first person in all his songs, "Bloody Mary Morning," "No Love Around," "I Still Can't Believe You're Gone," "It's Not Supposed to Be That Way," "Heaven and Hell," and "Pick up the Tempo." "Phases and Stages" uses an omniscient narrator ("things that we've all seen before / Let me tell you some more") as a frame before her first song and after his last one although "Washing the Dishes" is placed in the middle of the opening "Phases and Stages," and "Pick Up the Tempo" in the middle of the closing "Phases and Stages," another way of balancing the male/female sides.

This arrangement also suggests to me that even though "Pick Up the Tempo" is from a male perspective, it is also a cross-gender statement about getting over a bad phase of life and learning to cope and go on: "The singer ain't singin' and the drummer's been draggin' too long / Time'll take care of itself so just leave time alone / And pick up the tempo just a little and take it on home." The man is given more first-person songs on the album, but that makes sense since the composer is male. I think Willie deserves credit for assuming the woman's point of view in three songs and writing lyrics that are empathetic to her in all the rest. The woman's perspective is presented honestly and directly, unlike the manipulative, false representation of her feelings in "Good Hearted Woman." Instead there is an emotional balance of pain, blame, and survival in *Phases and Stages*.

The album was recorded not on a country label in a Nashville studio but on Atlantic, a label known for R&B, and at the Muscle Shoals, Alabama, studios, which are famous for R&B and rock 'n' roll, and produced by Atlantic Records' Jerry Wexler, one of the best-known producers in the business. Wexler and Muscle Shoals will be forever associated with the breakout years of R&B becoming rock 'n' roll from the early fifties on. The time from 1953, when Wexler first went to work for Atlantic, to 1974, when he produced *Phases and Stages*, was a period that included the invention of rock 'n' roll and later country music becoming more and more influenced by rock 'n' roll, an appropriate development since rock 'n' roll originally had been the illegitimate child of country and R&B.

CHAPTER 8

Come Back to Texas

From "Bogalusa Boogie"
to "Soy Chicano"

Cajun Music: "Laissez les bon temps rouler"

Growing up in Beaumont, I heard all about the Thibodeauxs and the Fontenots (two common Cajun family names mentioned in Hank Williams's "Jambalaya"). Southeast Texas is part of the Acadian cultural region because so many Cajuns migrated from Louisiana to Texas to work in the refineries and chemical plants and on oil pipelines. Cajuns were descended from French-speaking Acadians who were deported from Nova Scotia by British authorities in 1755. In 1765 they started to arrive in Louisiana, where they settled west of the Mississippi River and eventually spread throughout the southwestern part of the state. By the time I was growing up in the late forties and fifties, Cajuns were well established enough in southeast Texas that "Thibodeauxs and Fontenots" was a metonym for Cajun. Perhaps the term became a standard reference because of Hank Williams's hit country song "Jambalaya (on the Bayou)" (1952):

> Thibodeauxs, Fontenots, the place is buzzin'
> Kinfolk come to see Yvonne by the dozen
> Dressed in style, go hog wild, me oh my oh
> Son of a gun, we'll have big fun on the bayou.
> (Transcribed by the author)

Because of the large Cajun population, there are numerous Cajun restaurants in southeast Texas. When we lived in Beaumont during my high school and college years, we always ate Cajun food at Don's restaurant (the original was in Lafayette, Louisiana), and we continued to eat there every time we went back to visit family. When my parents retired and moved back to Beaumont, Don's was still our favorite place to eat out. I loved their fried shrimp, stuffed flounder, and as an adult, crawfish étouffée. My uncle JB married a Cajun girl (they were eventually divorced), so I have a half-Cajun cousin, Don, who still lives in Louisiana. My mother fixed shrimp gumbo regularly, and it was what I always asked her to cook when I came home for a visit. My mother's sister Evelyn had a wonderful recipe for shrimp creole, which I and my siblings have been using all our adult lives, Carol in Montana, Linda in California, Michigan, South Carolina, and New Jersey, and me in New York and Ohio.

We heard Cajun French around us in Beaumont and Port Arthur, later when we lived in Baton Rouge, and later still when my parents lived in Lake Charles while I was in college. I have vivid memories of us driving back and forth between Baton Rouge and Beaumont through Cajun country when I was in the eighth grade and stopping in Opelousas, Eunice, or Kinder to eat fried shrimp or buy sugarcane for us kids to suck on as we got restless during the drive. We heard Cajun music on the radio and sometimes on the jukeboxes in little joints where we stopped to eat.

Despite this exposure to the culture as a child and adolescent, I didn't buy any Cajun records until 1971, after I had become a professional folklorist and heard the music at the American Folklife Festival in Washington. A revival of Cajun music was going on because some younger Cajuns were starting to rediscover their own heritage, and folklorists, both within the community and at the Smithsonian Folklife Festival, helped to spread the music to the rest of the world as part of a vibrant folk music revival. I heard traditional musicians and singers such as the Balfa Brothers and Nathan Abshire when I worked at the Folklife Festival, and D. L. Menard at the National Folk Festival when it was at Cuyahoga National Park, south of Cleveland.

Later I became a fan of younger musicians such as Michael Doucet and Beausoleil when they played a concert in Columbus, and Steve Riley and the Mamou Playboys in Lafayette (see chapter 4). I was working at the 1976 Smithsonian Folklife Festival when a large group of Cajun musicians, dancers, and cooks performed there. Nathan Abshire was one of my favorites, a wonderful button accordion player who always seemed to be having a good time. You might say too good a time. Ralph Rinzler, who was the director of the festival, didn't want performers to drink onstage or backstage. I had noticed Nathan taking a few nips before he went on, but I thought he would stop once the official word came down. I was taking photographs of the performers as they played and went behind the stage to get a shot of the crowd. Sure enough, Nathan still had a flask sticking out of his back pocket. "Laissez les bon temps rouler."

This expression, which means "let the good times roll," is the name of a song and a traditional saying that suggests Cajuns as exotic other, an imagined concept that would include the stereotype of their propensity to drink, dance, and have a good time. Plenty of them do, but many outsiders think it is part of every Cajun who ever existed. When I started studying folklore and anthropology in graduate school and came across the term *exotic other*, I realized that Anglo-Texans' perception of Cajuns fit the image, perhaps not as exotic as that of African Americans (see chapter 2), but many of the stereotypes about Cajuns reflected a similar kind of primitivism, not primitive in any scientific empirical sense but the concept of primitive with an "ism" at the end—an image in one's mind about someone who is different ethnically or racially or from a lower socioeconomic class—basically a cultural stereotype.

One summer I worked with a Cajun who seemed to be playing with the stereotype that we Anglo-Texans had of him. We were working on a construction project at a small chemical plant near Port Acres between Beaumont and Port Arthur. This was one of the summer jobs my father arranged for me to help cover the costs of my education. Caffrey Courville (not his real name) was recently married and proud of his sexual relationship with his new wife. Every day he would tell us how many times he and his wife had done it the night before. If he forgot to mention it, someone would ask, "How many times last night, Caffrey?" He also boasted about how much he could drink and described his boisterous drinking with friends. I thought it was funny and didn't see the connection to his ethnic identity until several years later when I was studying the dynamics of ethnic-minority cultures' relationships with mainstream cultures.

He probably wasn't more sexual or a heavier drinker than any other man on the job, white or black, Cajun or Italian, but he seemed to enjoy playing with the stereotypes we had of him while also building up his own masculinity. Cajun music, like many types of ethnic dance music, reflects an image of people who like to drink, dance, and have a good time (including a sexual good time inherent in the dancing); this image then becomes a stereotype in the minds of outsiders who are attracted to the music and the dancing—"They all go native on a Saturday night" again.

If you listen to enough Cajun music and understand French or bother to look up translations of the lyrics, you realize that the content of songs covers not just having a good time but all phases of life including the prospect of death. A good example is the traditional Cajun song "Les flames d'enfer" (The flames of hell). It has been recorded by Austin Pitre (who is sometimes listed as the composer) and the Evangeline Playboys, the Balfa Brothers, Beausoleil, Zachary Richard, and even British folk-rocker Richard Thompson. It sounds happy and you can dance to it, but the lyrics definitely aren't celebrating a life of drinking and having fun.

> Oh, dear mother pray for me, save my soul from the flames of hell
> Pray for me, save my soul, I am condemned to the flames of hell.
> I will cry, I will cry, I will cry, in the flames of hell.
> (Transcribed by the author)

The Catholicism of Cajuns overlaps with the Protestantism of southern fans of country music and gospel: these lyrics sound pretty close to the warnings I heard from preachers in the Church of Christ as I was growing up, and it was part of the message preached the night I confessed my sins and was baptized. Drinking, dancing, and "doing the dirty deed" were considered sinful activities that could condemn you to *les flames d'enfer*. Vernacular song traditions often contain both invitations to sin and the terrible consequences if you do, once again reflecting the error of stereotyping any ethnic/racial/ class group as being inherently hypersexual, alcoholic party people.

"Bogalusa Boogie": Zydeco on the Bayou

Most African American Creoles in Louisiana speak French as well as English. In southwestern Louisiana, they played their own African American Creole music, which overlapped in style and content with European American Cajun music and black blues and R&B. Black Creoles were descended from slaves who before and after emancipation mixed with French, Spanish, Anglo, West African, and Native American people. They were largely segregated from their white Cajun brethren, but they shared culturally with them, especially in music and cuisine. Their music in the nineteenth century was influenced by African American field hollers, work songs, spirituals, and dance music as well as Acadian French music. Blues became an influence in the late nineteenth and early twentieth centuries, but the form of black

Creole music that we hear today as zydeco didn't come to fruition until the late forties and early fifties under the strong influence of rhythm and blues.

Zydeco in turn began to influence modern Cajun music. Both now usually feature the accordion and amplified instruments such as the electric bass and guitars, and are now sung in Cajun French and English. White Cajun musicians have also been influenced directly by R&B and rock 'n' roll. In fact, the music of Cajun musicians like Zachary Richard clearly reflect rock 'n' roll in such songs as "Filé Gumbo," and the music of zydeco musicians like Keith Frank echo strains of Jamaican reggae as in "Co Fa."

These influences are a great example of the cultural process of creolization. Just as two different languages can blend together to form a new language, two different genres of music can also blend together and form something new. We now have Cajun bands such as the Pine Leaf Boys that feature black and white musicians, and black zydeco and white Cajun musicians often play together at concerts and festivals. This is another of those musical examples that undermine the whole idea of "purity" in vernacular music. Zydeco and Cajun were never pure; they both always contained elements of other musical cultures. Zydeco and Cajun are played in widely different cultural contexts across the United States and the world, but both are also still played within their own communities.

The earliest roots of zydeco spring from African American musicians playing their own version of Acadian music in the late nineteenth and early twentieth centuries. Black musicians such as Amédé Ardoin and Adam Fontenot were playing blues-influenced, "highly syncopated" accordions during that period. They influenced younger musicians such as Freeman Fontenot (accordion), Canray Fontenot (fiddle), and Alphonse "Bois-sec" Ardoin (accordion) who carried on the tradition well into the twentieth century, establishing a tradition that eventually produced the "modern" zydeco of Clifton Chenier and his contemporaries in the late 1940s, the sound and style called zydeco today.

In 1961, when I was in college in Beaumont, I heard something on the radio that sounded like a mixture of African American blues and Cajun music, but I had no name for it at the time. I bought the 45 rpm record of "Sugar Bee" with Cleveland Crochet listed as the performer. The song reached number eighty on the national charts, but it must have been in the top ten in southwestern Louisiana and southeast Texas given the number of times I heard it played on the radio that year. I thought the band was black because of the bluesy accordion and the R&B rhythm section. I assumed the singer was black and continued to think so for the next forty years.

While doing research in 2001, I finally discovered that the 1961 recording of "Sugar Bee" was played by a white Cajun band, although the band's name was not on the label, and it was sung by a white guy named Jesse "Jay" Stutes, who also played pedal steel guitar. Cleveland Crochet turned out to be the name of the fiddle player and bandleader. The band ordinarily played country-influenced Cajun music as its name, Hillbilly Ramblers, suggests, but on this particular recording the Ramblers were taking a stab at a rock 'n' roll hit with an African American–influenced vocal and instrumental style.

Was this some kind of ironic musical "color blindness" on my part? Does race have to alter our perceptions of music? I still think it's important to know the role of racial and cultural differences in the history of vernacular music, but one of the significant historical facts is how these distinctions were often transcended in the music itself. To me "Sugar Bee" is a classic instance of creolization in American vernacular music. I had been listening to R&B, blues, country, and rock music since junior high in the mid-fifties and thought I could identify genres on first listen, and, significantly, I thought I could easily tell the difference between a white singer and a black singer because my preference for the original black versions of R&B songs over the white rock 'n' roll covers was so strong. I must have had some imagined sense of the purity of black music that could easily be identified, and I wasn't aware of a process like creolization although the evidence was all around me. My mistaken attribution of blackness where there was whiteness illustrates how much the music was already thoroughly mixed and musical labels often misleading.

I heard the first "real" zydeco even earlier, and it was not by Cleveland Crochet but by one of the inventors of zydeco, Clifton Chenier (whose brother was named Cleveland). I bought a 45 rpm record "Bayou Drive" / "My Soul." It was on the Checker label, and I still have it in my collection. "Bayou Drive" is an instrumental recorded in Chicago in 1959, and I first heard it on local radio in Beaumont and bought the record in 1960. I didn't know what to call it then, but I loved the bluesy accordion, played by Clifton Chenier of course, the R&B tenor sax by Lionel Prevost, and the irresistible dance rhythms. I didn't know at the time how important Clifton Chenier was, that his life during the late forties and early fifties was, in many ways, the history of the invention of zydeco.

He was born in 1925 in Opelousas, the Louisiana town we used to drive through going from Baton Rouge to Beaumont in 1954. The young Clifton learned the rudiments of accordion from his father and developed them by listening to records before he started playing in public. He moved all over southwestern Louisiana, living in New Iberia for a while and playing in clubs around Lake Charles with his brother Cleveland on rub board (also called washboard because its original use was in washing clothes by hand—my mother had one when I was little). All these towns are within the core region of Cajun and zydeco musical culture. Chenier was first recorded in Lake Charles in 1954 and had numerous regional hits in the fifties. He became more widely known in the sixties with appearances at clubs and various festivals around the country as he started to make record albums.

My favorite LP by him is *Bogalusa Boogie* (Arhoolie 1076, 1976), which I bought when it first came out on Arhoolie, the label run by Chris Strachwitz, who made some of the best records of ethnic and regional music in the United States including Cajun, zydeco, conjunto, African American blues, and old-time country music (listen to the boxed set *Arhoolie Records 40th Anniversary Collection: 1960–2000*, CD 491, 2000, for some great examples of all these types of music). The music on *Bogalusa Boogie* is infectious, from Clifton's emotional down-home blues singing on "Quelque chose sur mon idee" (Something on my mind) and John Hart's rambunctious tenor sax solo on "Bogalusa Boogie" to the complex layers of rhythm provided by brother Cleveland Chenier's rub board playing and Clifton's joyous accordion on the traditional "Allons a Grand Coteau" (Let's go to Big Coteau).

I had been listening to his records for years, but I didn't hear Clifton Chenier in person until the mid-eighties a few years before his death in 1987. He was already ill with diabetes and sat on a chair in the middle of the stage at Crazy Mama's, a campus-area club in Columbus known for an eclectic mix of musical acts. He still played and sang with great skill and energy, and people were dancing as if they were in New Iberia or Port Arthur.

When I heard him live in the eighties, I knew about his Louisiana background, but I wasn't aware until recently that he lived and played in clubs in Port Arthur in the late forties, a period when my family was still living in Beaumont, fourteen miles from Port Arthur. Like other young men in southwestern Louisiana, he had moved to southeast Texas to work in the refineries and chemical plants. He drove trucks in the Port Arthur Gulf and Texaco refineries, which my family would drive through on our way to the beach. Thinking back on it, I like to imagine that Daddy passed Clifton

Chenier's truck as we sped down the highway through the refineries on to the Gulf of Mexico. From there, it was only about fifteen miles to McFadden Beach, which had dirty dark sand because it was within the area where the Mississippi and other rivers drained silt into the Gulf, and the current took it west and south along the beaches.

The first beach area we reached was called "Nigger Beach" by white people in the region because a stretch of it was used only by black people during those segregated times. The white beach was a little farther down the coastal highway where an invisible line separated black and white—no physical markers, but everybody knew where it was. There was an even "nicer" beach down the coast along the Bolivar Peninsula where the sand was whiter and white people had beach houses, but McFadden was a shorter drive from Beaumont and Port Arthur, and I went there often as a child in the late forties, as a teenager in the fifties, and as a college student in the early sixties, when the beach was still segregated even after desegregation had begun.

Segregation was a fact of life back then, but music was a lifeline that crossed the racial divide. I didn't hear Clifton Chenier's music until the early sixties, but my fascination with it was influenced by all those early experiences of living in the racially segregated South as I became conscious of the shared love of music across racial lines. The black radio station KJET was playing white singers like Neil Sedaka in the fifties and early sixties (I remember Sedaka's name because Boyd Brown, my favorite KJET disc jockey, pronounced it with an intrusive r, "Sedaker"). The white station KTRM was playing Ray Charles and Little Richard during that same period. Black and white teenagers were listening to some of the same music even though we couldn't dance together to it.

Later in life, when I was living in Columbus, integrated dancing was the norm—at private parties, outdoor concerts, festivals, and at many of the music bars I frequented. Several Cajun and zydeco concerts stand out. There was a Buckwheat Zydeco performance at Stache's on High Street north of the Ohio State campus. He was terrific singing and playing accordion, and his hot band had people dancing on the sides of the stage and behind the tables near the entrance. There was no dance floor as such, but plenty of dancing always happened at Stache's. It was the kind of place you could meet the performers at the bar as I had done with blues singer/guitarist Johnny Copeland from Houston and as I did that night with Stanley Dural, better known as Buckwheat Zydeco.

Born in Lafayette, where he played in local bands, he later went on the road playing keyboards with Fats Domino, Little Richard, Barbara Lynn (who was from my hometown, Beaumont), and Clarence "Gatemouth" Brown (who grew up in Orange, Texas, near Beaumont). After all that experience, he started playing zydeco and formed the Ils Sont Partis Band, made records, and started to tour—all the way to Columbus, Ohio, and Stache's. He was laid back and willing to talk to a slightly inebriated fan. As was my custom in such circumstances, I talked about back home in southeast Texas and southwestern Louisiana. I'm truly thankful for the opportunities I've had to kibitz with the kings of zydeco, Cajun R&B, blues, country, rock, and Tex-Mex conjunto music.

"Across the Borderline": Corridos and Conjunto Music

I first remember hearing Mexican music on the radio in 1950, when I was in the fourth grade. We had just moved to Bay City, Texas, which was farther down the coast from Beaumont, about halfway to the Mexican border, which explains why there were more Mexican American people there. I didn't speak Spanish, and when I heard singing in Spanish on the radio, it sounded faraway and exotic to me. Seeing lots of Mexican Americans on the streets of downtown Bay City was a new experience too. My hometown had only a small population of Mexicans in the late forties and early fifties; Beaumont was just about as far from the Mexican border as you could get and still be in Texas, 470 miles to be exact. I know because I drove it so many times when I was doing field research with the shrimpers along the Gulf Coast for my dissertation, starting at Sabine Pass, where you can look across the water and see Louisiana, and going all the way to Brownsville and Port Isabel, where the Rio Grande flows into the Gulf of Mexico.

Mexican music continued to sound faraway and strange, but gradually I began to learn more about Mexican people. There were Mexican kids in my classes at the Bay City elementary school. I especially remember one girl in my fourth grade class because I had a crush on her. I even gave Minnie a Valentine card. I still have the picture of our class, and there she is, dark hair, brown skin, and pretty, sitting in the middle of the middle row, and there I am standing in the row behind her, both of us with slight smiles on our faces. There are also three Mexican boys, but the other twenty-five children all appear to be Anglo-American. Black people also lived in Bay City, but they were segregated in their own school and neighborhood.

Mexicans were integrated in school, but there were deep prejudices against them. I heard them called "spics" by adults, and they were stereotyped as lazy even though most were hardworking people. I remember one incident when a Mexican woman was nursing her baby on a bench on the courthouse square, and someone who worked with my father thought this was the scandalous behavior of uneducated, lower-class people. For me, knowing Minnie must have been a significant counter to those kinds of prejudices; I saw with my own eyes how sweet and smart she was, and even though I never met her parents, I imagined them being like mine only darker.

While living in Bay City, I heard Mexican music on the radio when I or someone else was switching stations. I continued to hear the music on radio when we moved to Lake Jackson and nearby Houston (when I was in the fifth and sixth grades respectively) and later when we moved to Lakewood in Southern California for my seventh-grade year. But I still had little direct contact with Mexican American people, and none at all after we moved to Newark, Delaware, and later to Oakville, Ontario, in the mid- to late fifties. In college back in Texas in the sixties, I began eating at Mexican restaurants and hearing Mexican music there, and finally in graduate school living in Austin in the mid-sixties I met and got to know a few Mexican Americans and had opportunities to listen to their music more closely.

My folklore advisor and director of my dissertation at the University of Texas was Américo Paredes, a professor in English and anthropology and a poet, novelist, musician, and singer of Mexican songs. He had a profound influence on my professional life by establishing my sense of what a scholar/professor was supposed to be. He was a believer in and fighter for social justice, not only for Mexican Americans who had suffered discrimination but for any disenfranchised group. At the time, he seemed very formal and reserved, but he was kind to and supportive of me as he was with anyone who came to him for help. For instance, the fine San Antonio singer Tish Hinojosa was trying to track down the words to a song her mother sang, and when Professor Paredes learned of her search, he called and arranged to sing the song for her and taught her some other traditional songs he knew.

She described him in a way that captures his kindness as well as his sense of outrage about social injustice: "He's not a chip-on-his-shoulder kind of guy. He may carry it inside, and I'm sure that's what has fueled his passion all these years, but he's never shown it outside . . . . He's done it in a very dignified way, and he's probably stirred more waters that way, which is something we can all learn from." She recorded an album, *Frontéjas* (Rounder Records, CD 3132, 1995), which contains some of the songs he taught her as well as a song she wrote in his honor, "Con su pluma en su mano" (With his pen in his hand), based on the title of Paredes's book *"With His Pistol in His Hand."*

When Américo Paredes played his guitar and sang, he was still dignified but with a depth of emotion that almost made me cry the first time I heard him sing. Even though I had taken Spanish in high school and college, I usually didn't understand all the words of a Spanish song; the emotion came through in his voice and guitar playing. In 1968 he played at a Texas Folklore Society meeting in Alpine, Texas, where I presented one of my first scholarly papers. Papers were read during the day (including outdoors in Big Bend National Park), and at night we ate barbecue, drank, danced, and listened to society members sing and play guitars. I don't remember the songs that Professor Paredes sang, but they were beautifully played and very intense as they were every time I heard him sing.

I always called him Dr. Paredes until years later when I was a professor at Ohio State and saw him at an American Folklore Society meeting in San Antonio and took a chance on calling him Américo. He was fine with that, and we had a totally relaxed conversation, probably the first personal, nonacademic talk I ever had with him.

In *"With His Pistol in His Hand,"* he says that "borders and ballads seem to go together, and their heroes are all cast in the same mold." From him I learned about the Mexican border ballad, the *corrido*; and as I studied and taught the British and American ballad, I began to recognize the connection he spoke of. The ballad is in its most basic sense a song that tells a story, like the American ballads I discussed in chapter 7, "The Story of Charlie Lawson" and "Long Black Veil." Américo Paredes's book is an in-depth analysis of "El Corrido de Gregorio Cortez" within its historical and cultural context. The ballad is about an outlaw hero feared by American sheriffs who are trying to capture him for a big reward. Cortez is accused of killing the Major Sheriff, and "they set bloodhounds on him / but overtaking Cortez / was like reaching a star," and "they decided not to follow / because they were afraid of him."

In the country of El Carmen look what has happened;
The Major Sheriff died leaving Roman badly wounded.
They went around asking questions about half an hour afterward,
They didn't find out who killed him and the wrongdoer is Cortez.

They set the bloodhounds on him to overtake his trail,
Then said Gregorio Cortez with his pistol in his hand,
"Ah, how many cowardly rangers against one lone Mexican!"
But overtaking Cortez was like reaching a star.
(Paredes, "*With His Pistol in His Hand*," 168–69)

The story is similar to British and American ballads with outlaw heroes like "Robin Hood" and "Jesse James" but with decidedly Mexican border attitudes and ideals, which Paredes explains by placing the *corrido* in the social context of border conflicts between Mexico and the United States. "The Corrido of Gregorio Cortez" is based on an incident that took place in 1901, a time when border conflict was already sixty-five years old. The hero is based on an actual person, a "peaceful man who defends his right[s]." Still, like most hero ballads, the song romanticizes the image of Cortez in terms of his invincible nature: "overtaking Cortez was like reaching a star," and the Anglo sheriffs are all afraid of his prowess with a gun. He belittles them as cowards, three hundred Americans "against one lone Mexican!" He expresses the pride of Mexican people who are often denigrated by Anglo-Americans.

Professor Paredes introduced me to both the sound of Mexican folk music and the scholarly study of it, and I soon began to discover other Texas Mexican traditional singers and musicians. I first heard the great singer Lydia Mendoza in a documentary film on border music, *Chulas Fronteras* (soundtrack on Arhoolie Records, 30005, 1976), in which she sings two songs, "Mal hombre" and "Pero hay que triste." Her singing and guitar playing struck me in many of the same ways that Américo's did, soulful and heartbreaking. "Mal hombre" is a woman's intense complaint about a man's mistreatment of her, a topic that clearly and widely crosses cultural and ethnic boundaries.

I was still a young girl when, by chance, you found me,
And with your worldly charm you took away my innocence.
It was then that you did to me what all of your kind do to women

So don't be surprised now if I tell you to your face what you
    really are.
Cold-hearted man, your soul is so vile, it has no name.
You are despicable; you are evil, you are a cold-hearted man.
(Liner notes of *Chulas Fronteras*, Arhoolie Records 30005, 1976,
    Spanish language version, pp. 8–9)

Part of the intensity of the song comes from the woman directly addressing the man who had taken advantage of her youth and innocence. Her
singing presents a dramatic scene that directly expresses her courage in
confronting him. It is in many ways a feminist protest song, so direct and
personal that it doesn't become polemical. In fact, most of the music in
Chulas Fronteras reveals the emotional depth of Mexican American culture
in direct personal ways.

    The film impressed me so much that I bought the LP of the soundtrack,
which introduced me to other fine Mexican musicians. This was the first
time I heard the accordion playing of Flaco Jiménez, who is recognized as
one of the key second-generation figures in the history and development
of conjunto music. His father, Santiago Jiménez, was one of the founders
of the accordion style that was a defining feature of conjunto.

    Conjunto can be thought of as the Mexican and Mexican American cousin
of Anglo-American country music since the audience for both kinds of
music is made up of people from rural areas who have migrated to cities to
work in factories, refineries, and other industries. Both conjunto and country
are played in working-class bars where people drink, dance, and sometimes
get rowdy. Both traditions have songs that celebrate that way of life and are
about some of the same issues: love and breaking up, social life and politics,
heroes and villains, migration and missing home, regional identity and pride.
Poor rural southerners moved north to find jobs; Mexican Americans in
northeastern Mexico first moved across the Rio Grande to South Texas and
then spread north and east, wherever they could find jobs as migrant farm
or factory workers.

    Both groups missed their roots and wrote songs yearning for home and
loved ones. "Canción Mixteca" by Ramiro Cavazos and Conjunto Tamau-
lipas is a heartbreaking example.

    How far I am from the land of my birth, intense nostalgia invades
        my soul.

As I see myself so sad and alone like a leaf in the wind,
I just want to cry. I just want to die from this painful loneliness.
Oh, land of the sun, I long to see you!
Now that I'm so far away, I live without light, without love.
(Liner notes of *Chulas Fronteras*, p. 7)

"Cancion Mixteca" is similar to country and bluegrass songs like "Old Home Place," "Blue Ridge Mountain Blues," and "Home Sweet Home Revisited," all linked together by a sense of dislocation and loneliness.

Another link between Mexicano music and country is the mistreatment that migrants experienced in their new location. "Un mojado sin licensia" ("Wetback without a license") was written by Santiago Jiménez and played by his son Flaco.

All the way from Laredo to San Antonio I've come to marry
    Chencha,
But I haven't been able to do it because I'm a wetback
And I keep being asked for my license.
I thought I'd buy a car to take my love for a ride
And that night I wound up in the can cause I didn't have any
    lights or a license.
(Liner notes of *Chulas Fronteras*, p. 14)

He gets out of jail only to find Chencha with the gringo who sells licenses. He decides to go back to Laredo: "I've suffered enough shame."

In some ways this is a comic song about a sad sack whose fiancée cheats on him, but the Anglo license agent's ability to take advantage of him is a condemnation of the U.S. immigration system as totally unfair to the migrant worker. Also the use of the Anglo derogatory term *wetback* by the illegal immigrant undermines the stereotype by giving him a cause and a reason to protest.

Mexican Americans who fight against this institutional prejudice in the United States can become the heroes of migrant workers; in some cases songs are even written about them, as happened with the "Corrido de Cesar Chavez" (written by Rumel Fuentes, performed by Los Pinguinos del Norte).

What's your secret, Cesar Chavez? What have you given
    your people
That those who are stooped over have now raised their heads?

The weariness in their breasts is reflected in sad eyes.
The brutal work of the field enslaves even the mind.
(Liner notes of *Chulas Fronteras*, p. 10)

The rest of the song describes the brutal conditions of the poor women and children who work in the hot sun for the rancher's profit: "For the rich to become richer, the poor must become poorer." Chavez demands "only a decent wage . . . for the benefit of the people / without anger or violence."

Here there are echoes of the civil rights movement and Martin Luther King's organizing among black laborers—both Chavez and King were heroes to those they fought for. There are also shades of Woody Guthrie and Pete Seeger, who wrote similar protest songs in support of American workers. When these songs are strung together, they become a history of various disenfranchised folk groups.

Chicano became a widely used term in the sixties among Mexican Americans born in the United States to identify them as people who were proud of their race and ethnicity. As one song, "Chicano," proudly proclaims, "I am a Chicano."

Chicano, soy Chicano.
Cause I'm brown and I'm proud, and I'll make it in my own way.
Some people call me third world, but I know that it's the
real world
'Cause to me all I am is Mexicano.
. . . .
Some people call me violent cause I'm no longer the silent
pobrecito Mexicano.
(Liner notes of *Chulas Fronteras*, pp. 12–13)

This song was recorded by a conjunto band from Eagle Pass, Texas, Rumel Fuentes and Los Pinguinos del Norte, but in one of those cross-cultural ironies, it was written by an Anglo from San Antonio, Doug Sahm. How did a song written by an outsider from the perspective of a native come to be accepted and performed by a Mexican band?

Doug Sahm was born in San Antonio, a city steeped in Mexican tradition with a large population of Mexican Americans. Most of his songs were in English, but he wrote and sang several in Spanish, and there were Mexican Americans in most of his bands. Doug Sahm's rock band the Sir Douglas Quintet had another Anglo member, Augie Meyers, who was also born in

San Antonio, sang in Spanish, and played conjunto music. Doug even had a Spanish name as one of his many performing personas; "[Doug] Saldaña is the name the Mexicans gave me," he explains. "They said that I had so much Mexican in me that I needed a Mexican name."

Doug Sahm wrote "Chicano" in first person to directly express pride in being a Mexican American in a land that often looked down on Mexicans. Other songs from the perspective of migrant Chicanos put more emphasis on the degrading effects of racial/ethnic prejudice in the United States. For example, Freddy Fender, who is Mexican American despite his performing name, sings just such a song, "Across the Borderline," which was on Ry Cooder's soundtrack for the 1982 movie *The Border* (Backstreet Records, BSR 6105, 1982). Cooder, John Hiatt, and Jim Dickinson wrote the song, which when sung by Freddy Fender sounds like the perfect match of voice and lyrics.

> There's a place where I've been told
> Every street is paved with gold
> And it's just across the borderline
> And when it's time to take your turn
> Here's one lesson that you must learn
> You could lose more than you'll ever hope to find.
>
> When you reach the broken promised land
> And every dream slips through your hands
> Then you'll know that it's too late to change your mind
> 'Cause you've paid the price to come so far
> Just to wind up where you are
> And you're still just across the borderline.
> (Transcribed by the author)

Freddy Fender's country, R&B, and "swamp pop" style of singing fit effortlessly with the English and Spanish lyrics and Mexican migrant workers' point of view. Freddy's amazing voice emotionally expresses their loss of pride while still maintaining hope.

So we have an Anglo-American Doug Sahm writing a song about Mexican ethnic pride that was played by a Mexican American conjunto band, and Mexican American Freddy Fender singing a song about a Mexican migrant worker's loss of pride that was written by three Anglos. This is a complex mix of American vernacular music by songwriters, musicians, and singers who are from different cultures and speak different languages, coming together to create strikingly original works of art.

Texas Rock for Country Rollers: From the Sir Douglas Quintet to the Texas Tornados

Flaco Jiménez, Freddy Fender, Doug Sahm, and Augie Meyers were key figures in the blending of Mexican and Anglo music with rock 'n' roll and country to create a new kind of border music. After successful careers of their own, they all came together to form the Texas Tornados, which then carried an updated "Tex-Mex" sound to an even wider audience. Their story is complex, and we need to cover their individual backgrounds to make sense of the creolization process of musical mixing and mingling.

Both Freddy Fender and Flaco Jiménez started out playing in Mexican American bands who sang in Spanish, and both eventually crossed over into the national scene of country, rock, and folk groups who sang in English and Spanish. Flaco Jiménez's career in regional conjunto music led to his reputation as a brilliant accordion player, and as a result several nationally known Anglo singers asked him to play on their albums. Bluegrass/eclectic folk singer/songwriter/musician Peter Rowan featured Flaco on his album *Peter Rowan* (Flying Fish, 071, 1978). The songs Rowan composed for the album were influenced by Mexican music and reflected his youthful counterculture beliefs and values. Flaco's conjunto accordion added regional/cultural authenticity to two of the songs that were set on the border. The lyrics of both "Panama Red" and "The Free Mexican Airforce" justified and romanticized the smuggling of marijuana into the United States, as this excerpt from the latter song illustrates.

> In the city of angels a cowboy is cooling his heels
> Remembering that God gave us herbs and the fruits of the fields
> But a criminal law that makes outlaws of those seeking light
> Made the free Mexican air force, Mescalito riding his white horse
> Yeah the free Mexican air force is flying tonight.
> (Transcribed by the author)

The metaphor for smuggling marijuana works with the sound of Flaco's conjunto accordion to reinforce the regional cross-cultural belief in the benefits of marijuana.

On Rowan's next album, *Medicine Trail* (Flying Fish, 205, 1980), "Riding High in Texas" makes the same point.

> I'm riding high in Texas in my mind
> Sometimes I feel I've got to leave this crazy world behind
> Seems they're all just trying to fake us, so let the lone star take us
> And we'll go riding high in Texas in my mind.
> (Transcribed by the author)

Flaco's accordion is featured on two other songs on *Medicine Trail*. These are not set on the border, but the accordion emphasizes the sadness of the story in "River of Stone." Flaco's playing adds tenderness to a song being sung to "my little sleepy head" on Jimmie Rodgers's "Prairie Lullaby." Flaco also played on two Ry Cooder albums, where his accordion helps define the physical and emotional response inherent in the title of the first album, *Chicken Skin Music* (Reprise Records, MS 2254, 1976). On the next Ry Cooder album, *Show Time* (Warner Bros. Records, BS 3059, 1977), Flaco gives a border aura to "Viva Sequin / Do-Re-Mi" and "Volver, Volver."

Flaco's friend Freddy Fender (a natural alliteration) crossed over into American pop music and rock 'n' roll even earlier than Flaco. He was born Baldemar Huerta in San Benito, Texas, in 1936, and he started performing Mexicano music in the Rio Grande Valley in the 1950s. He was already mixing pop, country, and rockabilly elements while singing in Spanish, but he didn't make the transition into the mainstream until he changed his professional name to Freddy Fender (after the famous electric guitar). His success depended on more than a name change though; he was a hugely talented singer who established his reputation in country music with numerous hit records, including "Before the Next Teardrop Falls," "Wasted Days and Wasted Nights," "Secret Love," and "You'll Lose a Good Thing." Although these songs were all hits on the country music charts, the sound was steeped in what was called "swamp pop" music, a sound associated with the region I came from in southeast Texas and southwestern Louisiana.

I first heard swamp pop when I was in high school in Beaumont and later when I returned to southeast Texas to start college in the late 1950s. I was immediately attracted to songs like Jivin' Gene and the Jokers' "Breaking Up Is Hard to Do"; Rod Bernard's "This Should Go on Forever"; Cookie and the Cupcakes' "Mathilda"; Barbara Lynn's "You'll Lose a Good Thing"; and Phil Phillips's "Sea of Love." And these are just the ones I can remember off the top of my head. Singer Rod Bernard's son, Shane K. Bernard, wrote a very good book on swamp pop, *Swamp Pop: Cajun and Creole Rhythm and Blues*, whose subtitle defines the genre. As the younger Bernard points out, "swamp pop grew out of intense, sustained interaction between Cajuns and black Creoles" in southeast Texas and southwestern Louisiana. So how did Freddy Fender, from near the Mexican border at the other end of the Texas Gulf Coast, come to be influenced by swamp pop? Part of it was through recording his first hits in Houston for producer Huey "The Crazy Cajun" Meaux's record label. He was also directly influenced by Cajun singers Rod Bernard and Joe Barry, who were also recorded by Huey Meaux.

To pick up the other musical threads of Freddy and Flaco's development, we can swing back to southwest Texas and the stories of the other two Texas Tornados, Doug Sahm and Augie Meyers. They were born in San Antonio, where they were childhood friends. Doug was a child prodigy who once played with Hank Williams at the age of ten. Both Doug and Augie were deeply influenced by the Mexican music that surrounded them in San Antonio. Doug had several Mexican American musicians in his bands over the years; one early example: John Perez played drums and Rocky Morales saxophone in Sahm's 1960s and '70s band the Sir Douglas Quintet, which also included Augie Meyers on Farfisa organ.

The name Sir Douglas Quintet was an invention of—you guessed it— Huey Meaux, who produced the band's first records in the late sixties. The idea was to make the teenage public think they were a British band like the Beatles or the Rolling Stones, but their sound was not an imitation but rather an original mix of the music they grew up with in Texas. Their unique sound eventually produced two international hits, the first in 1965, "She's about a Mover," and the second in late 1968, "Mendocino." They continued to record and expand their repertoire, which included a cover of Freddy Fender's "Wasted Days."

I don't think most rock critics realized the complex musical roots of their music, but music writer Chet Flippo was one of the first to explain not only the tradition behind it but also to recognize the broad international influence it had on the rock music that followed. This quote is from his album liner notes to *The Best of the Sir Douglas Quintet* (Takoma, TAK 7086, 1980).

When I was listening to [Doug Sahm's cover of the Freddy Fender song] "Wasted Days" it hit me pretty quick that he [Doug] was New Wave or Nuevo Wavo back in the Sixties. When you listen to Sir Doug doing

"Mendocino" or "Texas Me" you can tell pretty quickly that Elvis Costello patterned both his vocals and his band after SDQ and so did many new wave bands . . . that have fashioned their sound around the Quintet's rolling chicano rhythms and its pumping Farfisa organ and its blues guitar breaks. It sounds deceptively simple but only the originals can really pull it off. Doug unconsciously [I disagree; he was conscious of the multiple sources of his sound] fused Texas, C&W, Western swing, Texas blues, Tex-Mex, South Texas German polkas, and everything else he heard, like Ornette Coleman's jazz, and he finally became, in his own words, too "far out" to be Top-40.

It is worth adding that the band was also influenced by psychedelic rock after moving to the West Coast in the mid-sixties. There you have it: the creative creolization of an incredible variety of different kinds of music by a band that then had a direct influence on the invention of a new style of rock music in the mid-seventies, and that "New Wave" sound still influences rock 'n' roll today.

You don't have to take the word of a critic for Doug Sahm's influence; singer/songwriter Elvis Costello himself has recommended Sir Douglas Quintet's "Too Many Dociled Minds" (*The Complete Mercury Masters*, Hip-O Select, B4002496-02, 2005) in a list of "five records you may enjoy," adding,

> For a brief time I was actually a "Mercury Recording Artist," and was proud to be in the company of Sir Doug, one of the Great Knights of Texas. In fact, I met Doug Sahm at a Flaco Jimenez gig in London during the last century. He was still full of wit and wonder. I wish I'd had a chance to see him play around the time he recorded fantastic records like this one and "Can You Dig My Vibrations."

When Costello refers to Sahm as a "Great Knight," it is, I think, a reference to Doug's first band, the Knights, an indication of Elvis Costello's knowledge of obscurities in rock history.

In the seventies and eighties Doug did a series of recordings under his own name, many with Augie but some not. One of the great albums he did in this period was *Doug Sahm and Band* (Atlantic, SD 7254, 1973), which has a who's who of musicians backing him up: Augie Meyers and Flaco Jiménez of course, Bob Dylan, Dr. John, David Bromberg, David Fathead Newman, Wayne Jackson, to name a few. The songs include his usual mixture of different genres—covers of Charlie Pride's country hit "Is Anybody Going to San Antone"; Bobby "Blue" Bland's R&B hit "Your Friends"; Bob Dylan's "Wallflower," with Bob helping out on vocal; T-Bone Walker's blues classic "Papa Ain't Salty"; Willie Nelson's "Me and Paul," plus three originals written by Doug. He also used the name Sir Doug and the Texas Tornados on albums such as *Texas Rock for Country Rollers* (ABC Dot, DOSD-2057, 1976) and just his name on several blues and R&B records including *Hell of a Spell* (Takoma, TAK 7075, 1980), whose title song is actually a reggae number, and *Juke Box Music* (Antone's Records, ANT 0008, 1988).

In 1981 Doug and Augie came back together as the Sir Douglas Quintet with some other key Texas musicians on *Border Wave* (Takoma, TAK 7088), which is one of my favorite rock 'n' roll albums of all time. I liked their early hits "She's about a Mover" and "Mendocino" when they first came out as singles, but I became a devoted Sir Douglas Quintet fan with *Border Wave*. The band is real tight; it sounds as if all the musicians have been playing together for years. Doug, Augie, Alvin Crow, Johnny Perez, Speedy Sparks, and Doug's son Shawn are definitely simpatico, sharing a love of the music and a dedication to getting it right. They play and sing with joyful abandon even when they are describing a love affair gone wrong or criticizing their own wild behavior. And on this album, their Tex-Mex sound reaches its peak—perfect energetic blending of country music, blues, R&B, conjunto, and rock 'n' roll.

Six of the ten songs on the album were written by Doug (one with Johnny Perez); the rest by Alvin Crow, Ray Davies, Butch Hancock (see the Flatlanders below), and Rocky Erickson (of the legendary Texas rock band the 13th Floor Elevators). Despite the different songwriters, there is a unified vision—all of them describe a particular way of life from a young male perspective, and the album suggests that the ideal location for this way of life is down on the border. I don't think it was intentionally a "concept album," but Doug's personality as leader, and the similar Texas assumptions of all the other songwriters, except for British-born Ray Davies, contributed to the unified view.

Central to this perspective is the idea of masculine freedom, to continue to live the life they grew up with and heard about within that masculine culture, which was projected in country, blues, R&B, and rock 'n' roll songs—freedom to have sex with different women, to get drunk and raise hell, and to ignore responsibilities that polite society expected of them. In many ways, these are the same attitudes and behaviors associated with rockabilly singers and songwriters from the 1950s (see chapter 3) except for the decidedly southwestern and especially Texas-border setting. The regional emphasis can be seen in the title of the album and in the two songs that refer directly to the border.

"Down on the Border" is the third cut on the first side of the album and works to focus the action on the border even though it starts in New York City.

> With a trembling hand and a shaky voice, she said I had to leave
> New York.
> With ya crawlin' out of corners, stop a hidin' in the dark.
> I wanna go down South where all the people laugh and play.
> I got my hands on some bread, we can leave out right away.
> Hey, down on the border, down on the border.
> (Transcribed by the author)

The first two times Doug sings "down on the border," it's in a normal voice; the second two, he almost screams it, and after each line Augie responds with doodle-de-do on the organ. The lyrics and his screaming emphasize the confusion of being in New York, but Augie's organ phrase anticipates the pleasures of arriving down South. They have to get out of the dark corners of New York City and return to where *all* the people laugh and play. His girlfriend may be a Yankee, but she accepts his need to escape the city and return to his Texas stomping grounds.

"Border Wave," the last song on side 2 also functions to unify the album by returning to the Texas-Mexico-border setting.

> Take a little time just to satisfy my mind and go back to
> the border
> Sit out on the pier and drink some Lone Star beer and try to
> get my mind in order.
> Too much rock 'n' roll lay heavy on my soul, gonna kick back
> right away
> Well the girls are screamin', record cats are schemin'
> Cause they're gonna call it border wave.
> . . . .
> Border wave, border wave
> That's what they call the song now
> Sittin' with Lupe in the local cantina
> Floatin' the days away.
> (Transcribed by the author)

The border becomes an almost mystical place to restore your sense of well-being, a place to "get your mind in order" by simply doing what comes naturally: "sit out on the pier and drink some Lone Star beer" or sit "with Lupe in the local cantina." "Floatin' the days away" gives a sense of a weight being lifted off you just because you're in this curative place and enjoying the resulting peaceful state of mind. Perhaps surprisingly, rock 'n' roll itself is something to get away from. Doug recognizes the negative side of the music business—when he's going all over the country playing one-night stands, the crowds and loud music and pressure become "too much for [his] soul." In a clever twist, he refers to the naming of the album, which makes it what a literary critic might call a meta-album: "record cats are schemin' / Cause they're gonna call it border wave." A song about singing rock 'n' roll acknowledges the process of its own creation. Metafiction has been around a long time, but how many rock 'n' roll albums refer to themselves as record albums?

The Sir Douglas Quintet continued to perform and record for several years, but in 1990 Doug and Augie got together with Flaco Jiménez and Freddy Fender to form a new group, the Texas Tornados. This was a "super group" in the sense that all four were recognized as outstanding singers and musicians before they recorded together. They played an astounding mix of conjunto, country, blues, R&B, and rock 'n' roll—creolization at its most creative and complex. Freddy Fender's soulful R&B singing, Flaco Jiménez's heartfelt conjunto accordion playing, Augie Meyers's Vox and Hammond B3 organ, accordion, guitar, and piano playing and singing, and Doug Sahm's singing and guitar and piano playing were all essential elements of their blended sound.

When Doug Sahm died of a heart attack at age fifty-eight on November 18, 1999, that, of course, was the end of the Texas Tornados. Each member of the band was essential to its sound, and the Tornados couldn't go on playing without all four. Freddy Fender died in 2006, and Augie and Flaco continue to record separately.

"West Texas Waltz": The Flatlanders

Another all-time favor-right (as Merle Haggard used to pronounce it) Texas all-star band is the Flatlanders. A couple of years ago, I went to hear them at Valley Dale Ballroom, an old music venue in Columbus that goes back to the swing band era. The Flatlanders are three Texas singer/songwriter/musicians who are all products of Lubbock—Joe Ely, Jimmie Dale Gilmore, and Butch Hancock. Their first recording as the Flatlanders was made in 1972 but didn't come out as an album until 1990; it was called *More a Legend than a Band* (Rounder Records CD SS 34). My first Joe Ely LP was *Honky Tonk Masquerade* (MCA Records, MCA-2333, 1978) followed by *Down on the Drag* (MCA Records, MCA 3080, 1979) and *Musta Notta Gotta Lotta* (MCA Records, MCA-815, 1981). He did three Butch Hancock songs on *Honky Tonk Masquerade*, "Boxcars," "Jericho (Your Walls Came Tumbling Down)," and "West Texas Waltz," and one Jimmie Dale Gilmore song, "Tonight I Think I'm Gonna Go Downtown."

He continued to record many of their songs on subsequent albums along with plenty of his own. Having heard songs they wrote, I was a Butch Hancock and Jimmie Dale Gilmore fan before I heard them sing. Later I bought two Jimmie Dale LPs: *Fair & Square* (Hightone Records, HT-8011, 1988), which had songs by both Joe and Butch, and *Jimmie Dale Gilmore* (Hightone Records, HT-8018, 1989), which had four Butch Hancock songs (two of them cowritten with Jimmie Dale). Then I started buying Jimmie Dale's CDs *After Awhile* (Elektra, 9 61148-2, 1991), *Spinning around the Sun* (Elektra, 9 61502-2, 1993), *Come on Back* (2005). I have two of Butch's CDs, *Own & Own* (Sugar Hill Records, SH-CD-1036, 1991), with Joe as producer on four cuts and Jimmie Dale and Joe as backup singers on several songs, and *Eats Away the Night* (Sugar Hill Records, SH-CD 1048, 1995). Joe, Jimmie Dale, and Butch clearly had been collaborating on one another's albums while also recording as the Flatlanders, which helps to explain their tight harmonies and solid instrumental sound.

I had seen them all together as the Flatlanders in 2009 at another venue and loved it, but their show at Valley Dale in 2012 was even better. I was with my friend Larry Doyle, and as is our custom, we'd had a beer at my house before going to the concert and a few more after we got there. After the opening act finished, there was an intermission, and I went to the restroom. I knew it was in the right-hand corner near the stage, but I must have walked past it and found myself in a big, open area behind the stage. I saw two guys talking and asked them where the restroom was. As I got closer I recognized them: Jimmie Dale Gilmore and Butch Hancock chatting with each other. I introduced myself, told them I was from Beaumont, Texas, and that I had gone to the second grade in Levelland near Lubbock. I don't know if being fellow Texans had anything to do with it, but they were open and friendly. Butch was more talkative, and after a few minutes Jimmie Dale wandered off.

Butch and I talked about Austin, where we had both lived for a time, and I mentioned some of the songs he had written; we talked quite a bit about one of my favorites, "Junkyard in the Sun." I mentioned that I was a folklorist and how that was connected to my being a fan of their music, and Butch asked me, "Do you know Archie Green?" "Do I know him? He was a good friend of mine, stayed at our house when he first came to Columbus to teach at OSU. In fact, he loaned us some money to help with the down payment on our house. He was one of my folklorist heroes, one of my mentors when I was first starting out." I asked Butch how he happened to know Archie. "I can't remember exactly how we met," he replied. "But I saw him several times over the years." I said, "Once you've met him, you never forget him." Archie was one of the great folklorists of the twentieth century, someone who kept us on the right track regarding our commitment to the people we studied. He was an old leftist who kept the traditions of Woody Guthrie alive; he wrote a wonderful book on the folk music of workers, *Only a Miner: Studies in Recorded Coal-Mining Songs.* (For more on Archie, see chapter 1.)

Our talk about Archie reminded me of another folklorist connection with Butch: one of my folklorist friends had said she dated Butch when she was in graduate school in Austin, but he didn't remember her when I mentioned her name. The next day I remembered that she had dated Jimmie Dale Gilmore. I wish my memory was better; it might have made for a more personal conversation with Jimmie Dale. But Butch and I had an engrossing talk for about fifteen minutes before I heard the band warming up and said that I had better get back to my seat (after hurriedly going to the restroom on the way). I love it when things like that happen, and I think talking to Butch made me enjoy their show even more.

I get to see lots of Texas performers in Ohio, and when I go back to Texas, I try to see whoever happens to be playing while I'm there. My brother, David, has been very helpful in finding good concerts while I'm in Houston. A few years ago, we went with a group of seven family members, including two of David's daughters and one daughter's teenage kids, to the beach on Bolivar Peninsula, where we always went as kids. Luckily one of our favorite Texas country singers, Max Stalling, was playing at the Stingaree, which was our favorite seafood restaurant when our parents took us to Crystal Beach. The restaurant is on the Intercoastal Canal and is built on pilings, as are most of the beach houses to protect them from the rising tide when hurricanes hit.

Nowadays they have a bar on the ground floor underneath the restaurant, a relatively small space that is open to the canal on one side. Max Stalling and his band were in fine form that night, and we all danced on the small dance floor right in front of the band. They played some of my favorite Max Stalling songs: "Running Buddy," "Travelin' Light," "Dime Box, Texas," "Heat of the Wide Afternoon," and "Cowboy from Catrina," all from the album *Wide Afternoon*. David and his girlfriend Tiffany go to see Max often enough to have gotten to know him. After the show, David introduced me to him, and we had a nice chat about his music and the possibility of him coming to Ohio to play.

Since I don't get back to Texas more than once a year, I try to see my favorite Texas singers and bands when they come to Columbus. Over the years I've seen plenty, including the Flatlanders, the Texas Tornados, George Strait, Willie Nelson, Johnny Copeland, Rodney Crowell, and Tish Hinojosa.

"Come Back to Texas"

It's no accident that this book starts in Texas and ends there as well. The music that I grew up with as a child and teenager made such a deep impression on me that it's part of who I am today. I've been living in Ohio for almost fifty years, but my musical imagination was formed in Texas, so deeply embedded in me that what I heard back then is still in my soul today. My record and CD collection is wide and varied and reflects the rhythm and blues, jazz, rock 'n' roll, Cajun, zydeco, and conjunto that I heard while I was growing up. Through the music I have learned about race, class, gender, ethnicity, politics, and history—all through the experiences of listening to music and the various contexts in which I heard it. That's really the basis of this whole book.

And that cultural process continues. I'm still learning about new music, which often emanates from Texas. A few years ago, a friend and former student, Charley Camp, sent me a compilation CD he had put together with new recordings he thought I would like. He's aware of my Texas background and how connected to it I am even after living in Ohio all these years. One song especially showed how well he knows me and my tastes in music. It was recorded by a band with an absurdly funny name, Bowling for Soup, from Denton, Texas, where I lived for two years while working on my MA degree at North Texas State University, where the guys in this band also went to school (see chapter 5). The song expresses through comic lyrics and driving rock 'n' roll music the reasons to "Come Back to Texas."

"OHIO (COME BACK TO TEXAS)"

She said she needed a break
A little time to think
But then she went to Cleveland
With some guy named Leland
That she met at the bank.

There's nothing wrong with Ohio
Except the snow and the rain.
I really like Drew Carey
And I'd love to see the Rock 'n' Roll Hall of Fame.

Come back to Texas
It's just not the same since you went away
Before you lose your accent
And forget all about the Lone Star State.
There's a seat for you at the rodeo
And I've got every slow dance saved
Besides the Mexican food sucks north of here anyway.
(Transcribed by the author)

Going back in time, I felt as if this song was sung by one of my former girlfriends in Texas trying to get me to return. I wondered, Do the Bush twins want me back? I doubt it; I voted against their father in both his presidential elections. Maybe Willie Nelson wants me back; I've been a fan since the first song I heard him sing back in the late sixties. I have to admit that there *is* a lot of rain and snow blowing in from Lake Erie. On the other hand, I've had good Mexican food in Cleveland, and I'm sure Leland would agree (talk about a cheap—but funny—rhyme). And I'm a charter member of the Rock 'n' Roll Hall of Fame and go there all the time. I've heard some blow-me-away blues, R&B, and rock 'n' roll there. But the biggest reason is that my wife, Roseanne, is from Cleveland, and I love her hometown almost as much as I love her.

Still, the song works well to tempt any Texan back home by listing some Texas pleasures: Mrs. Beard's fruit pies (as a kid anyway), Blue Bell ice cream, and rodeos (especially the Houston Fat Stock Show and Rodeo). I lost a lot of my Texas accent growing up in so many other parts of the country (and Canada), but I still say *y'all* a lot, and I still love Texas music.

Notes

For readers who want to know more about a particular genre or performer, I mention some books and articles that I have found useful and entertaining to read as I listened to music over the years.

CHAPTER 1. They All Go Native on a Saturday Night: Civilized versus Native in American Vernacular Music

A good starting place for more information on country music is Paul Kingsbury, ed., *The Encyclopedia of Country Music: The Ultimate Guide to the Music* (New York: Oxford University Press, 1998). For instance, it contains a good short introduction to the career of Red Foley.

p. 3: The most thorough detailed biography of Hank Williams that I have read is *Sing a Sad Song: The Life of Hank Williams* (Urbana: University of Illinois Press, 1981) by Roger M. Williams, but the most entertaining to read is Chet Flippo's *Your Cheatin' Heart: A Biography of Hank Williams* (Garden City, NY: Dolphin/Doubleday, 1985).

p. 7: One of the best articles on the history of the concept of the folk is by my old friend William A. "Burt" Wilson: "Herder, Folklore, and Romantic Nationalism," in *Folk Groups and Folklore Genres: A Reader*, ed. Elliott Oring (Logan: Utah State University Press, 1980), 21–36, which is, in fact, a wide-ranging introduction to the study of folklore, as are Barre Toelken's *The Dynamics of Folklore* (Logan: Utah State University Press, 1996), and Jan Harold Brunvand's *The Study of American Folklore: An Introduction*, 4th ed. (New York: W. W. Norton, 1998).

pp. 9–10: My favorite book on Woody Guthrie is *Woody Guthrie: A Life* by Joe Klein (New York: Ballantine, 1980). Guthrie's autobiography *Bound for Glory* (New York: E. P. Dutton, 1943) is also a good read, but as Klein and others note, Woody's version of his life sometimes contains "tall talk," traditional exaggerations that he slips into at times. The edition I read is a Dutton paperback published in 1968 with a wonderful introduction by Pete Seeger written in 1967 soon after Woody died of Huntington's chorea, "a progressive degeneration of the nervous system." Pete said that when he heard of Woody's death his first thought was "Woody will never die, as long as there are people who like to sing his songs." They were still singing his songs when I wrote this in 2014. A very good article on Woody is Richard A. Reuss, "Woody Guthrie and His Folk Tradition," *Journal of American Folklore* 83, no. 329 (1970): 273–303.

p. 11: John Steinbeck's comments about Woody appear in Joe Klein's *Woody Guthrie: A Life* (Crystal Lake, IL: Delta, 1981), 160.

pp. 12–15: Two excellent well researched books on the folk music revival, including detailed consideration of Woody Guthrie and Pete Seeger, are Robert Cantwell, *When We Were Good: The Folk Music Revival* (Cambridge, MA: Harvard University Press, 1996), and Benjamin Filene, *Public Memory and American Roots Music* (Chapel Hill: University of North Carolina Press, 2000). For a variety of approaches to the folk revival, see the collection of essays edited by Neil V. Rosenberg, *Transforming Tradition: Folk Music Revivals Examined* (Urbana: University of Illinois Press, 1993). A good summary of Woody Guthrie's politics and his influence on the folk music revival can be found in Mike Marqusee, *Wicked Messenger: Bob Dylan and the 1960s* (New York: Seven Stories Press, 2005), 16–31. More recently a very good book on Bob Dylan within the broader context of the folk revival is Elijah Wald, *Dylan Goes Electric!* (New York: Dey St., an imprint of William Morrow, 2015).

p. 16: Bob Dylan's statement about Harry Belafonte is from his memoir *Chronicles*, vol. 1 (New York: Simon and Schuster, 2004), 69.

p. 17: Archie Green, *Only a Miner: Studies in Recorded Coal-Mining Songs* (Urbana: University of Illinois Press, 1972). Archie lobbied Congress full time without pay. When he finally ran out of funds, he tried to find a job to make enough money to return to Washington. He and I discussed his situation at an American Folklore Society meeting, and I was able to convince the English Department at Ohio State to hire him to teach folklore for a quarter. He stayed at our house and at Bill Lightfoot's house until he found an apartment within walking distance of the campus. He made a tremendous impression on his students and was able to make enough money to return to Washington. Archie was someone you never forget.

pp. 17–19: I discuss the concept of authenticity in my book *The Man Who Adores the Negro: Race and American Folklore* (2008), 14–15, 120–25, 139–41, 189–91; several of my examples are folk singers. Two essential folklore studies on authenticity are Richard Handler and Jocelyn Linnekin, "Tradition, Genuine or Spurious," *Journal of American Folklore* (1984), 97: 273–90; and Regina Bendix, *In Search of Authenticity: The Formation of Folklore Studies* (1997).

CHAPTER 2. **Yes Indeed: Race, Revival, and Rock 'n' Roll**

bell hooks is one of the African American scholars who had a profound influ-ence on my approach to the study of race, especially in her book *Black Looks: Race and Representation* (Boston: South End Press, 1992). An earlier influence was one of my professors at the University of Texas, Roger D. Abrahams. He introduced me to the study of African American folklore in his seminars as well as in his books, especially *Deep Down in the Jungle: Negro Narrative Folklore from the Streets of Philadelphia* (Chicago: Aldine, 1970); *Positively Black* (Englewood Cliffs, NJ: Prentice Hall, 1970); and *The Man of Words in the West Indies: Perfor-mance and the Emergence of Creole Culture* (Baltimore: Johns Hopkins University Press, 1983). Also significant was a book by John W. Roberts, one of my former graduate students, *From Trickster to Badman: The Black Folk Hero in Slavery and Freedom* (Philadelphia: University of Pennsylvania Press, 1989). My own book on race and cultural representations of African American culture is *The Man Who Adores the Negro: Race and American Folklore* (Urbana: University of Illinois Press, 2008). Another book of mine has three chapters on elderly African Americans, *Listening to Old Voices: Folklore, Life Stories, and the Elderly* (Urbana: University of Illinois Press, 1992), 25–102.

I've read quite a few books on R&B and early rock 'n' roll from the late forties and early fifties; this was the music I heard on the radio during my early teenage years. The first book was Charlie Gillett, *The Sound of the City: The Rise of Rock and Roll* (New York: Outerbridge and Dienstfrey, 1970). I think it provided my basic sense of the history of R&B and rock. Others include Carl Belz, *The Story of Rock* (New York: Harper Colophon, 1971); Arnold Shaw, *Honkers and Shouters: The Golden Years of Rhythm and Blues* (New York: Collier Books, 1978); and Peter Guralnick, *Feel Like Going Home: Portraits in Blues and Rock 'n' Roll* (London: Omnibus Press, 1971). Many other books on early rock 'n' roll and R&B have been published since then, but the ones listed here influenced me more directly and deeply than any others.

A thorough overview of gospel music with coverage of all the major figures is Tony Heilbut's *The Gospel Sound: Good News and Bad Times* (New York: Simon and Schuster, 1971). Heilbut has a chapter on Thomas A. Dorsey (56–71) and another on Mahalia Jackson (89–106). Michael H. Harris has written an entire book on Dorsey, *The Rise of Gospel Blues: The Music of Thomas Andrew Dorsey in the Urban Church* (New York: Oxford University Press, 1992).

Two old but still useful introductions to traditional Anglo-American folk songs and the British tradition they sprang from are Albert B. Friedman, ed., *The Viking Book of Folk Ballads of the English-Speaking World* (New York: Penguin Books, 1982); Roger D. Abrahams and George Foss, *Anglo-American Folksong*

Style (Englewood Cliffs, NJ: Prentice Hall, 1968). For the folk music roots of early country music, see Bill C. Malone, *Country Music, U.S.A.*, rev. ed. (Austin: University of Texas Press, 1985), 1–76. Studies of African American blues tradition in the Appalachia and the Piedmont regions include Cecelia Conway, *African Banjo Echoes in Appalachia: A Study of Folk Traditions* (Knoxville: University of Tennessee Press, 1995), and Barry Lee Pearson, *Virginia Piedmont Blues: The Lives and Art of Two Virginia Bluesmen* (Philadelphia: University of Pennsylvania Press, 1990).

pp. 23–24: Ray Charles collaborated with David Ritz to produce *Brother Ray: Ray Charles' Own Story* (New York: Dial Press, 1978). He speaks directly to the reader in the introduction: "I'm pleased to have you come along with me, pleased that you're interested enough to sit there and listen to me tell my story" (xii). This gives a good idea of what reading the book is like—relaxed, informal, and very personal, full of intimate details about his life.

p. 24: On the concept of primitivism, see Marianna Torgovnick, *Gone Primitive: Savage Intellects, Modern Lives* (Chicago: University of Chicago Press, 1990).

p. 31: Toni Morrison, *Playing in the Dark: Whiteness and the Literary Imagination* (Cambridge, MA: Harvard University Press, 1992). This is one of the most brilliant books of literary criticism I've ever read, a great novelist writes a great critical book. My favorite novels by her are some of the earliest, *Song of Solomon*, *Beloved*, and *The Bluest Eye*. I devote a chapter to Mollie Ford in my book *Listening to Old Voices: Folklore, Life Stories, and the Elderly* (Urbana: University of Illinois Press, 1992), 25–42.

p. 34: For John Cephas and Archie Edwards, see Pearson, *Virginia Piedmont Blues*. For Dink Roberts, Odell Thompson, and Joe Thompson, see Conway, *African Banjo Echoes in Appalachia*.

p. 35: The quotation from Robert Cantwell is taken from his "When We Were Good: Class and Culture in the Folk Revival," in *Transforming Tradition: Folk Music Revivals Examined*, ed. Neil V. Rosenberg (Urbana: University of Illinois Press, 1993), 44. Rosenberg's collection of essays provides many diverse approaches to the folk music revival. Robert Cantwell's book length study is also essential, *When We Were Good: The Folk Revival* (Cambridge, MA: Harvard University Press, 1996), 2–10, 316–18. For more on the folk revival in general, see the notes to chapter 6.

pp. 37–40: Bruce Pegg, *Brown-Eyed Handsome Man: The Life and Hard Times of Chuck Berry* (New York: Routledge, 2002).

pp. 40–41: John Goldrosen, *Buddy Holly: His Life and Music* (Bowling Green, OH: Popular Press, 1975).

CHAPTER 3. **Let's All Get Dixie Fried: Sexuality, Masculinity, Race, and Rockabilly**

A useful reference for rock 'n' roll fans is Holly George-Warren and Patricia Romanowski, eds., *The Rolling Stone Encyclopedia of Rock and Roll* (New York: Rolling Stone Press, 2001).

Some of my analysis of rockabilly is from an article I wrote, "Hillbilly Hipsters of the 1950s: The Romance of Rockabilly," *Southern Quarterly* 22, no. 3 (Spring 1984): 79–92. The books I've cited previously on the early history of rock 'n' roll have sections on rockabilly.

I've done extensive research on masculinity as it relates to folklore and American literature. The scholarly sources I found useful include Michael Kimmel, *Manhood in America: A Cultural History*, 2nd ed. (New York: Free Press, 2006); Elizabeth Lunbeck, *The Psychiatric Persuasion: Knowledge, Gender and Power in Modern America* (Princeton, NJ: Princeton University Press, 1994); and Sheila Whiteley, ed., *Sexing the Groove: Popular Music and Gender* (London: Routledge, 1997).

The books that have helped me understand white mimicry of black masculinity are Eric Lott, *Love and Theft: Blackface Minstrelsy and the American Working Class* (New York: Oxford University Press, 1993); David R. Roediger, *The Wages of Whiteness: Race and the Making of the American Working Class* (London: Verso, 1991); and Susan Gubar, *Race Changes: White Skin, Black Face in American Culture* (New York: Oxford University Press, 1997).

p. 46: I taught *On the Road* several times over the years and read three biographies of Jack Kerouac in the late seventies and early eighties: Ann Charters, *Kerouac: A Biography* (New York: Warner Paperback Library, 1974); Dennis McNally, *Desolate Angel: Jack Kerouac, the Beat Generation, and America* (New York: Random House, 1979); and Gerald Nicosia, *Memory Babe: A Critical Biography of Jack Kerouac* (New York: Grove Press 1983).

p. 46: The quotation about Gene Vincent is from George-Warren and Romanowski, *Rolling Stone Encyclopedia of Rock and Roll*, 1037.

p. 46: An early biography of Elvis Presley is Jerry Hopkins, *Elvis: A Biography* (New York: Warner Paperback, 1972). A much more thorough and in-depth biography is Peter Guralnick's two-volume set, *Last Train to Memphis: The Rise of Elvis Presley* (Boston: Bay Back Books, 1994) and *Careless Love: The Unmaking of Elvis Presley* (Boston: Little Brown, 1999). A much shorter but still worthwhile biography by the always-engaging southern fiction writer Bobbie Ann Mason is *Elvis Presley* (New York: Penguin Books, 2003). Music critic Greil Marcus has an imaginative analysis of Elvis's cultural significance, "Elvis: Presliad," in his book *Mystery Train: Images of America in Rock 'n' Roll Music*, rev. ed. (New York: E. P. Dutton, 1982), 141–209.

p. 49: A good biography of Carl Perkins is David McGee, *Go, Cat, Go!* (New York: Hyperion Press, 1996). For the life of Jerry Lee Lewis, see Joe Bonomo, *Jerry Lee Lewis: Lost and Found* (New York: Continuum Books, 2009); and Nick Tosches, *Hellfire* (New York: Grove Press, 1982).

p. 49: The Eric Lott quotation is taken from his *Love and Theft*, 52.

p. 51: The definition of boogie is from Harold Wentworth and Stuart Berg Flexner, eds., *The Dictionary of American Slang*, 2nd supplemented ed. (New York: Crowell, 1975), 54.

p. 51: bell hooks discusses the contrasting associations of blackness versus whiteness in *Black Looks: Race and Representation* (Boston: South End Press, 1992).

p. 51: The Alan Lomax quotation is taken from his *The Land Where the Blues Began* (New York: Dell, 1993), xix.

p. 51: The John W. Rumble quotation is taken from *The Encyclopedia of Country Music*, 176.

p. 52: I used two sources for information about Emmett Miller: Charles Wolfe, "Emmett Miller," in *The Encyclopedia of Country Music*, ed. Paul Kingsbury (New York: Oxford University Press, 1998), 345; and John Morthland, liner notes, *Okeh Western Swing* (Epic LP EG37324, 1982).

p. 52: Emmett Miller's recording of "Lovesick Blues" can be accessed at https://archive.org/details/EmmettMiller-21-26.

p. 54: For more on the role of Sun Records in the birth of rockabilly, see Colin Escott and Martin Hawkins, *Catalyst: The Sun Records Story* (London: Aquarius Books, 1975); Guralnick, *Last Train to Memphis*; and Craig Morrison, *Go Cat Go! Rockabilly and Its Makers* (Urbana: University of Illinois Press, 1996).

p. 55: The Bill Lightfoot quotation is taken from William E. Lightfoot, "The Three Doc(k)s: White Blues in Appalachia," *Black Music Research Journal* 23, no. 1/2 (Spring–Autumn 2003): 167–93, here 184.

p. 55: For more on Lesley Riddle and the Carter Family, see Barry O'Connell, "Step by Step: Lesley Riddle Meets the Carter Family; Blues, Country and Sacred Songs," in liner notes to *Dock Boggs: His Twelve Original Recordings* (Folkways RBF 654, 1983).

p. 56: Nick Tosches discusses Jerry Lee Lewis's version of "Drinkin' Wine Spo-Dee-O-Dee" in *Hellfire*.

p. 56: The "nice sweet jacket" quotation is taken from Jack Kerouac, *On the Road* (New York: New American Library, 1957), 168.

p. 58: The Carl Perkins interview is by Ron Weiser, "Interview with Carl," *Rollin' Rock*, 26 (1978): 16–17; quotation on 16. I don't remember where I found this journal, but if you're a Carl Perkins fan, the interview is worth looking for.

p. 61: The Bill Malone quotations are taken from his "Honky-Tonk Music," in Kingsbury, *Encyclopedia of Country Music*, 245–46: "The honky-tonk was essentially," 246; "the ambience and flavor," 245.

p. 61: The quotation beginning "a glorious manhood" is from Elizabeth Lunbeck, *The Psychiatric Persuasion: Knowledge, Gender and Power in Modern America* (Princeton, NJ: Princeton University Press, 1994), 245.

p. 62: The Greil Marcus quotation is from his *Mystery Train: Images of America in Rock 'n' Roll Music*, rev. ed. (New York: E. P. Dutton, 1982), 169.

p. 65: Nick Spitzer's article concentrates on Louisiana Cajuns and Creoles, but the concept of creolization has much broader applications. His field research in southwestern Louisiana was broad and thorough. He even talked to my mother, who lived in southeast Texas just across the border from Louisiana, an area considered a part of the Cajun/Creole cultural region. She called me in Ohio to tell me how much she enjoyed talking to him. Nicholas R. Spitzer, "Monde Creole: The Cultural World of French Louisiana Creoles and the Creolization of World Cultures," *Journal of American Folklore* 116, no. 459: 57–72.

p. 65: James Baldwin's wise and beautiful statement appears in his essay "Here Be Dragons," in *The Price of the Ticket: Collected Non-Fiction, 1948–1985* (New York: St. Martin's /Marek, 1985), 690.

CHAPTER 4. Take Me Higher: Dancing, Drinking, and Doing Drugs

p. 72: "Brown Bottle Blues" is a country song recorded in 1942 by Slim Harbert & His Boys. It's on the LP *Okeh Western Swing*.

p. 79: "Don't You Know We're Riding on the Marrakesh Express" is on David Crosby, Stephen Stills, and Graham Nash's album *Crosby, Stills, and Nash* (Atlantic, SD 8229, 1969).

p. 80: Zap Pow's "This Is Reggae Music" leads off the album of the same name (Island Records LP, ILPS 9251, 1974). It's a terrific collection that features some of the best Jamaican singers and musicians. The second cut is by the Wailers, "I Shot the Sheriff," followed by Joe Higgs, "The World Is Upside Down"; Jimmy Cliff, "Hey Mr. Yesterday"; the Maytals, "Funky Kingston"; Lorna Bennett, "Breakfast in Bed"; the Maytals, "Louie, Louie"; Owen Gray, "Guava Jelly"; the Heptones, "Book of Rules"; and the Wailers again, "Concrete Jungle." The Wailers' lead singer was the biggest reggae star of all, Bob Marley. A good compilation of his songs is the CD *Legend* (Island Records 901-1, 1984). Another great introduction to reggae music is the soundtrack to the film *The Harder They Come* with Jimmy Cliff's "You Can Get It If You Really Want," "Many Rivers to Cross," "The Harder They Come," and "Sitting in Limbo," as well as other reggae classics like "Rivers of Babylon" by the Melodians and "Pressure Drop" by the Maytals. One of the leading producers in reggae was Leslie Kong. His *The King Kong Compilation* (Mango, MLPS-9632, 1981) includes Desmond Dekker and the Aces' "Israelites," the Maytals' "Monkey Girl," and the Melodians' "Sweet Sensation." You may have noticed how many times the Maytals are represented on these collections; a large part of their success was due to their leader and lead singer, Toots Hibbert.

pp. 81–85: Stephen Wade, a musicologist who reviewed the manuscript for this book, pointed out something that prompted my explanation of the negative consequences of alcohol and drug abuse: "Is there a way of sometimes connecting the personal behavior to deeper truths or wider currents?" I took this to include an honest description of how alcohol and drugs had affected me personally.

CHAPTER 5. *Blues and the Abstract Truth:*
From Blues to Jazz

I've read quite a few books on jazz, but that doesn't make me an expert. I'm really more of a fan than a critic or scholar. But for what it's worth, here are a few books on jazz that have helped me understand where the music came from and the cultural and social context in which it developed: James Lincoln Collier, *The Making of Jazz: A Comprehensive History* (New York: Dell, 1979); Bill Kirchner, ed., *The Oxford Companion to Jazz* (New York: Oxford University Press, 2000); Gary Giddens, *Visions of Jazz: The First Century* (New York: Oxford University Press, 1998); James Lincoln Collier, *Duke Ellington* (New York: Oxford University Press, 1987); Mark Tucker, *The Duke Ellington Reader* (New York: Oxford University Press, 1993); and Rob van der Bliek, ed., *The Thelonious Monk Reader* (Oxford: Oxford University Press, 2001). I know, all but one book was published by Oxford University Press. I didn't do this on purpose; Oxford just happens to have a lot of good, accessible books on jazz.

p. 90: Quotation from Charles Keil is taken from his *Urban Blues* (Chicago: University of Chicago Press, 1966), 1.

p. 90: I still have thirteen old LPs by B. B. King going back to the old Crown and Kent labels that I bought at drugstores or discount stores in the black neighborhood in Beaumont, followed by his breakout albums on ABC (Paramount, Bluesway, etc.). My favorite Bobby Bland LPs are *Two Steps from the Blues* on the Duke label (DLP 74, 1961, later reissued on a number of labels) and *Here's the Man Dynamic Bobby Bland*, also on Duke (DLPS 75, 1962)—twenty-three cuts of some of the best R&B you'll ever hear, not a clinker on either of them. Little Junior Parker's *Driving Wheel* (Duke, DLP 76, 1962) isn't as even, but it has some great performances on it. Duke Records was located in Houston, so it was as if the records were made next door.

p. 92: Quotations from Alan Lomax are taken from his *The Land Where Blues Began* (New York: Pantheon, 1993): "Sexually active at ten," 89; "The couples, glued together," 364. For further analysis of blues and blues singers in the cultural context, see Jeff Todd Titon, *Early Downhome Blues: A Musical and Cultural Analysis* (Urbana: University of Illinois Press, 1977).

p. 94: Not much was known about Robert Johnson when *King of the Delta Blues* was released in 1961 on Columbia; as Frank Driggs says in the liner notes, "Robert Johnson is little, very little more than a name on aging index cards and a few dusty master records in the files of a phonograph company that no longer exists," but since then more research has been done on his life. Peter Guralnick in *Searching for Robert Johnson* (New York: Plume, 1989) uses the new research and his own emotional/intellectual response to the music to create an excellent essay on Johnson. A two-CD boxed set, *Robert Johnson: The Complete Recordings* (Sony Legacy, C2K 64916), was released in 1990.

p. 95: I've read two biographies of Janis Joplin. The first was *Buried Alive: The Biography of Janis Joplin* (New York: Bantam Books, 1974) by Myra Friedman, a writer in the music business who worked for record companies and for Janis's manager, Albert Grossman, from 1968 to 1970. She interviewed the most important people in Janis's life, and the book is full of intimate details about her. Even more intimate is *Love, Janis* (New York: HarperEntertainment, 2005) by Laura Joplin, Janis's sister—a loving biography but also very well researched.

p. 97: The Francis Edward Abernethy quotations are taken from a book he edited, *The Texas Folklore Society, 1943–1971* (Denton: University of North Texas Press, 1994), 213.

p. 98: My favorite Lightnin' Hopkins LPs are *Country Blues—Lightnin' Hopkins* (Tradition Records, TLP 1035, 1959) and *Autobiography in Blues* (Tradition Records, TLP 1040, 1960), both of which were recorded and have liner notes by Mack McCormick; and *Lightnin' Hopkins Down Home Blues* (Prestige, PR1086, 1964), with bass and drums backup. Alex Govenar, one of my former OSU students, wrote a fine book about him, *Lightnin' Hopkins: His Life and Blues* (Chicago: Chicago Review Press, 2010).

p. 100: Mance Lipscomb told his life story to Glen Alyn, who published a book, *I Say Me for a Parable: The Oral Autobiography of Mance Lipscomb, Texas Bluesman* (New York: W. W. Norton, 1993).

p. 113: For more about Billy Harper and his music, see http://www.billyharper.com.

CHAPTER 6. I Was So Much Older Then: Folk Revival into Rock 'n' Roll

There are several useful books on the folk revival. I think the best one is by someone I know and like, Bob Cantwell, officially Robert Cantwell, author of the book *When We Were Good: The Folk Revival* (Cambridge, MA: Harvard University

Press, 1996). He knows the subject well and has written a detailed and thoroughly developed analysis that concentrates more on American cultural ideas than on the history of the revival. That history you can find in other books such as Benjamin Filene, *Romancing the Folk: Public Memory and American Roots Music* (Chapel Hill: University of North Carolina Press, 2000); Robbie Lieberman, *"My Song Is My Weapon": People's Songs, American Communism, and the Politics of Culture* (Urbana: University of Illinois Press, 1989). A good collection of essays on folk revivals is Neil V. Rosenberg, ed., *Transforming Tradition: Folk Music Revivals Examined* (Urbana: University of Illinois Press, 1993). The University of Illinois Press has a superb series titled Music in American Life. Judy McCulloh, former executive editor at the press, was a folklorist, a leader in folk music scholarship, and a key figure in publishing books in this series. She died July 13, 2014, just as I was in the middle of writing this book, and I want to acknowledge how important she was in helping me and other authors who write about vernacular music and American folklore. She was more than an editor to the writers she worked with; she was also a good friend.

Political and protest songs are covered in these books on the folk revival. Another valuable study of political songs is by Richard A. Reuss. Dick was a friend whom I got to know at American Folklore Society meetings. He developed a respiratory disease and died at the age of forty-six in 1986. He wrote his dissertation on political folk songs, but unfortunately it was not published until after his death with the help of his wife, JoAnne, *American Folk Music and Left-Wing Politics, 1927–1957* (Lanham, MD: Scarecrow Press, 2000). His papers are housed at the Indiana University Archives; the archives' website has this to say about him: "Richard A. Reuss was well-respected as a pioneering scholar of the folksong revival: Scholars of and participants in the folksong revival appreciated Reuss for his detailed knowledge, his intellectual honesty and his gracious and helpful responses to their requests for facts, analysis, citations and reviews" (http://www.libraries .iub.edu/archives). He deserves more attention from protest song scholars.

p. 119: The only book I've read about Joan Baez focuses on her relationship with Dylan, and it is one I highly recommend: David Hajdu, *Positively 4th Street: The Lives and Times of Joan Baez, Mimi Baez Farina, and Richard Farina* (New York: North Point Press, 2002). As the title indicates Hajdu places the subjects in a social, cultural, and historical context while still providing a fairly deep and complex view of their individual personalities. It is a revealing and engaging read.

p. 123: For more on "the new aesthetic," see Ellen J. Stekert, "Cents and Nonsense in the Urban Folksong Movement: 1930–66," in Rosenberg, *Transforming Tradition*, 84–106. There are three other articles in *Transforming Tradition* on "the new aesthetic"; see 123–75.

p. 125: There must be hundreds of books about Bob Dylan, but I am going to list only a few that I have found especially good. First of all, if you are a Dylan fan, you have to read his book about himself, *Bob Dylan Chronicles, Volume One* (New York: Simon and Schuster, 2004). As you might expect from him, the book is hard to classify; not strictly speaking an autobiography, it contains lots of details about how he feels about his songs, almost like a book of self-criticism, not negative but in the sense of analyzing his own works. And there are plenty of details about his life. It is well written too, a poet's prose describing his own life. For lots of details, read the long and sometimes boring biography by Robert Shelton, *No Direction Home: The Life and Music of Bob Dylan* (New York: Beech Tree Books, 1986). Shelton has the advantage of having known Dylan from his early days in Greenwich Village, so there is an intimacy in the point of view. But some sections, unfortunately, read more like record reviews than biography; Shelton comments on all the individual songs in sometimes obvious ways.

For critical studies of Dylan songs, I like the two books I used when I taught the Dylan course at Ohio State. For a study of Dylan's songs placed in the cultural context of the 1960s, read Mike Marqusee, *Wicked Messenger: Bob Dylan and the 1960s* (New York: Seven Stories Press, 2005). As a folklorist who values cultural context as absolutely necessary for understanding a text, be it a novel, poem, folk, or rock song, I prefer Marqusee's approach to Christopher Ricks's literary-textual approach in *Dylan's Visions of Sin* (New York: HarperCollins, 2004). Still, Ricks is a good literary critic, and he reveals different erudite meanings in the songs by treating them as poems. For a variety of approaches, see the collection of essays edited by Neil Corcoran, *Do You, Mr. Jones? Bob Dylan with the Poets and Professors* (London: Pimlico, 2003). Most critical books on Dylan cover a wide variety of his songs, but Greil Marcus devotes an entire book to one song, *Like a Rolling Stone: Bob Dylan at the Crossroads* (New York: Public Affairs, 2006). If a song ever required a whole book of analysis, "Like a Rolling Stone" is it. A very good, more recent book is *Dylan Goes Electric! Newport, Seeger, Dylan, and the Night That Split the Sixties* (New York: Dey Street, 2015). I heard the author, Elijah Wald, give a talk at Ohio State in 2016, and I liked it so much I bought the book.

pp. 136–38: John A. Lomax and Alan Lomax, *American Ballads and Folk Songs* (New York: Macmillan, 1934); Alan Lomax, *Cowboy Songs and Other Frontier Ballads* (New York: Macmillan, 1938).

p. 140: For a discussion of Woody Guthrie's draft avoidance in the Second World War, see Joe Klein, *Woody Guthrie: A Life* (New York: Ballantine, 1980), 265–66.

CHAPTER 7. **The Night They Drove Old Dixie Down: Bluegrass, Folk Rock, and Outlaw Country**

The first bluegrass book I bought was written by bluegrass musician Bob Artis and called *Bluegrass: From the Lonesome Wail of a Mountain Love Song to the Ham-*

mering Drive of the Scruggs-Style Banjo, the Story of an American Musical Tradition (New York: Hawthorn Books, 1975). It's still a good one, although it was followed by several histories that were more analytical, more detailed, and more in-depth. Folklorist Neil V. Rosenberg wrote *Bluegrass: A History* (Urbana: University of Illinois Press, 1985), and it remains one of the best books about the genre. Another book came out around the same time, Robert Cantwell's *Bluegrass Breakdown: The Making of the Old Southern Sound* (Urbana: University of Illinois Press, 1984). It was also a history but a more ambitious examination of the cultural meaning of the music as well. A quote from the dust jacket gives some sense of this quality: Cantwell "explores in depth the historical background, the commercial origins, the internal workings, as well as the cultural and social significance of this 'old time music.'" Neil Rosenberg also put together a beautiful book on bluegrass with photographer Carl Fleischhauer, *Bluegrass Odyssey: A Documentary in Pictures and Words, 1966–86* (Urbana: University of Illinois Press, 2001). It has amazing photographs that capture the emotional atmosphere at a bluegrass performance whether in a small club or a big outdoor festival. The text describes some of that scene from the first-person perspectives of the creators' own fieldwork—a creative combination with the photos. Much of their fieldwork was done in Ohio, and there are some great pictures of a bluegrass bar in Columbus that I frequented back in the seventies, the exterior of the Blue Grass Palace on Parsons Avenue and an interior shot of people dancing to Lake Brickey's band (see the bluegrass section of this chapter).

p. 145: For more about the Comet Bluegrass All-Stars, see http://www.comet bluegrass.com.

p. 151: I learned that the Bluegrass Banjo Pickers were the Osborne Brothers from Rosenberg, *Bluegrass*, 266.

p. 152: The *New York Times* quote about Charlie Lawson is from Henry M. Belden and Arthur Palmer Hudson, eds., *Folk Ballads from North Carolina*, The Frank C. Brown Collection of North Carolina Folklore 2 (Durham, NC: Duke University Press, 1952).

p. 152: For a discussion of the evolution of the Country Gentlemen, see Rosenberg, *Bluegrass*, 158–61.

p. 154: The quotations about Tony Rice are from Tim Stafford and Caroline Wright, *Still Inside: The Tony Rice Story* (Kingsport, TN: Word of Mouth Press, 2010), 160–61.

p. 158: I ran across two books on the Byrds: Johnny Rogan, *The Byrds: Timeless Flight Revisited* (London: Rogan House, 1998); and Christopher Hjort, *So You Want to Be a Rock 'n' Roll Star: The Byrds Day-by-Day (1965–1973)* (London: Jawbone Press, 2008).

p. 159: The illustration for *Sweetheart of the Rodeo* is made up of two Jo Mora posters, the *Evolution of the Cowboy* and *Sweetheart of the Rodeo*. For more on

Mora, see *The Year of the Hopi: Paintings and Photographs by Joseph Mora, 1904–'06* (Washington, DC: Smithsonian Institution, 1979); *Jo Mora: Artist and Writer* (Monterey, CA: Monterey Museum of Art, 1998); and *Back to the Drawing Board with Artist Jo Mora* (Monterey, CA: Monterey History and Art Association, 2003).

p. 162: Waylon Jennings didn't like the term *outlaw country*, but no other name emerged to cover the music he and the rest played. Jan Reid has an entertaining book whose title suggests another name, *The Improbable Rise of Redneck Rock* (New York: Da Capo Press, 1977), but that didn't really catch on either. A more theoretical scholarly book by Barbara Ching uses another term to identify a broader category of country music, *Wrong's What I Do Best: Hard Country Music and Contemporary Culture* (Oxford: Oxford University Press, 2001). She includes Waylon and Willie in *hard country* but also Hank Williams, Buck Owens, and Dwight Yoakam—a wide net over time and different styles. I'll stick with *outlaw country* and Waylon and Willie and Billy Joe.

CHAPTER 8. Come Back to Texas: From "Bogalusa Boogie" to "Soy Chicano"

Barry Jean Ancelet is a folklorist who knows as much about Cajun music as anybody. Check out his book *The Makers of Cajun Music* (Austin: University of Texas Press, 1984). He gives the history of the music, describes the cultural context in which it exists, and provides a first rate bibliography on Cajun culture and history. The book also has numerous photographs of Cajun musicians at work and play; it has been updated and expanded and has a new title, *Cajun and Creole Music Makers* (Jackson: University Press of Mississippi, 1999). Another Cajun insider, Ann Allen Savoy, has written *Cajun Music: A Reflection of a People* (Eunice, LA: Bluebird Press, 1984). There is also an excellent article by Nicholas Spitzer, a folklorist friend of mine, "Cajuns and Creoles: The French Gulf Coast," in "Long Journey Home, Folklife in the South," special issue, *Southern Exposure* 5, nos. 2–3 (Summer and Fall 1977): 140–55.

I'm aware of only two books on zydeco: Michael Tisserand, *The Kingdom of Zydeco* (New York: Arcade Publishing, 1998); and Pat Nyhan, Brian Rollins, and David Babb, *Let the Good Times Roll* (Portland, ME: Upbeat Books, 1997), which covers Cajun music as well. You can also find information on zydeco at http://andrethierry.com/zydeco/ and on Clifton Chenier at http://www.allmusic.com/artist/clifton-chenier-mn0000159337.

Besides Américo Paredes's *"With a Pistol in His Hand": A Border Ballad and Its Hero* (Austin: University of Texas Press, 1971), several other publications on the *corrido* are useful: John Holmes McDowell, "The Corrido of Greater Mexico as Discourse, Music, and Event," in *"And Other Neighborly Names": Social Process and Cultural Image in Texas Folklore*, ed. Richard Bauman and Roger D. Abrahams (Austin: University of Texas Press, 1981), 44–78.

Inez Cardozo-Freeman, a former student and still close friend, wrote her dissertation on a *corrido* composer who lived in Toledo, Ohio; based on that field research, she also wrote two significant articles on how the *corrido* was carried far from the Texas-Mexico border by immigrant Chicanos: "Arnulfo Castillo, Mexican Folk Poet in Ohio," *Journal of the Ohio Folklore Society* 1, no. 1 (1972): 2–28; and "Creativity in the Folk Process: The Birth of a Mexican Corrido," in *El romancero hoy: Nuevas fronteras* (Madrid: Editorial Gredos, 1979), 205–14.

I learned what I know about conjunto by reading the notes on the back of LPs until Manuel Peña's article "The Emergence of Conjunto Music, 1935–1955" came along in a book edited by Richard Bauman and Roger D. Abrahams, *"And Other Neighborly Names": Social Process and Cultural Image in Texas Folklore* (Austin: University of Texas Press, 1981), 280–99, which also includes the article by John McDowell on *corridos* cited above.

p. 170: For a discussion of the Acadians' settlement in the South, see Ancelet, *Makers of Cajun Music*, 19–20.

p. 173: For more on creolization, see Spitzer's "Cajuns and Creoles."

p. 174: For the early forerunners of zydeco, see Ancelet, *Makers of Cajun Music*, 23. Ancelet discusses their influence on pp. 73–87.

p. 175: There is an album containing both songs, *Bayou Drive* (P-Vine Special–PLP-6035, Chess–PLP-6035, 1985).

p. 176: I compiled a CD of my favorite Cajun and zydeco songs that illustrates the complex nature of the music. Remembering the drives that my family made back and forth between Louisiana and Texas, I called it "Beaumont to Baton Rouge: A Cajun Zydeco Melange."

1. David Greely, "La malheureuse"
2. D.L. Menard, "Wildwood Flower"
3. Bruce Daigrepont, "Laissez faire"
4. Beausoleil, "Les flames de-enfer" (The flames of hell)
5. Steve Riley and the Mammou Playboys, "La danse de Mardi Gras"
6. The Louisiana Aces, "Lacassine Special"
7. Jo-El Sonnier, "Jole blon"
8. D. L. Menard, "Je peux pas t-oublier"
9. Hackberry Ramblers with Rodney Crowell, "Pipeliner Blues"
10. Moon Mullican, "New Jole Blon"
11. Cleveland Crochet, "Sugar Bee"
12. Buckwheat Zydeco, "I'm on a Wonder"
13. Boozoo Chavis, "Lula Lula Don't You Go to Bingo"
14. Nathan and the Zydeco Cha Chas, "Outside People"

15. Clifton Chenier, "Quelque chose sur mon idee"
16. Zachary Richard, "Filé Gumbo"
17. Beau Jocque and the Zydeco Hi-Rollers, "Give Him Cornbread"
18. Clifton Chenier, "Bayou Drive"
19. Steve Riley and the Mamou Playboys, "Ca tu dis et ca tu fais sont pas pareils"
20. Keith Frank and the Soileau Zydeco Band, "Co Fa"

I'm fairly sure you can still find all the CDs on which these performances are recorded. The wide variety of songs range from the Carter Family–influenced "Wildwood Flower" by D. L. Menard, to the deeply traditional Cajun fiddle tune "La malheureuse" played by David Greely. The music ranges from the rock 'n' roll sound of "Filé Gumbo" by Zachary Richard to the bluesy "I'm on a Wonder" by Buckwheat Zydeco; from Jo-El Sonnier's French-language singing of "Jole blon" to Moon Mullican's fractured French rendering of the same song. From the very Cajun Hackberry Ramblers playing with the non-Cajun Rodney Crowell's countrified singing on "Pipeliner Blues" to Clifton Chenier's absolutely R&B instrumental "Bayou Drive." Enjoy!

pp. 179–80: The Tish Hinojosa quotation is from the *Austin American States-man*, May 6, 1999, A12.

p. 180: Paredes's comment about borders and ballads is from his *"With a Pistol in His Hand,"* xii.

pp. 180–81: Regarding the basis of "The Corrido of Gregorio Cortez," see Paredes, *"With His Pistol in His Hand,"* 150.

p. 181: I have two books on Lydia Mendoza on my folklore shelves; together they give a pretty complete story of her life. *Lydia Mendoza's Life in Music* (Oxford: Oxford University Press, 2001), coauthored by Yolanda Broyles-González and Mendoza, is based on an interview of Mendoza by Broyles-González, which is presented as an oral autobiography in both Spanish and English translation. It also includes a section titled "Background and Analysis," written by Broyles-González, and a CD of her music. The other book is *Lydia Mendoza: A Family Autobiography* (Houston: Arte Público Press, 1993). The book's coauthors, Chris Strachwitz, of Arhoolie Records fame, and James Nicolopulos, interviewed Mendoza, family members, and other people who were familiar with her life and career.

p. 182: Manuel H. Peña discusses Santiago Jiménez in his "Emergence of Conjunto," 280–99. It is worth noting that the book in which this essay appears, Bauman and Abrahams, *"And Other Neighborly Names,"* is dedicated to Américo Paredes.

p. 185: The Doug Sahm quotation is from "The Doug Sahm Pages," http://www.laventure.net/tourist/sdq_hist.htm.

p. 186: I read a good biography of Doug Sahm recently. It contains lots of information about Doug's life and the histories of his various bands, but there are some gaps, and it seems to have been written hurriedly. Jan Reid wrote it with Doug's son, Shawn Sahm. I like the title, *Texas Tornado: The Times and Music of Doug Sahm* (Austin: University of Texas Press, 2010).

The Texas Tornados' first CD was simply called *Texas Tornados* (Reprise, 9 26251-2, 1990), and it's one of their best, crackling with the energy of all four talents coming together, with Doug, Freddie, and Augie doing lead vocals and Flaco playing accordion on every cut. They made several other CDs; the ones I have are *Zone of Our Own* (Reprise, 9 26683-2, 1991), *Hangin' on by a Thread* (Reprise, 9 45058-2, 1992), *4 Aces* (Reprise, 9 46197-2, 1996), and *Live from the Limo Vol. 1* (Frontera Records, 7243 8 47751 2 4, 1999), but their first CD contains the essence of their sound. The first two songs, "Who Were You Thinkin' Of" ("when we were makin' love last night") and "(Hey Baby) Que Paso" set the tone for the album. Although not written by Doug, "Who Were You Thinkin' Of" fits perfectly with the sardonic complaint songs he sings on *Border Wave* (Takoma, TAK 7088, 1981). "(Hey Baby) Que Paso" was written by Doug (with Bill Sheffield).

Doug's son, Shawn, put together a tribute album for his father and Freddy Fender that featured the surviving members Augie and Flaco, *Esta Bueno!* (Proper Records, PRPCD060, 2010).

p. 188: The Shane K. Bernard quotation is from his *Swamp Pop: Cajun and Creole Rhythm and Blues* (Jackson: University Press of Mississippi, 1996), 65. For his discussion of Cajun influences on Freddie Fender, see 64–65. Shane's father, Rod, sang one of swamp pop's biggest hits, "This Should Go on Forever."

p. 189: The Elvis Costello quotation is from "Spectacle Report: Elvis Costello's Favorite Songs," on *Sundance TV* (blog), http://www.sundancechannel.com/blog/2009/12/spectacle-report-elvis-costellos-favorite-songs.

p. 194: Archie Green, *Only a Miner: Studies in Recorded Coal-Mining Songs* (Urbana: University of Illinois Press, 1972).

Index

McClinton, Delbert, 75
McConville, Leo, 52
McCormick, Mack, 100
McDaniel, Luke, 159
McDowell, Fred, 99
McGhee, Brownie, 31, 55
McGhee, George, 55
McGhee, Stick, 55–57, 75
McGuinn, Roger, 157–58, 160
Meaux, Huey "The Crazy Cajun," 188
Meinerding, Brad, 145
Menard, D. L., 171
Mendoza, Lydia, 181–82
Merritt, Mitchell, 103
Mexican Americans: in Bay City, TX,
    178–79; conjunto, 5, 13, 42, 150, 178,
    182–83, 186–87; racial status, 178–79,
    183–84; Ry Cooder advocacy for,
    134; Sir Douglas Quintet influences,
    184–86, 188–92; and Tex-Mex music,
    66, 186, 189–92
Meyers, Augie, 184–86, 188–92
Miller, Emmett, 52
Miller, Mitch, 118, 124
Mingus, Charlie, 84, 114–15
minstrelsy, 49–50, 52, 138–39
Mitchell, Blue, 109
mixtapes, 74
Modern Jazz Quartet, 114–15
Monk, Thelonious, 109–12
Montgomery, Wes, 109
Moore, Johnny B., 75, 77
Morales, Rocky, 188
Morris Brothers, 153
Morrison, Toni, 31, 33
movies. *See* film(s)/movie(s)
MP3s, 110–11
Mullen, Benjamin Harrison "Big Daddy"
    (grandfather), 6–10
Mullen, "Big Mama" (grandmother), 8
Mullen, Carol "Sissy" (sister), 1, 3, 36, 73,
    120, 171. *See also* Smith, Carol and Bob
Mullen, David "Bubba" (brother), 1–2, 4,
    38–39, 73–74, 88, 104, 109, 194
Mullen, Mama (mother), 1, 3, 6, 72–73,
    97–98, 104
Mullen, "Moon" ("Daddy," father), 1–3, 6,
    10–11, 38–39, 72–73, 79, 108

Mullen, Pat (chronology): Beaumont,
    TX (1940–1947; *see* Beaumont, TX);
    Levelland, TX (1947), 1–3, 11, 138; Dev-
    on, AB, Canada (1949), 3, 52; Bay City,
    TX (1950), 22, 117–18, 178; Baytown,
    TX, and Horace Mann High School
    (1954), 23, 36, 47, 67; Istrouma Junior
    High School, Baton Rouge (1954),
    47; Newark, DE (1954–1965), 4, 8–9,
    12, 22, 25–26, 38, 41, 54; Beaumont,
    TX (1956–1957; *see* Beaumont, TX);
    Blakelock High School (Oakville, ON,
    Canada, 1957), 4, 31, 35, 41–43, 66–67,
    104–5; Lamar Tech College (1959; *see*
    Lamar Tech College); North Texas
    State University (1964), 13–14, 86,
    112–13, 195; University of Texas (1965),
    79, 96–99, 113, 126–27
Mullen, Roseanne (wife, née Rini), 16, 18,
    74, 114, 169, 196
Mullican, Moon, 72
Mulligan, Gerry, 110, 115
Mullins, Moon, 72
murder ballads, 155
Murvin, Junior, 139

Nager, Larry, 145
"native" music. *See* civilized vs. native
    music
Near, Holly, 15
Nelson, Oliver, 111
Nelson, Ricky, 49
Nelson, Willie, 13, 30, 73, 75, 162–63,
    166–69, 195–96
New Christy Minstrels, 118
New Lost City Ramblers, 124
Newman, David "Fathead," 114–15
New South, 154–55
New Wave rock, 188–89
Nixon, Richard, 11
nostalgia, 10, 39–40
novelty songs, 23

O'Brien, Parry, 43
Ochs, Phil, 118
Odetta, 31, 118
Orbison, Roy, 54
Osborne Brothers, 151

PATRICK B. MULLEN is professor emeritus of English and folklore at the Ohio State University. His books include *The Man Who Adores the Negro: Race and American Folklore* and *Listening to Old Voices: Folklore, Life Stories, and the Elderly.*

The University of Illinois Press
is a founding member of the
Association of American University Presses.

Text designed by Jim Proefrock
Composed in 11.25/14 Adobe Jenson Pro
with Archer display
at the University of Illinois Press
Cover designed by Jim Proefrock
Cover image: Musical instruments image
©iStock.com / Bill Oxford

University of Illinois Press
1325 South Oak Street
Champaign, IL 61820-6903
www.press.uillinois.edu